CATHY GLASS

THE MILLION COPY BESTSELLING AUTHOR

Saving Danny

Trapped and alone in a
dark and terrifying world,
Danny doesn't understand
why he must leave home

HARPER
element

Certain details in this story, including names, places and dates,
have been changed to protect the family's privacy.

HarperElement
An imprint of HarperCollins*Publishers*
1 London Bridge Street
London SE1 9GF

www.harpercollins.co.uk

First published by HarperElement 2015

1 3 5 7 9 10 8 6 4 2

Text © Cathy Glass 2015
Illustrations © Nicolette Caven 2015

Cathy Glass asserts the moral right to
be identified as the author of this work

A catalogue record of this book is
available from the British Library

ISBN 978-0-00-813049-7

Printed and bound in Great Britain by
Clays Ltd, St Ives plc

MIX
Paper from
responsible sources

FSC
www.fsc.org   FSC™ C007454

FSC™ is a non-profit international organisation established to promote
the responsible management of the world's forests. Products carrying the
FSC label are independently certified to assure consumers that they come
from forests that are managed to meet the social, economic and
ecological needs of present and future generations,
and other controlled sources.

Find out more about HarperCollins and the environment at
www.harpercollins.co.uk/green

Saving Danny

Also by Cathy Glass

Acknowledgements

A big thank-you to my family; my editor, Holly; my literary agent, Andrew; and all the team at HarperCollins.

Chapter One
Lost and Frightened

I t was dark outside, and cold, at five o'clock on Tuesday, 1 February. I was expecting a six-year-old boy to arrive with his social worker at any moment. Indeed, I'd been expecting them for the last hour. Danny was coming into foster care and Jill, my support social worker, had given me some details about him over the phone two days previously. As well as being six, I knew he was an only child who had learning difficulties and challenging behaviour, which included meltdowns, tantrums and aggression, and his parents – unable to cope any longer – had approached the social services. Danny was coming into care under a 'Section 20', also known as accommodated or voluntary care, where the parents agree to the move and retain full legal parental rights. The hope was that Danny would eventually be able to return home.

I was in the kitchen preparing dinner. My children – Adrian, fifteen, Paula, eleven, and Lucy (soon to be adopted), thirteen – were upstairs in their bedrooms, hopefully doing their homework before they watched television or generally relaxed. As I worked I listened out for the doorbell signalling the arrival of Terri, Danny's social worker, with little Danny.

1

Saving Danny

If all had gone to plan Danny's mother would have taken some of his clothes and toys to his school at the end of the day, where she would have met with Terri, explained to Danny that he was coming into foster care and said goodbye. It would have been an emotional and upsetting parting for mother and son, but they would be seeing each other regularly. Jill was going to arrive with the placement information forms once Terri and Danny were here. However, when the telephone rang I guessed things weren't going smoothly. Experience had taught me to expect last-minute changes, even if the move was planned, as Danny's was.

'I've just heard from Terri, Danny's social worker,' Jill said. 'There's a problem. Danny became very distressed when they told him he was coming into care, even though Terri handled it sensitively and stressed he'd be seeing his mother regularly. Apparently he kicked his mother and ran off screaming. He's somewhere in the school grounds. Terri and the staff at the school are looking for him. Hopefully they've found him by now. His mother was too upset to stay and went home. Terri has asked if you can go to Danny's school and collect him. She thinks he'll feel a bit better once he's met you.'

'Yes, of course,' I said. 'I'll leave straight away. It should take me about fifteen minutes.' I knew from the information Jill had already given me where Danny's school was.

'Thank you,' Jill said. 'Can you let me know when you're home with Danny? If it's too late for me to visit I'll come tomorrow.'

'All right. Will do.'

We said a quick goodbye and I hurried out of the kitchen and upstairs to where my children were. Thankfully they were old enough now to be left for short periods. When they were younger and I was called out at short notice, as a single-parent foster carer I had to take them with me, which at times was quite disruptive for them. Now, however, I knocked on each of their bedroom doors, stuck my head round and said, 'Jill's just telephoned. I have to collect Danny from school. Can you keep an eye on the dinner, please? I should be back in about an hour.'

They knew Danny was coming to stay and that plans in fostering could change without much notice, so their responses were: 'Yes,' 'OK,' and 'See ya later,' followed by a chorus of 'Bye, Mum.'

Downstairs again, I quickly slipped on my shoes and coat and, grabbing my bag and keys, headed out the front door. I felt the adrenalin kick in and my pulse quicken as I jumped into my car and then drove in the direction of Danny's school. Poor little mite, I thought. He went to school as usual this morning, expecting to return home to his parents at the end of day, and then his mother and a social worker arrived to tell him he's going to live with a foster carer – a complete stranger. How devastating, especially for a child like Danny, who already had problems. Little wonder he'd run off. I hoped he'd been found and was calmer now.

I turned into Yew Road where Danny's school was and the first thing I saw was a police car parked outside, with its lights casting a moving glow over the front of the school building and nearby houses. With a stab of fear I thought the police's presence must have something to do with Danny. I parked in the road, a little back from the police car, and got out. His school, Yew Primary, like many in the area, had a small tarmac playground at the front and grass playing fields at the sides and rear, which were flanked by shrubs and trees. As I hurried along the pavement and then across the front play-ground I could see torch lights flickering over the playing fields to the right of the building and hear voices calling, 'It's OK, Danny! There's nothing to be frightened of!' and 'Danny, are you there?' So Danny hadn't been found and was still out there in the cold and dark.

I went in the main door, which was no longer security locked as it would have been during the day, and then through the empty reception and into the corridor beyond. All the lights were on, but it was eerily quiet and empty. I didn't know the building, but the layout was clear. It was single storey and I hurried along the corridor towards the door that led out to the playing fields. All the classrooms I passed were empty. School finished at 3.30 and I assumed the staff that hadn't gone home were probably on the playing field looking for Danny. I pushed open the door at the end of the corridor and stepped outside. A security light flashed on overhead. I could see three torch beams flickering along the edges of the fields as they searched the shrubbery, and male and female voices were calling Danny's name. Then one female voice came closer.

'Can I help you?' she asked, stepping out of the dark to stand beside me.

'I'm Cathy Glass, Danny's foster carer.'

'Hello. I'm Terri, Danny's social worker,' she said. 'Thank you for coming. It's a nightmare. I called the police. There are two officers as well as some of the staff looking for him. The police and the caretaker have the torches, but there's no sign of Danny. Goodness knows where he is.' In the light of the security lamp I could see Terri looked very stressed and worried, with good reason. She was average height, mid-

4

thirties, with short brown hair, and was dressed in a quilted winter jacket and jeans.

'How long has he been out here?' I asked.

'Nearly an hour now. He has his coat on, thank goodness – or did have, when he fled. It all seemed to be going well, but when his mother began to say goodbye to him, he flipped. He kicked her and ran off crying and screaming. He's been out here ever since.'

'Is it possible he's not in the school grounds?' I asked, concerned.

'We've searched the building twice,' Terri said. 'The police have said once we've finished searching the grounds, if we haven't found him they'll widen the search and bring in the police helicopter. He could have got out of the school grounds, but it's unlikely. He would've had to scale a six-foot-high fence, which runs all around the perimeter.'

'What can I do?' I asked.

'Help search,' Terri said. 'We're taking it in sections. Come with me.'

I went with her across the dark, damp playing fields as torch beams flickered in the shrubbery like ghostly will-o'-the-wisps. Without a torch visibility was only a few metres, and then all you could see were shadows. I wished I'd brought a torch, but then I hadn't known Danny was still out here. I followed Terri to a section of the perimeter where no one else was searching and we began peering in and around the bushes, all the time calling Danny's name. 'Danny' echoed in the darkness behind us as the others searching also called his name. We were concentrating on any movement, sound or irregular dark shadow that could be a young boy hiding, huddled small with fear, but there was nothing. I felt a growing dread that he had managed to leave the school grounds, for I knew from experience that when a child is very distraught they can scale heights and run distances they wouldn't be able to normally. Terri must have been thinking the same thing, for after a few minutes she turned from where she was looking and said, 'I think we need to bring in the police helicopter now and look outside the school.'

Yet just as we turned to head back to the school, a male voice came from the far side of the playing field: 'Found him!'

'Thank God,' Terri gasped.

We hurried across the dark field in the direction of the voice. The others were doing the same – those with torches had their beams pointed a little ahead, lighting their way. As we drew close to where the voice had come from I saw that it was one of the police officers who had found Danny. His torch was tucked under his arm, and he was holding Danny against his chest. All I could see of Danny was the back of his head and coat.

'Thank you so much,' Terri said to the officer.

'Well done,' his colleague said to him.

The other searchers had arrived and we formed a small circle around the officer and Danny. 'You're OK now, son, aren't you?' the officer said gently to Danny.

Danny didn't reply. His face was buried in the officer's jacket and his little hands, knuckle-white, gripped his lapels for all he was worth.

'Thank goodness we found you,' Terri said, taking a step closer to Danny.

'Good boy,' another female voice added.

'We'll go into your school now,' the police officer holding Danny said in a calm and reassuring voice. 'Then, if you're all right, you can go home.'

'To his foster home,' Terri corrected.

Danny didn't speak or move.

'So you're going to stay with a foster carer,' the officer said, trying to reassure him 'That'll be nice.'

Danny didn't say anything and remained motionless. The officer turned and began towards the school, and the rest of us followed. As we entered through the door at the rear of the building Danny chanced to peep out and I caught sight of his little round face with pale cheeks and blue eyes wide with fear.

'Hi, love,' I said gently. 'I'm Cathy, your foster carer.'

He buried his head in the officer's jacket.

Inside the school we congregated in one of the classrooms. We could see each other properly now with the lights on. Three members of staff who'd been on the field helping in the search said that now Danny had been found they'd go home. Terri thanked them and they called goodbye as they left. Then the caretaker said he'd go and start to lock up and would we let him know when we were going.

'Thanks, Sam,' a young woman said. Then she introduced herself to me. 'I'm Sue Bright, Danny's teacher.'

'Hello. Cathy Glass, Danny's foster carer,' I said with a smile.

The police officer carrying Danny sat on one of the children's school chairs while the other officer stood by the closed classroom door – possibly to stop Danny if he tried to run off again, although that didn't seem likely. He remained very quiet and still, with his face buried in the officer's chest so that only his mop of blond hair was visible.

'Danny,' Terri said, squatting down beside him. 'Are you OK?'

Danny didn't respond.

'I expect you're hungry,' she said. 'Cathy, your foster carer, is going to take you home in her car soon and give you a nice hot dinner. Then, when you've had a sleep, she'll bring you to school tomorrow and you'll see your mother.'

Danny remained motionless. He didn't acknowledge that he had heard Terri or even that she was there.

'Danny,' his teacher, Sue, now said, stepping forwards. 'It's getting very late. All the other children have gone home. We're all going home too. You are going to Cathy's house for tonight and then we'll see you tomorrow in school.' She came across as very caring and had spoken to him gently, but he didn't respond.

'We've got a meeting here tomorrow at nine o'clock,' Terri now said to me.

I nodded, more concerned with getting Danny home than a meeting in the morning.

'Danny, time to go home with Cathy,' Terri said, touching his hand.

Danny snatched his hand away and tucked it beneath his coat but didn't say anything or look up. The police officer standing by the door answered his radio and we heard a female voice at the control centre ask if he and his colleague could attend an RTA (road traffic accident). The officer replied that they could, as Danny had been found safe and well. When he'd finished he joked to us: 'That was my mum telling me dinner was ready,' and I smiled.

8

Lost and Frightened

'Danny, time to go with Cathy now,' Terri said again. 'I'll phone your mother and tell her you're safe, then she'll come to school to see you in the morning.'

Danny still didn't move or speak. Clearly he had to come with me, so Terri lightly lifted his arm and began easing him away from the officer. Danny didn't resist. I stepped forward ready to take him and Terri and the officer lifted Danny into my arms. As soon as his little body touched mine he wrapped his legs tightly around my waist, grabbed my coat sleeves and buried his head in my chest. I breathed a sigh of relief now that I had him safe. It was just a matter of getting him into my car and home. Some six-year-olds are quite heavy, and being of a slight build myself I would have had difficulty carrying them, but Danny was as light as a feather – too light for a child of his age, I thought.

'We'll see you to your car,' said the police officer who'd been holding Danny.

'Thank you,' I said.

'Here's his bag,' Terri said, passing a large canvas holdall to the officer.

'I'll phone your mother now,' Terri said to Danny, staying behind. 'See you in the morning.'

'See you tomorrow in school,' his teacher said to us as we began towards the classroom door.

'Yes, see you tomorrow,' I replied.

Danny didn't make a sound, but his legs tightened around my waist and his fingers gripped my coat. 'It's going to be OK,' I reassured him. 'There's nothing to worry about.'

The officer standing by the classroom door held it open for me and I carried Danny out of the classroom and along the corridor. His teacher and social worker stayed behind. I would see them both at the meeting in the morning. The officers came with me and opened the main door and I stepped outside into the cold and dark again. Danny tightened his grip further and I held him close and talked to him gently, reassuring him that everything would be all right. I passed my car keys to the officer and he unlocked my car and opened the door. The officer holding Danny's bag put it on the passenger seat and then they waited while I lifted Danny into the child's car seat. He was still clinging desperately to me and I had to gently release his grip, all the time talking to him reassuringly. Once in the car seat he didn't look at me but pulled his head down into his coat. I fastened his seatbelt, checked it and then straightened. The officers said goodbye to Danny before I closed the rear door.

'Doesn't say much, does he?' the officer who'd been holding him remarked.

'He's scared stiff,' I said. 'Thank you for your help.'

'You're welcome.' He handed me my keys and began towards the police car.

I opened the driver's door and climbed in. Before I started the engine I turned and looked at Danny. 'Try not to worry, love,' I said. 'It's going to be all right.'

But Danny pulled his head further down into his coat, and I thought the sooner we were home the better.

Chapter Two

Meticulous

As I drove I glanced in the rear-view mirror to check if Danny was all right, but he kept his head down, buried deep in his coat, so I couldn't see his face. I talked to him in a calm and reassuring manner, but he didn't reply or say anything – not once. Even when I told him he'd be able to have ice cream and chocolate pudding for dessert, which would have elicited a response from most children, there was nothing from him. Nothing to say he'd even heard. I was relieved when we arrived home.

'We're here,' I said to him as I pulled onto the drive.

I cut the engine, got out and walked round to the passenger side where I took Danny's holdall from the seat and hooked it over my shoulder. I then opened Danny's door, which was child-locked. 'We're here, love,' I said again.

Danny remained silent and sat very still; he didn't even raise his head to have a look at his new surroundings as I thought he might.

'It's OK,' I said. 'There's nothing for you to worry about.' I released his seatbelt.

As I slipped my arms around his waist to lift him out he leapt at me, wrapping his arms tightly around my neck and his legs around my waist as he had done before. I manoeuvred him out of the car and then pushed the door shut with my foot.

'This is my home,' I said. 'It's going to be your home too, for a while.'

I carried him across the drive to the front door and went in. 'My son and my two daughters live here too,' I said as I closed the door. 'They're looking forward to playing with you.'

Nothing. Danny clung to me in desperation, his head in my shoulder. I set his holdall on the floor, then lowered him into the chair by the telephone table. His arms and legs were still wrapped around me, so I had to gently release them.

'Let's take off our coats and shoes and then we'll have something to eat,' I said. I could smell the casserole I'd left in the oven and I hoped one of the children had remembered to switch it off.

Danny was sitting where I'd put him on the chair, motionless and with his chin pressed into his chest. I was starting to find his silence and complete lack of reaction to anything I said worrying. I knew from Jill that there were concerns about his language skills and general learning development, but there'd been no mention of deafness. Danny's prolonged silence and indifference to the noises around him suggested a child who couldn't hear. He wouldn't be the first child I'd fostered who had hearing loss – either from birth or as a result of a trauma to the head – that hadn't been diagnosed.

I took off my shoes and hung my coat on the hall stand. Then I began undoing the zipper on Danny's coat, but as I did so he suddenly pulled back and hugged his coat tightly to him, clearly not wanting to take it off. 'Are you cold?' I asked

12

him. He didn't feel cold and the car had been very warm. He didn't reply but clutched his coat to him as if for protection. 'OK, let's take off your shoes first then,' I said easily.

I knelt down and unstuck the Velcro first from one shoe and then the other, and slid them off. Danny didn't object, and I paired his shoes with ours beneath the coat stand. 'We'll leave your shoes here, ready for morning,' I explained, but he didn't respond.

Danny's shoes, coat and what I could see of his school uniform beneath his coat appeared to be quite new and of good quality, unlike many of the children I'd fostered, who'd arrived in rags and with their toes poking through worn-out trainers. I now made another attempt to take off his coat, but he clung to it.

'All right, love,' I said. 'Leave it on for now, although I think you're going to be hot in the house. The heating is on.'

Danny didn't answer, nor did he look at me. He kept his chin down, his little face expressionless. But any thoughts I'd entertained about him being deaf now vanished. Upstairs Paula opened her bedroom door. Danny heard it and looked up anxiously. 'That's Paula,' I said to him. 'One of my daughters.'

He lowered his head again.

'Come and meet Danny,' I called to Paula, and she came downstairs. 'He's feeling a bit lonely at present, but I'm sure he'll be fine once he gets to know us all.'

'Hello, Danny,' Paula said softly, going up to him. 'How are you?'

His head was down but he gave the smallest of nods. It was the first sign of recognition from him and I was pleased. 'Well done, Paula,' I said.

'The dinner was ready, Mum, so I switched off the oven,' she said.

'Thanks, love. I was longer than I thought I'd be.'

'And Jill telephoned,' Paula said. 'Lucy answered it. Jill thought you'd be back and asked if you would phone her when you returned.'

'Yes, I'll phone her now,' I said.

Lucy and Adrian called 'Hi' from the landing and then returned to their rooms to finish their homework. They'd come down and meet Danny properly later. I looked at Danny. He was going to have to get off the chair now and come with me.

'Danny, we're going into the living room,' I said. 'There are some toys in there for you to play with. I'll unpack your bag later.' I'd sorted out a selection of age-appropriate games and puzzles for him to play with that afternoon.

Danny didn't move or say anything.

'Come on, love,' I said, gently taking his arm. 'You can't stay here.'

Paula was looking a bit concerned. Most children arrived with something to say – some had plenty to say. I eased him off the chair, took his hand and led him gently down the hall and into the living room.

'He's still got his coat on, Mum,' Paula said.

'Yes, he's going to take it off later, aren't you?' I said to Danny, but there was no response.

Now he was standing I could see just how small he was. I'd previously fostered a four-year-old girl, Alice, whose story I told in *I Miss Mummy*, but Danny, two years older, was about the same size as her, and definitely well below the average height and weight for a boy of his age. Perhaps his parents were of small stature, I thought, which could account for it.

Meticulous

Danny looked at the toys in the centre of the living room but didn't immediately go to them as most children would have done, so I led him over. 'Do you like building bricks?' I asked, pointing to the Lego. 'Perhaps you'd like to build a car? Or a castle, or a boat, or a house?' I suggested.

He didn't say anything but did squat on the floor by the toys, where he just sat staring at them.

'I need to phone Jill,' I said to Paula.

'I'll play with him,' she offered.

'Thanks, love.'

Paula knelt on the floor beside Danny while I sat on the sofa and picked up the handset from the corner table. It was after office hours, so I keyed in the number for Jill's mobile and she answered straightaway.

'It's Cathy. Danny's with me,' I said. 'We've just got in.'

'Is everything OK?' Jill asked.

'I think so. It took a while to find him. The police were there. But he's safe now. I'll give him some dinner soon.' I couldn't say too much as Danny was within earshot, and I didn't want to leave him so soon after arriving and phone from another room.

'Is Terri with you?' Jill asked.

'No, she stayed behind to telephone Danny's mother and tell her Danny had been found. There's a meeting at school first thing in the morning. At nine o'clock.'

'That's the first I've heard of it,' Jill said. 'I won't be able to attend. I've got a child's review booked in at nine-fifteen. It's been in the diary for a month.'

It was more important for Jill to attend a child's review than the meeting at Danny's school, and Jill knew that as an experienced foster carer I'd be all right to attend the meeting without her, otherwise she would have arranged for another support social worker from the fostering agency to accompany me.

'No worries,' I said. 'I'll let you know what happens.'

'Thanks. I'll visit you and Danny tomorrow after school,' Jill said. 'Four o'clock?'

'That's fine. We'll be home by then.'

'And you've got everything you need for tonight?' Jill asked.

'I think so. Danny's come with a holdall. Terri didn't say he had any allergies or special dietary requirements, so I assume there are none.'

'There's nothing in the essential information forms,' Jill confirmed. 'And he hasn't come with any medication?'

'Not as far as I know, no.'

'All right, well, good luck then, see you tomorrow.'

We said goodbye. I replaced the handset and looked at Danny. He was now watching Paula put together the pieces of Lego but wasn't making any attempt to join in, although Paula was encouraging him. It was 6.30, and I really needed to get the dinner on the table. Danny was calm, so I asked Paula if she could stay with him while I went into the kitchen. I went over to Danny to tell him what was going to happen. When a child first arrives I find it helps them if routines, practices and expectations are explained as they arise. Households vary and what is obvious and familiar to members of one household won't be to another. It helps them to settle in if they have a routine and know what to expect.

'Danny,' I said, squatting down so I was in his line of vision (although he didn't make eye contact), 'it's nearly time for our dinner, so I'm going into the kitchen to finish making it. Then we'll all sit at the table and eat. Paula is going to stay here with you, while I'm in the kitchen. All right?'

He didn't look at me or acknowledge me, but I now knew he could hear, so I continued. 'If you need anything, tell Paula. Do you need the toilet yet?' I thought to ask.

Danny gave a small shake of his head.

'OK. Good boy. When you do, ask Paula or me, and I'll show you where it is.' Usually, I took a new child on a tour of the house soon after they'd arrived so that they knew where everything was, and normally they were inquisitive and ready to have a good look around, but Danny wasn't. He was clearly struggling with all the changes, so I thought I'd leave the tour for another time. He was a child who needed to take things very gradually, one step at a time.

'Do you want a drink?' I asked him as I stood.

He gave another little shake of his head.

'I'll leave the door open so you can hear me in the kitchen,' I said. I went to touch his shoulder – a little reassuring physical contact – but he moved out of reach. Not rudely, just showing he didn't want to be touched, which I understood. I hoped that would change in future when he got to know me, for if there was ever a child who looked in need of a hug, it was Danny.

As I worked in the kitchen I could hear Paula talking to Danny, encouraging him to play, but there was nothing coming from Danny. I would learn more about his language delay and general development at the meeting at his school the following morning, when I would also meet his mother.

Once dinner was ready I went into the living room where Paula and Danny were sitting on the floor as I'd left them.

Paula had built a small house out of Lego, complete with windows, a door and a potted plant on the doorstep. Danny appeared not to have even touched the Lego. There were other games and toys within his reach, but he hadn't attempted any of them, despite Paula's encouragement.

'Very nice,' I said to Paula, admiring her house.

She grinned. 'I've always liked Lego.'

'I know. Dinner's ready,' I said to them both. 'I'll call Adrian and Lucy.'

I left the living room and went to the foot of the stairs where I called up to Adrian and Lucy. They replied that they'd be down straightaway. I returned to the living room where, to my slight surprise, Danny was slowly undoing the zipper on his coat. Then he began struggling out of it – difficult while sitting down. Paula instinctively reached out to help him, but he pulled away from her. She looked at me and I motioned for her not to worry. Fiercely independent, Danny struggled out of his coat and then clutched it protectively to his chest.

'Danny, we're going to eat now,' I said, going over to him.

He didn't look at me or reply, but he did stand up.

'Wotcha!' Lucy said to Danny, as she bounced into the living room. 'I'm Lucy, Cathy's other daughter. How are you doing, Mister?'

Danny didn't look at her.

'I was a foster child once,' Lucy said, trying to reassure him. 'So I know how you feel. But you'll be fine here, I promise you. You'll be well looked after and will soon feel at home.'

Bless her, I thought, although Lucy's arrival as a foster child had been very different to Danny's. She'd been older

18

and had been grateful for the stability that being in care offered. I wondered if Danny would respond to her approach, but he didn't; he just clutched his coat and stared at the floor. He looked so lost and alone I dearly wished I could reach out and hug him, as I'm sure Paula and Lucy did too, but clearly Danny was nowhere near ready for that yet.

'Let's eat,' I said.

Lucy turned and led the way into the kitchen-cum-dining room with Paula following and then Danny and me. Danny was still clutching his coat.

'This is where you sit,' I said to Danny, drawing out the chair. We tended to keep the same places at the table, partly from habit but also because it helped the children I fostered to settle in if they knew where to sit. It became known as their place, and some even wrote their name on a piece of paper and stuck it to the back of the chair.

Danny was standing by his chair, still holding his coat. 'Shall I put your coat with ours in the hall?' I asked him.

He shook his head.

'Hang it on the back of your chair then,' I said, 'so it doesn't get food down it. It's a nice coat. You don't want it spoilt.'

Thankfully, Danny did as I asked and very slowly and meticulously draped his coat around the chair-back, and then spent time adjusting and straightening it.

'That's cute,' Lucy said, watching him. Indeed it was, but it was also a little odd. Most boys of Danny's age would have happily thrown their coat on the floor, not spent minutes perfecting its position. Adrian still dumped his coat on the floor sometimes if he was in a hurry.

'Sit down now,' I said to Danny, for having arranged his coat to his satisfaction he was still standing by the chair.

There was a small delay, as though he was processing or considering what I'd asked him to do, before he climbed onto his chair.

Adrian arrived and said, 'Hi, Danny,' as he took his place at the table.

Danny lifted his head slightly in Adrian's direction but didn't look at him.

'This is my son Adrian,' I said to Danny.

'Hi, Danny,' Adrian said again, but Danny still didn't reply.

'It's bound to take Danny a while to get used to us all,' I reassured everyone.

I served dinner and then sat in my place at the end of the table. Danny and Paula sat next to each other, to my right, and Adrian and Lucy to my left. We all began eating except little Danny, who sat motionless with his hands in his lap, staring at the contents of his plate. I'd given him a spoon as well as a knife and fork, but he made no attempt to pick up any of them. 'It's chicken and vegetable casserole,' I said. 'Try some. I'm sure you'll like it.'

'It's nice,' Lucy encouraged.

'Yummy,' Paula said.

Danny didn't move or make any attempt to start eating.

'Come on, love,' I said. 'You need to eat something,' I picked up his spoon and placed it on the edge of his plate, ready for him to use.

After a moment he slowly picked up the spoon, but instead of dipping it into his food to start eating he set it down again. He repositioned it precisely beside his plate and then picked it up again. Independent, or resenting my help? I didn't know. My children had seen this, but they knew better than to comment. Nor did they say anything about what Danny did next. Having picked up his spoon, he didn't use it to start eating but began separating out the various components of the casserole. He arranged them in little heaps around the edge of his plate so that after a while there was a little pile of chicken pieces, another of diced potatoes, another of sliced carrots, and a mound of peas. You couldn't really call it 'playing' or 'toying' with his food – it was too exact and precise for that. My children and I watched mesmerised – surreptitiously, of course, so Danny didn't notice.

'Are you going to eat it now?' I asked him eventually.

Danny gave a small nod and then, using his spoon, began eating his food, one pile at a time. First the chicken, then the potatoes, carrots and peas. It wasn't how one would normally eat a casserole, but the important thing was that Danny was eating. He finished it all and then spent some minutes scooping up the gravy until his plate was clear.

'Good boy,' I said.

He was the last to finish, and I now stood and began gathering together the dirty dishes. As I did, Danny finally spoke. He said one word: 'George.'

Chapter Three

George

W̲e all looked at him. We couldn't help it. Danny suddenly speaking had taken us all by surprise.

'George?' Paula and I chorused together.

'Who's George?' Lucy asked.

'George,' Danny repeated. 'George. George.'

'Tell me who George is,' I said, 'and I can help you.'

Danny stared around the room and then towards the kitchen as though he was looking for something or someone. 'George,' he said again, louder. 'George!'

'Danny, who is George?' I asked, trying to make eye contact with him.

But he didn't look at me or reply. He was staring around searchingly, clearly looking for something, but what or who? He was also growing increasingly anxious in his demands for George. 'George! George!'

'Is George a person?' I asked him.

He didn't reply.

'A toy, maybe?' I suggested. 'Is George a toy in your hold-all?' I was envisaging a favourite toy packed by his mother that went everywhere with Danny and he couldn't be separated from. But Danny shook his head vigorously.

'George!' he shouted again. Sliding off his chair, he ran into the kitchen and to the back door. I went after him.

'Danny, who is George?' I asked again.

'George!' he said, facing the back door as though George could be outside. 'George! George!' Danny was very agitated now and close to tears.

'Danny, there's no one out there, love,' I said, going up to him. 'George isn't out there. Tell me who George is and I can help you.'

Danny turned from the door and looked around him, bewildered. Then he threw himself onto the floor, face down, and began sobbing and beating the tiles with his fists and feet. I knelt beside him and placed my hand lightly on his arm, but he wriggled out of reach and sobbed louder. Adrian, Paula and Lucy had fallen silent at the table and were looking at him, very worried.

'George!' Danny cried at the top of his voice as if he thought George might be able to hear him. 'George!'

'Danny, calm down,' I said, staying close to him. 'I'll do what I can to find George.'

But he didn't calm down; he continued sobbing loudly, crying out for George and beating the floor as his upset began to escalate into a tantrum. Sometimes, when a young child has a tantrum, holding them close and soothing them can ease them out of it, while older children often have to work through it before they can be held. Danny was so little and vulnerable my instinct was to pick him up, but given his resistance to physical contact I wasn't sure this was the right thing to do.

'Danny,' I said, lightly touching his arm again, 'can you tell me who George is?'

George

There was a small pause before he cried, 'No!' and thrashed around on the floor even more.

'I can't help you unless I know what it is you want,' I said more firmly.

'George!' Danny yelled at the top of his voice.

At that moment Toscha, our rather lazy cat, perhaps intrigued by the commotion going on indoors, leapt in through the cat flap. Danny suddenly fell quiet – from shock, I think – and, sitting bolt upright, stared at Toscha. She threw him a disparaging glance and then sauntered over to her food bowl.

'Not George!' Danny cried, pointing to Toscha.

'No. That's Toscha, our cat,' I said.

'Not George!' Danny cried again as though it was her fault.

'No, our cat,' I repeated. Danny got onto all fours and crawled to the cat flap and pushed it open.

'Is there something you want to see outside?' I asked.

Danny nodded vigorously.

'Can you bring me Danny's coat and shoes, please?' I called to Adrian, Lucy and Paula. I was wearing slippers, but Danny only had on his socks. Paula stood and went into the hall for Danny's shoes while Lucy unhooked his coat from the chair and brought it to me.

'Thank you,' I said with a reassuring smile.

Danny was calmer now he knew he was going outside, although what he expected to find out there I'd no idea – I could foresee another tantrum when he was disappointed.

'Do you want me to get your coat, Mum?' Paula asked, arriving with Danny's shoes.

'No thanks, love. We won't be out there for long. It's cold.'

Saving Danny

I set Danny's shoes on the floor beside him. 'Shall I put them on for you or do you want to do it?' He took first one and then the other, quickly stuffing his foot in and doing up the Velcro. 'Good boy,' I said. 'Now stand up and put your coat on.' I held his coat out ready for him. There was a moment's pause, as though he was processing or considering what I'd asked him to do, and then he slipped his arms into each of the sleeves and drew his coat around him.

'I want you to hold my hand when we go out into the garden,' I said to him. 'It's dark and there's a step outside. I don't want you falling.' Also, not knowing what Danny wanted to do in the garden, I was concerned he might be thinking of running off and hiding again as he had done at school.

Danny didn't offer me his hand, so I repeated that he needed to hold my hand before we went into the garden. After another pause he did as I'd asked. 'Good boy,' I said, taking every opportunity to praise him.

I opened the back door. The light from the kitchen shone out illuminating the step, and I helped him over it. Once outside Danny began looking around again anxiously. 'George?' he asked. 'Where George?'

'I don't think we're going to find George here,' I said gently.

'George,' Danny repeated. Still holding my hand, he led me round the back where we stood on the patio facing the house. He pointed to the wall beneath the kitchen window. 'George?' he asked, puzzled. 'George?'

'Did you think George would be here?' I asked him. He nodded. 'I'm sorry, love, he's not. I expect he's at your house. Who is George?'

George

Danny opened his mouth as if to answer, but it was as though he couldn't find the right word, so he said something else instead – 'George needs dinner' – and his eyes filled with tears.

Then it dawned on me. 'Is George an animal?' I asked.

Danny gave a very small nod.

'Is George your pet who lives outside?'

Danny nodded. 'George needs feeding.'

'I expect your mother has given George his dinner,' I reassured him. 'What type of animal is George?'

Danny looked around, bemused, apparently unable to find the right word.

'Does George live in a cage?' I asked, narrowing down the possibilities.

Danny nodded.

'Is he a rabbit?'

Danny turned to me, and for the first time since I'd collected him from school and brought him home he made eye contact. 'Yes. George Danny's best friend,' he said so sadly I could have wept.

'All right, love,' I said. 'I understand. Let's go inside and I'll explain.'

Danny still had his hand in mine and he slowly turned away from the place where he thought George would be. He looked lost and utterly defeated as he allowed me to lead him back indoors.

Danny's assumption that George had come with him to live with us was, I felt, logical for a child of six. Danny had come to stay, so why shouldn't his beloved pet and best friend have come too? It would have helped Danny if his mother or his social worker had explained to him more fully about

27

coming into care – or perhaps they had, for I was realizing that Danny was a child with very special needs who not only had difficulty with language but seemed to have great difficulty processing information as well. I wondered if he'd been assessed.

Danny appeared slightly dazed by what had happened and let me help him out of his coat and shoes without protest. Paula took them into the hall. He was too preoccupied with George's absence to notice that his coat had gone to hang with ours on the coat stand. I explained to Adrian, Lucy and Paula that George was Danny's much-loved pet rabbit, which he had hoped had come with him. I could see from their expressions that they were as moved as I was by Danny's upset, for they appreciated the bond that existed between pets and their owners from having Toscha with us for so many years.

'Come on, Danny,' I said. 'Let's go and sit down and I'll try to explain what's going on.'

I took him into the living room where I asked him to sit on the sofa. He clambered on and I sat next to him, close but not touching, which, to a child such as Danny who wasn't naturally tactile, could have felt threatening and like an invasion of his personal space.

'No George?' he asked sadly, without looking at me.

'No, love, George isn't here. He's at your house, safe and warm. I'm sure your mother will have given him his dinner.'

Danny shook his head and tried to say something, but nothing came out.

'Do you usually feed George?' I asked him.

He nodded.

'After you've had your dinner?' I asked. From the way Danny had left the table and started looking for George as soon as he'd finished his dinner, I thought it was probably a routine.

He nodded again.

'Danny, I need you to listen carefully to what I am going to tell you. My name is Cathy and I'm a foster carer. I look after children to help their parents. You'll still see your mummy and daddy, and you'll be going to school as normal. But you are going to live with me for a while. Your mummy and daddy love you, and George loves you too. You mustn't worry about any of them. They are all safe.' I'd no idea what Danny understood about coming to live with me, but I knew from experience that many children who came into care fretted and worried that something dreadful had happened to their parents and any loved ones they'd left behind. Once they'd seen them again at contact they were usually reassured. 'Your mummy and daddy are safe at home, and George is safe in his hutch,' I said.

'George here,' Danny said.

'No, love, George isn't here. He's at your house.'

'George here,' Danny repeated, growing anxious again. I was puzzled that he was still asking as clearly he'd seen for himself that George's hutch wasn't outside.

'No, love. George is at your house,' I said again.

'No! George here!' Danny cried more insistently. It was then I realized that 'George here' now meant something different and was no longer a question.

'You want George here?' I asked.

He nodded.

'I understand.'

This was a difficult one, because pets don't usually accompany a child into care. Reasons for this include that it isn't always practical, members of the foster family may have allergies to animal fur, the animal might be unsafe (this usually applies to dogs), or the parent(s) might not want the pet to go with the child, which is understandable as they can be as attached to it as the child. But this was a little rabbit we were talking about that lived in a hutch outside. None of us were allergic to fur and I didn't mind pets, so I decided not to immediately rule out the possibility of George coming to stay with us, but neither was I going to give Danny false hope.

'I'll talk to your mother about George when I see her tomorrow at school,' I said to Danny.

'Need George,' Danny said despondently with his head down. I felt so sorry for him.

'I understand,' I said. 'We'll see what your mother says tomorrow.'

This was the best I could offer and it seemed to reassure Danny a little, for he climbed off the sofa and went over to the games and puzzles that were still laid out on the floor. Kneeling down, he began to play with the Lego. I was pleased; this was a good sign. When a child feels relaxed enough to play it shows they are less anxious and starting to settle in.

However, as I watched Danny picking the Lego bricks out of the box and laying them on the floor, I saw that he wasn't using them to build a house or car or any other object; he was arranging them end to end in a line. After a few minutes it was clear he was creating a multicoloured line of bricks, and I saw a pattern emerging from the different brick sizes and colours he was using: large white, small pink, large yellow, small red, blue, green, etc. I watched, impressed, as he concentrated hard and carefully selected each brick from the box and added it to the line. When the pattern had repeated three

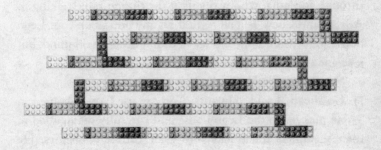

times he placed a large blue brick at right angles to the previous red brick to turn the corner, then added a green one at right angles to that and started creating a second line running parallel to the first with an identical repeating pattern. I'd never seen a child use Lego like this before, so intricate and precise. Maintaining the pattern he completed a third and then a fourth line, then halfway through the fifth line he ran out of red and blue bricks. He looked at the house Paula had previously built, which was an arbitrary arrangement of red, yellow and blue bricks.

I immediately realized what Danny wanted and called through to Paula, who was still at the dining table talking to Adrian and Lucy. 'Is it all right if Danny breaks up your Lego house so he can use the bricks?' I didn't think she'd mind, but it seemed right to ask her.

'Sure,' she called back easily.

'Go ahead,' I said to Danny. 'You can use Paula's house.'

He picked up the Lego house and carefully dismantled it, then separated the bricks into their different colours. He completed a fifth and sixth line of bricks in the same sequence. There were six bricks left over and he returned those to the box. He then carefully put the lid on the box and pushed it away, out of sight, as though he didn't want to be reminded of the rogue bricks that hadn't fitted in. He sat back and contemplated his work. It had taken him about fifteen minutes.

'Well done,' I said, going over. 'That's a fantastic pattern.'

I called to Adrian, Lucy and Paula to come and see what Danny had made and they dutifully traipsed in. But once they caught sight of his innovative use of Lego their expressions changed to surprise and awe as they admired the impressive six-line sequenced pattern. Here was a child with learning difficulties and very limited language skills producing a complex pattern.

'That's better than my house,' Paula said kindly.

'It's the work of a genius!' Lucy declared.

'Where did you get that idea from?' Adrian asked, obviously impressed.

Danny didn't answer.

I assumed Danny would be pleased with the praise and admiration he was receiving – most children would be – and that he would show it by smiling, but he didn't. His face remained expressionless, as it often was, and he continued to stare at the Lego pattern.

'Very good,' I said again. 'We'll leave it there while we have some dessert.'

'What is for dessert, Mum?' Adrian asked.

And before I could answer, without looking up, Danny said, 'Ice cream and chocolate pudding.'

'That's right, Danny,' I said. 'Well done. We're having ice cream and chocolate pudding. Let's go to the table and have some now.'

Although Danny hadn't acknowledged me when I'd mentioned dessert earlier in the car, he'd clearly taken it in and remembered what I'd said. His words had come out so quickly and on cue it was as though he'd had them ready at the forefront of his mind, for when they might be needed, whereas it seemed that if I said something new to him there was a delay before he responded, as though he needed time to process the information.

Leaving the Lego, Danny stood and we went into the kitchen-cum-dining-room where the children returned to the table and I went to the kitchen. I heated the chocolate pudding and spooned it into the dessert bowls, then added a generous helping of ice cream on top of each pudding. My children and I loved it served this way so that as the ice cream melted it created a delicious combination of taste and texture, hot and cold. I assumed Danny would like it too – all the other children we'd fostered had – but as the rest of us began eating Danny spent some time scraping the ice cream from the top of his pudding before he made a start. Then he ate the ice cream first, followed by the pudding.

'Do you prefer your ice cream separate?' I asked him.

He gave a small nod.

'I'll remember that for next time,' I said. 'If I forget you must tell me.'

It was only a small point but accommodating a child's preferences, likes and dislikes helps them settle in and feel part of the family. Danny finished all his pudding and scraped his bowl clean. I was pleased he'd eaten a good meal. He was very slim and needed to put on some weight.

It was after seven o'clock now and I thought I should start Danny's bedtime routine. He was only six years old and he'd had a very traumatic day. I was sure that once he'd slept in his room and enjoyed a good night's sleep everything wouldn't seem so strange to him and he'd start to feel better. I explained to him that it was time for bed and that I'd take him upstairs and help him get ready. He didn't look at me as I spoke – his gaze was down – but he seemed to be concentrating and taking it all in. I asked him if he'd like a bedtime story before we went up, but he shook his head.

'Would you like to see the other rooms in the house now?' I asked. He'd only been in the living room and the kitchen-cum-diner.

Danny shook his head again, but then asked, 'George?'

'George is in bed,' I said, hoping this was the right answer. 'And you'll see Mummy tomorrow at school,' I added.

'Daddy?' he asked.

'I expect Daddy's at your house.' I didn't know if this was true, but it seemed a reasonable assumption given that Danny lived with both his parents and it was evening. Danny accepted this.

'Would you like to say goodnight to Adrian, Paula and Lucy?' I asked him. He looked away awkwardly and didn't reply, so they said goodnight to him.

I offered Danny my hand to hold but he didn't take it, so I led the way into the hall. As we passed the living room he looked in to check on the Lego. 'We can leave the Lego as it is until tomorrow,' I said.

He gave a small nod, and then came with me down the hall. Adrian had previously taken Danny's holdall upstairs and placed it in his bedroom. As we passed the spot in the hall where the holdall had been Danny stopped and pointed.

'Your bag is in your bedroom,' I said.

Then he pointed to his coat, now hanging with ours on the coat stand. 'Your coat is with ours ready for when we go out in the morning,' I said.

He wasn't reassured and began waving his arms agitatedly.

'What's the matter?' I asked. 'Your coat will be safe there.'

He flapped his arms more vigorously and then began rocking back and forth on his heels while making a low humming noise, clearly heading for another tantrum.

'Enough, Danny,' I said firmly. 'I need to know what you want so I can help you.'

He started tugging at his coat, so I assumed he wanted it, but it was too high up for him to unhook.

'OK. Stop,' I said. 'I'll reach it down for you once you're calmer,' and I waited for him to relax. While giving him his coat wasn't an issue – he could take it upstairs with him if it made him feel more secure – I didn't want him to think that throwing a tantrum would get him what he wanted. He had some language skills and he needed to use them.

Gradually Danny grew still and became less agitated, so I took his coat from the stand and gave it to him. He didn't put it on or clutch it protectively to his chest as he had done before; instead, he began reaching up to the coat stand again.

'Do you want to hang it up yourself?' I asked, having seen many toddlers do this.

Danny nodded.

'Would you like me to lift you up so you can reach it?'

He nodded again.

He let me put my hands around his waist, and I lifted him up until he was high enough to hook his coat onto the stand. Then I set him on the floor again.

'Thank you,' he said quietly, without looking at me.

'You're welcome. It's always best to try to tell me what you want, then I'll know and can help you.'

I offered him my hand to hold to go upstairs but again he refused it, using the banister rail for support instead. Upstairs I showed him where the toilet was and asked him if he needed help. He shook his head, so I waited outside. I heard the toilet flush and then the taps run. He came out and I led the way to his bedroom.

'This is your bedroom,' I said. 'I hope you like it. It will be better once you've got your things around you.'

George

Danny didn't comment, nor did he look around the room, but he went to his holdall and unzipped it. At the top lay a soft-toy rabbit, which he picked up and held lovingly to his cheek.

'George,' he said with a small sigh, and for the first time since he'd arrived I saw him smile.

Chapter Four

Precise

I was upstairs for two hours helping Danny get ready for bed. He didn't have a huge amount in his holdall – there was a couple of changes of clothes, pyjamas, a towel and wash bag – but Danny insisted on unpacking it all himself, and he was very precise. First he spent some time deciding which drawers to put his clothes in, then he spent a long time arranging them and rearranging them until, mindful of the time, I began chivvying him along. Once he was satisfied that his clothes were in the right drawer and positioned correctly he spent more time arranging his soft toy rabbit on the pillow, repositioning it in a number of different places.

'It won't ever be quite the same as at your house,' I said, for clearly Danny couldn't replicate exactly what he had at home.

But Danny continued until he was satisfied, and then finally changed into his pyjamas, neatly folding the clothes he'd taken off and placing them squarely at the foot of his bed, as I guessed he did at home. Eventually we went round the landing and into the bathroom. I showed him where everything was, and he spent some time arranging his towel and wash things beside ours. He was probably the most precise and self-sufficient six-year-old I'd ever come across, yet at the same time there was a vulnerability about him that was younger than his years.

'You can have a bath tomorrow evening,' I told him. 'There isn't time tonight. A good wash will be fine for now.'

Danny didn't object and I placed the childstep in front of the hand basin so that he could comfortably reach into the bowl. He then spent some moments repositioning the step, squaring it, before he was satisfied and finally stood on it. I put the plug into the sink and turned on the taps. Danny turned them off, and then on again, wanting to do it himself.

'The water is hot,' I said, turning down the hot tap. 'I need to help you with this.' His face set; he didn't like my interference, but he was six, and in some things he had to accept my help for his own safety. 'Hot water can burn you,' I told him.

He didn't reply but stared blankly at the sink. I ran the water and checked the temperature. 'That's fine now,' I said. 'Do you want me to wash your face, or can you do it?'

There was pause before he picked up his flannel, folded it in half and half again, carefully submerged it in the water, squeezed it out and began washing his face. 'Good boy,' I said.

As Danny washed and dried his face and then cleaned his teeth, I saw there was something measured, almost ritualistic, in the way he performed the tasks. I guessed he carried them out exactly the same way every evening. In cleaning his teeth he carefully unscrewed the cap of his toothpaste, set the cap to one side, squirted a precise amount of paste onto his toothbrush, put down the brush, screwed the cap back on the paste and then began cleaning his teeth. Such exactness was very unusual for a child, and of course it was a slow process. I realized we would have to start the bedtime routine earlier in future. When Danny brushed his teeth the movement was so regular that it created a little rhythm as the brush went back and forth over his upper front teeth, then the left and right, and the same on his lower teeth. But he appeared content, as though he enjoyed the feel of it. I began to think he could continue indefinitely, so eventually I said, 'You've done a good job, Danny. You can rinse out now.'

There was a pause before he did as I'd asked. Then he patted his mouth dry on his towel and returned it to the rail, where he spent some moments squaring it before he was satisfied. I wondered how much of his precise and ritualistic behaviour was because he was anxious and how much was just part of Danny. He was certainly an unusual little fellow, and I clearly had a lot to learn about him.

It was now nearly nine o'clock, and while I'd been upstairs Adrian, Lucy and Paula had come up and were in their rooms getting ready for bed. As Danny and I went round the landing I pointed out everyone's bedrooms, but he didn't want to look in.

'If you need me in the night, call out and I'll come to you,' I said. 'There is a night light on the landing, but I don't want you wandering around by yourself. So call me if you need me.' I told all the children this on their first night, although given Danny's lack of language I doubted he would call me. I was a light sleeper, though, and usually woke if a child was out of bed. We continued into his bedroom. 'Do you want your curtains open or closed?' I asked him, as I asked all children when they first arrived.

Danny didn't reply and looked bewildered. 'They are closed now,' I said. 'Are they all right like that?'

He gave a small shake of the head and then went over to the curtains and parted them slightly.

I smiled. 'Good boy. I'll know what you want next time. Do you sleep with your light on or off?' This was also important for helping a child settle.

Danny didn't say anything but went to the light switch and dimmed it.

'That's fine,' I said. 'Is there anything else you need before you get into bed?'

He shook his head and climbed into bed, then snuggled down. He pulled the duvet right up over his head and drew the soft-toy rabbit beneath it.

'Won't you be too hot like that?' I asked him.

There was no reply.

I tried easing the duvet down a little away from his face so he could breathe, but he pulled it up over his head again.

'All right then, love. I'll say goodnight.' It was strange saying goodnight without being able to see his face. Often a child wanted a hug or a goodnight kiss, or, missing home, asked me to sit with them while they went off to sleep. Clearly Danny didn't want any of these.

'Night then, love,' I said to the lump in the duvet that was Danny. Silence. 'Do you want your door open or closed?' I asked before I left.

There was no answer, so I left the door slightly ajar and came out. I'd check on him later. Yet as I went round the landing to Paula's room I heard Danny get out of bed and quietly close his door. He had known what he wanted but hadn't been able to tell me. Whether this was from poor language skills, shyness or some other reason I couldn't say.

Once I'd checked that Paula, Lucy and Adrian were OK and getting ready for bed, I went downstairs. I would go up later when they were in bed to say goodnight. I was exhausted, but I knew I should write up my fostering notes before I went to bed while the events of the day were still fresh in my mind. All foster carers in England are asked to keep a daily log in respect of the child or children they are looking after. They record any significant events that have affected the child, the child's wellbeing and general development, as well as any appointments the child may have. It is a confidential document, and when the child leaves the foster carer it is sent to the social services, where it is held on file.

I sat on the sofa in the living room with a mug of tea within reach and headed the sheet of A4 paper with the date. I then recorded objectively how I'd collected Danny from school and the details of how he was gradually settling in, ending with the time he went to bed and his routine. I placed the sheet in the folder I'd already begun for Danny, and which would eventually contain all the paperwork I had on him. I returned the folder to the lockable draw in the front room and went upstairs to say goodnight to Paula, Lucy and Adrian. Then I checked on Danny. He was still buried beneath the duvet and, concerned he would be too hot and breathing stale air, I crept to the bed and slowly moved the duvet clear of his face. He was in a deep sleep and didn't stir. His cheeks were flushed pink, and his soft-toy rabbit lay on the pillow beside him. Danny looked like a little angel with his delicate features relaxed in sleep and his mop of light blond hair.

I checked on him again at 11.30 before I went to bed, and then when I woke at 2 a.m. Both times he was fast asleep, flat on his back, with his face above the duvet and soft-toy George beside him. I didn't sleep well – I never do when a child first arrives. I subconsciously listen out for the child in case they are upset. But as far as I was aware Danny slept soundly, and he was still asleep when my alarm went off at 6 a.m. I checked on him before I showered and dressed, then again before I went downstairs to feed Toscha and make myself a coffee. At 7 a.m., after I'd woken Adrian, Lucy and Paula, I knocked on Danny's door and went in. He was awake now, still lying on his back but with his arm around the soft toy and staring up at the ceiling.

'Good morning, love,' I said, going over to the bed. 'You slept well. Did you remember where you were when you woke?'

His gaze flickered in my direction, but he didn't make eye contact. Then he spoke, although it wasn't to answer my question.

'For breakfast I have cornflakes, with milk and half a teaspoon of sugar,' he said.

I smiled. He had clearly prepared this speech, and I wondered at the effort that must have gone into finding the correct words and then keeping them ready for when they were needed.

'That sounds good to me,' I said. 'I want you to wash and dress and then we'll go down and have breakfast.'

I looked at his little face as he concentrated on what I'd said and tried to work out if a response was needed, and if so, what.

'So the first thing you need to do is get out of bed,' I said. I appreciated that Danny needed clear and precise instructions. There was a moment's pause before Danny pushed back the duvet and got out of bed. 'Good boy,' I said. 'The next thing you need to do is go to the toilet and then the bathroom so you can have a wash.'

43

Danny turned, not towards the bedroom door but to where his clothes were at the foot of the bed. He stared at them anxiously.

'Do you usually put your clothes on first?' I asked him.

He nodded.

'That's fine, but you'll need clean clothes. I'll wash those.' I usually replaced the child's clothes with fresh ones when they took them off at night, but I hadn't had a chance the previous evening. I went to the chest of drawers where Danny had put his clean clothes and opened the drawer. Danny arrived beside me, wanting to take out what he needed himself.

'I'll put your dirty clothes in the laundry basket,' I said.

He shook his head and, setting down his clean clothes, picked up the dirty ones, again clearly wanting to do it himself. 'OK. I'll show you where to put your laundry,' I said. But Danny went ahead. I followed him round the landing and then waited just outside the bathroom while he put his clothes into the laundry basket. He'd obviously remembered seeing it the night before.

'Good boy,' I said.

He used the toilet and then we returned to his bedroom. I was on hand to help if necessary. Before he began dressing Danny laid out his clothes on the bed in the order in which they would go on. His vest at the top, beneath that his school shirt, then his jumper, pants, trousers and socks. I wondered if this was a system he'd thought of to help him dress or if it had been devised by his parents. Special needs children often struggle with sequencing tasks like this that appear simple to the rest of us; they can easily put their vest on over the top of their shirt, for example. Danny's system worked. Slowly but surely he dressed himself and didn't need my help.

'Well done,' I said as he finished.

He didn't reply but now concentrated on folding his pyjamas – precisely in half and half again – and then tucked them neatly under his pillow. He carefully positioned his soft toy, George, on his pillow and then drew up the duvet so just the little rabbit's face peeped out. After that he spent some moments readjusting the duvet until I said, 'Time to go downstairs for breakfast now.'

He finally stopped fiddling with the duvet and came with me. At the top of the stairs I offered him my hand, and for a second I thought he was going to take it, but then he took hold of the handrail instead. Because Danny was quite small he navigated the steps one at a time, as a much younger child would. He then came with me into the kitchen-cum-diner and went straight to his place at the table.

'Good boy,' I said again.

Adrian came down and took his place at the table. 'Hi, Danny,' he said. 'How are you?'

Danny didn't answer but did look in Adrian's direction.

'Toast and tea?' I asked Adrian, which was what he normally had for breakfast during the week.

'Yes please, Mum.'

In the kitchen I dropped two slices of bread into the toaster, poured Danny's cornflakes into a bowl, added milk and sugar and then placed the bowl on the table in front of him. He picked up his spoon and began eating, clearly used to eating cornflakes. 'What would you like to drink with your breakfast?' I asked Danny.

There was silence. His spoon hovered over his bowl and he concentrated hard before he said, 'I have a glass of milk with my breakfast.'

I poured the milk, gave it to Danny and then joined him and Adrian at the table. The girls came down and said hello to Danny, then poured themselves cereal and a drink. As we ate, Lucy and Paula tried to make conversation with Danny, asking him what he liked best at school and what his favourite television programmes were. He didn't answer, and I could see he was growing increasingly anxious at their questions, although of course they were only trying to be friendly and make him feel welcome. Danny appeared to be a child who needed to concentrate on one task at a time, and he finally stopped eating.

'I think Danny is finding our talk a bit much first thing in the morning,' I said as diplomatically as I could.

'I know the feeling,' Adrian added dryly.

'Watch it,' Lucy said jokingly, poking him in the ribs.

But the girls understood what I meant and not usually being great conversationalists themselves first thing in the morning, they left Danny to eat. Once I knew more about Danny's difficulties I'd be better equipped to explain them to Adrian, Lucy and Paula, and also to deal with them myself. At present I was relying on common sense and my experience as a foster carer.

As the children finished eating they left the table one at a time to go upstairs and carry on getting ready for school. I waited with Danny while he emptied his bowl of cornflakes and then drank his glass of milk.

'Good boy,' I said. 'Now it's time for you to go upstairs so you can wash and brush your teeth.'

'George?' he asked questioningly, glancing towards the back door.

'Do you feed George in the morning?' I asked.

He nodded.

'Your mummy will feed George today,' I said. 'I'll talk to her about George when I see her this morning at school.'

He accepted this, slid from his chair and then followed me down the hall and upstairs. In the bathroom he completed the tasks of washing and brushing his teeth in the same order and with the same precision as he had the previous evening.

Adrian, Lucy and Paula left for their respective secondary schools, calling goodbye as they went. Then, once Danny had finished in the bathroom, we went downstairs, where I told him we needed to put on our shoes and coats ready to go to school. I went to unhook his coat from the stand, but he put his hand on my arm to stop me. 'Of course,' I said, smiling. 'You want to do it yourself.'

I lifted him up and he unhooked his coat, then struggled into it, finally accepting my help to engage the zipper. He sat on the floor to put on his shoes, and when he'd finished I praised him. He put so much effort into everything he did, it was important he knew when he'd done well. He didn't have a school bag; I assumed it had been left at school.

'We're going outside, so hold my hand, please,' I said as I opened the front door.

He did as I asked and we went to my car on the driveway. I opened the rear door and Danny clambered into the child seat and then fastened his own seatbelt. I checked it was secure, closed his door and went round and climbed into the driver's seat. As I drove I reminded Danny what was going to happen that day (as far as I knew); that we were going to school where he would see his mother, and I was going into a meeting. Then at the end of the day I would collect him from school and bring him home with me. I didn't mention that Jill was visiting us at 4 p.m., as I thought it might overload him with information; I'd tell him after school. He didn't reply, but I knew he was taking it all in – his gaze was fixed and serious as he concentrated.

Although I was slightly anxious about meeting his mother for the first time, I was also looking forward to it. I would learn more about Danny, and hopefully I'd be able to work with his parents with the aim of eventually returning Danny home. Having looked after Danny for only one night, I appreciated how his parents might have struggled. Caring for Danny was hard work, and I'd had plenty of experience looking after children – many with special needs. Some parents are very angry when their child or children first go into care, although given that Danny had been placed in care voluntarily I didn't think that was likely. I thought his parents would probably be upset rather than angry, and I was right – although I was completely unprepared for just how upset Danny's mother would be.

Chapter Five

Absolute Hell

The school building and surrounding trees and shrubbery seemed a lot more welcoming now it was light than it had the evening before in darkness. Some parents were already in the playground chatting to each other while their children played before the start of lessons. I was planning on going straight into school with Danny that morning as the meeting started at nine o'clock, but as we entered the playground I heard Danny's name being called. I turned and saw a woman rushing towards us in tears. I guessed it was Danny's mother, Reva. She scooped him up and, holding him to her, buried her head in his shoulder and sobbed.

'Shall we go inside?' I suggested, touching her arm reassuringly. 'It'll be more private.' I could see others in the playground looking and I felt Danny's reunion with his mother – and her grief – needed some privacy.

'Yes, please,' Reva said quietly.

She carried Danny and we walked towards the main door. As we approached, it opened from inside and Sue Bright, Danny's teacher, came out. 'I've been looking out for you,' she said. 'Come in. We can use the medical room, it's free.'

'Thank you,' I said.

We followed Sue down a short corridor, turned left and entered the medical room, which was equipped with a couch, three chairs, a sink and a first-aid cupboard. Danny's mother sat on one of the chairs and held Danny on her lap, close to her. 'He must have missed me so much,' she said through her tears. 'He never normally lets me touch him.'

Danny said one word in a flat and emotionless voice: 'Mum.'

'Would you like some time alone?' Sue asked Reva.

'Yes, please,' she said.

'We'll come back in a few minutes when school starts,' Sue added.

I left the medical room with Sue and she closed the door behind us. 'Has he been very upset?' she asked me, concerned.

'More quiet and withdrawn, really,' I said. 'But he slept well, and has been eating.'

Sue nodded. 'Danny is often withdrawn in school; that's one of his problems.'

'Has there been an assessment?' I asked.

'Not yet.' She paused. 'Would you mind waiting until the meeting to talk about this? It's complicated and I need to see to my class soon.'

'That's fine, of course,' I said.

'Thanks. His social worker, Terri, is on her way. She'll be about five minutes. Once school starts Danny can join his class, and then we can have our meeting. We'll use the staff room. It'll be empty once school begins. We're only a small school and a bit short of space. Are you all right to wait here while I bring my class in from the playground?'

'Yes, go ahead.'

'I'll be about ten minutes.'

Absolute Hell

Sue disappeared around the corner and I waited in the small corridor outside the medical room. While I waited I looked at the children's art work that adorned most of every wall. Although it was only a small school it came across as being very friendly and child-centred. Danny's teacher, Sue, seemed really kind and caring, as had the other staff I'd briefly met the evening before. My thoughts went to Danny's mother, Reva, who unlike Danny was quite tall, but also slender. She was in her late thirties and was dressed smartly in a grey skirt and matching jacket. I felt sorry for her. She was so upset; she and her husband must have had a sleepless night, counting the hours until they could see Danny again. Her husband wasn't with her, but Terri had said there was going to be regular contact, so he would see Danny before too long.

A whistle sounded in the playground signalling the start of school, and presently I heard the clamour of children's voices as they filed into the building and went to their classrooms. Then Sam, the caretaker I'd briefly met the evening before, appeared at the end of the corridor. 'How's the little fellow doing?' he asked cheerfully.

'He's doing all right,' I smiled.

'Good for you. You foster carers do a fantastic job. I know – I was brought up in care.' And with a nod and a smile he went off to go about his duties. That was a nice comment, I thought.

Five minutes later the school was quiet as the first lesson began. Sue appeared with Terri and we said good morning. 'How's Danny been?' Terri asked.

'Quiet,' I said. 'But he ate and slept well, and we only had one tantrum.'

'Good. Have you met his mother, Reva?'

'Just briefly in the playground. She's very upset.'

Terri nodded. 'Shall we get started then? I have to be away by ten-thirty as I have another meeting at eleven.'

Sue knocked on the door to the medical room and she and Terri went in, while I waited at the door. I could see Danny was now sitting on a chair beside his mother. They both had their hands in their laps, and were quiet and still.

'Danny, I'll take you to your class now,' Sue said gently.

Danny obediently stood.

'Say goodbye to your mother,' Sue said.

'Goodbye,' Danny said in a small, flat voice and without looking at her.

'Goodbye, love,' she called after him. 'I'll see you later.'

Danny didn't reply or show any emotion but walked quietly away with his teacher.

'Will you show Reva and Cathy to the staff room?' Sue said to Terri. 'I'll join you there once I've taken Danny to his class.'

'Bye, love,' Danny's mother called again as he left, but Danny didn't reply.

'How are you?' Terri now asked Reva as she stood, looping her handbag over her shoulder.

She shrugged and dabbed her eyes with a tissue.

'You've met Cathy,' Terri said to her.

She nodded, tears glistening in her eyes.

'Hello, Reva,' I said with a smile.

I could see the family resemblance between her and Danny – the same mouth and eyes.

'I did my best for him,' she said as we left the medical room. 'Really I did, but I've failed.' Her tears fell.

'You haven't failed,' I said. 'Danny is a lovely boy, but I can appreciate just how much it takes to look after him.'

'You don't blame me then?' she said, slightly surprised.

'No, of course not.'

'No one blames you,' Terri added. 'I've told you that.'

'My husband does,' Reva said.

'For what?' Terri asked.

'Having an autistic son.'

Reva and I went with Terri to the staff room where we settled around the small table that sat at one end of the room and waited for Sue. The staff room was compact, with pigeonhole shelving overflowing with books and papers, and pin boards on the walls covered with notices, leaflets and flyers. On a cabinet stood a kettle beside a tray containing mugs and a jar of coffee. But like the rest of the school the staff room emanated a cosy, warm feeling, easily making up for what it lacked in size. Reva, sitting opposite me, had dried her eyes now, but I could see she wasn't far from tears. Terri, to her right, had taken out a notepad and was writing. I felt I needed to say something positive to Reva to try to reassure her.

'Danny did very well last night,' I said. 'Our house was obviously all new to him, but he coped well. He ate dinner with us and then played with some Lego.'

'Terri said it took ages to find him on the playing field,' Reva said despondently. 'Danny's good at running off and hiding. You'll need to be careful.'

'I'll remember that,' I said. Although I'd rather guessed that might be the case.

'You'll have to lock all your doors and windows or he'll run off outside and you'll never find him,' Reva said.

'Don't worry,' I reassured her. 'My house is secure. He'll be safe.' Foster carers are not allowed to lock children in the house even for their own safety, but I knew that Danny couldn't reach to open the front and back doors, and I would be keeping a close eye on him. 'I like his method of dressing,' I said to Reva, again focusing on the positive. 'Did you and your husband teach him to do that?'

'I did,' Reva said softly.

Terri looked at us questioningly and I explained how Danny had laid out his clothes in the order he should put them on.

'Very good,' Terri said. 'Does that work for him at school too – after games?' she asked.

'I think his classroom assistant helps him,' Reva said.

The door opened and Sue came in carrying a file. 'Sorry to keep you,' she said. 'Danny is with his class now.' She smiled at Reva as she sat next to me.

'Are we expecting anyone else?' Terri asked.

'My support social worker can't make it,' I said. 'I'm seeing her later so I'll update her then.'

'Is Danny's father joining us?' Terri now asked Reva.

'No,' she said, but she didn't add why.

'Let's get started then,' Terri said. 'I thought this meeting would give us a chance to discuss how we can best help Danny. The three of us and his father are the key people in Danny's life right now. I'll make a few notes as we go, but I want to keep this meeting informal. I'm in the process of drawing up a care plan, and as a child in care Danny will have regular reviews.' She glanced at Reva. 'We'll talk about contact arrangements later. Cathy, as Reva didn't have a chance to meet you before Danny came to you, perhaps you'd like to start by telling her a little about your family and home life?'

'Yes, certainly,' I said. I sat slightly forward and looked at Reva as I spoke. 'I have three children – a boy, fifteen, and two girls, thirteen and eleven, and a cat, Toscha. She doesn't bite or scratch. I'm divorced and have been fostering for over fifteen years now. I live in …' I briefly described my house and then my family's routine, and the types of things we liked to do at the weekends. 'Danny will, of course, be included in all family activities and outings,' I said. 'Whether it's a visit to a local park or to see my parents. Danny's bedroom is at the rear of the house and overlooks the garden, so it is quiet and has a nice view. He'll be able to play in the garden when the weather is good. Last night before Danny went to bed I showed him where my bedroom was in case he needed me in the night, but he slept through. It was a good idea packing his toy rabbit, George,' I concluded positively, smiling at Reva. 'That helped him to settle.'

'Did he ask for the real George?' Reva asked.

'Yes. I had to show him he wasn't outside.'

Terri looked at us, puzzled.

'George is Danny's pet rabbit,' Reva said to Terri. 'They're inseparable. I did tell Danny he couldn't take him to Cathy's. I think that was one of the reasons he kicked me and ran off and hid yesterday.'

I looked at Terri. 'I know it's not usual fostering practice,' I said, 'but I was thinking that if Reva and her husband agreed then perhaps George could come and stay with us too? He means so much to Danny. It could help him settle.'

'Oh, would you?' Reva cried. 'I'd be so grateful. Danny loves his rabbit more than anything – probably more than he loves me.'

'Are you sure that's all right?' Terri asked me.

'Yes. I don't mind pets, and George lives in his hutch outside.'

'Danny likes to bring him into the house sometimes,' Reva said. 'But he doesn't make much mess.'

'I'm sure it will be fine,' I said.

'If it doesn't work out you can always return it to Reva,' Terri said.

I met Reva's gaze and we both knew that wasn't an option. It would be devastating for a child like Danny to be allowed to have his beloved pet stay and then have to return him home while he remained in care. He wouldn't cope.

'It'll be fine,' I said again.

'Well, if you're sure,' Terri said. 'I'll leave the two of you to make arrangements at the end of this meeting to collect George.'

'Thank you,' Reva said to me.

I thought the meeting had got off to a good start and that George was now one less thing for Reva to worry about, but then her face clouded and she began to cry.

'I'm sorry,' she said, taking a fresh tissue from her handbag. 'You're all being so nice to me and trying to help. I really don't deserve it.'

'Of course you deserve it,' Terri said. 'We all want to help you and Danny. You must stop blaming yourself. It's not your fault Danny is as he is.' Then to Sue, Terri said, 'Would you like to tell us a bit about how Danny is doing in school? I expect Cathy will want to help him with his homework.'

'We don't actually set Danny homework as such,' she said. 'More targets to work towards, in line with his individual education plan. Reva has a copy of the plan and I can have one printed for Cathy, if that's all right with Reva?'

Reva nodded.

Sue made a note of this and then said, 'Danny has been in this school a year. He arrived after his parents moved into the area with his father's job. At present Danny is working towards a reception-level standard. He is difficult to assess educationally because of his communication difficulties, but he is about two to three years behind his peer group. He tries his best but finds the core subjects of English, maths and science very challenging, although I adapt all the work to suit his needs. He does like art, especially drawing, painting and creating patterns. He's very good at making patterns. Danny has communication and language difficulties – both receptive and expressive – so we have to pace his learning to fit him. His teaching assistant, Yvonne, is good with him and has endless patience. Danny is uncoordinated and finds games lessons difficult, but he likes a good run around the playing field.'

'Yes, I noticed that last night,' Terri said dryly.

I smiled.

'Tell them about his meltdowns,' Reva now said.

Sue looked at me. 'Danny can become frustrated when he is unable to express himself or there is too much going on for him, and he has a "meltdown". Yvonne and I have become adept at spotting the warning signs and can sometimes distract him to avoid it, but not always. He'll lie on the floor, scream and shout and lash out at anyone who goes near him. It's very upsetting for him, and for us to witness.'

'He does it at home as well,' Reva said. 'And in public, in the street and in shops. Everyone stares. I know they blame me for not controlling him properly, but I don't know what to do.' She was close to tears again.

'As an experienced and specialist foster carer you'll be able to cope with Danny's behaviour, won't you?' Terri said to me.

'Yes,' I said confidently, although I was feeling far from confident inside.

'Danny finds it difficult to make friends,' Sue continued. 'The children in the class are very tolerant of him and kind, but he doesn't have a proper friend. He doesn't understand how to make friends, although Yvonne has tried to show him. In the playground he keeps close to her or one of the other assistants. He can easily become overwhelmed by all the noise and activity, so we often bring him in early. He eats his lunch with the other children in the dining hall, but he takes a long time and is usually the last to finish.' My heart clenched as I imagined little Danny sitting all alone in a big dining room while the other children were outside playing. 'Yvonne or one of the other assistants stays with him until he's finished,' Sue said. 'There are a lot of unknowns with Danny and at times he's very difficult to reach. The school would like the educational psychologist to assess him so that we're all in a better position to help him meet his full potential. But we need the parents' permission for that assessment.'

Which begged the question: why hadn't his parents given permission?

Terri turned to Reva. 'Is your husband still not happy with Danny being assessed?'

'He won't,' Reva said. 'He is ashamed. He refuses to admit anything is wrong with Danny.'

'I'll have a chat with him and explain why it's important Danny is assessed,' Terri said, making a note. Then looking at Sue she said, 'Is that everything for now?'

'I think so.'

'Thank you,' Terri said. Then she turned to Reva: 'Would you like to say a bit about Danny? Perhaps tell Cathy about his likes and dislikes, and his routine. Anything you think may help her look after Danny.'

'Yes,' Reva said. 'I've made a few notes.' She unhooked her shoulder bag from the back of her chair and, opening it, slid out a thick wodge of papers. 'This is Danny's daily routine,' she said, passing it across the table to me. 'It never alters.'

'Thank you,' I said, taking it. I began flipping through. Usually a parent will say a few words about their child's routine, very occasionally they'll give me some notes, but never in all my years of fostering had I seen anything this detailed before: twenty-three pages of A4 paper covered in small print.

'Perhaps you could read it later,' Terri said, aware of the volume of paperwork.

I nodded and smiled at Reva. 'Thank you. This will be helpful.'

'Is there anything you want to add to what you've written?' Terri asked Reva.

I assumed there wouldn't be, given the detail in the paper-work, but Reva said, 'Yes. That's just Danny's routine. Cathy also needs to know what it's like looking after Danny. I mean, what it's *really* like.' She paused, and I saw her bottom lip tremble. 'It's been hell,' she said. 'Absolute hell. It's a night-mare looking after Danny. I know it's my fault, and some days I wish he'd never been born.' Her face crumpled into tears.

Chapter Six

Prisoners

My heart went out to Reva. She was clearly carrying a huge burden of guilt and self-blame for Danny's problems, and appeared to be at her wits' end, and close to breaking point. Terri, Sue and I tried to reassure her, but her feelings of inadequacy were too deeply ingrained, and I wondered how much of this was a result of her husband's attitude. Reva's previous comment about him blaming her for having an autistic son weighed heavily in my thoughts. The last thing the poor woman needed was to be blamed by her partner; she needed all the help and support she could get.

Presently Reva dried her eyes and was composed enough to continue. 'Danny cried a lot as a baby. I thought all babies cried, but my husband, Richard, said his other two children hadn't cried as much as Danny did. He was married before. Danny's my only child, so I had nothing to compare him to. But I became exhausted – up most of the night, every night. Danny didn't seem to need much sleep. I read all the books I could find on parenting. I felt I must be doing something wrong, and if I'm honest Danny's crying scared me. It seemed as if he wanted something and I should be able to work out what it was. He was out of control when he screamed, even as a baby, and there was nothing I could do to help him.'

'Didn't you have anyone you could talk to?' Terri asked.

'Not really. I discussed it with my mother when we spoke on the phone, but she said babies often cried for no reason. She lives over a hundred miles from us, so we don't see her very often. She's not a hands-on grandmother. Richard's job was very demanding – it still is – and I'd given up work to look after Danny, so I got up in the night and did most of the parenting. I do now. I tried to keep Danny quiet, because if Richard went to work tired he couldn't function. I couldn't function either. I asked the health visitor about Danny's crying and she said it was nothing to worry about, that it was probably a bit of colic. The gripe water she recommended didn't help, and Danny kept crying for large parts of every day and most nights until he was eighteen months old. Then it suddenly stopped and he became very quiet and withdrawn. He had some language by then and was starting to put words together into little sentences – you know the sort of thing: "Daddy go work", "Danny want biscuit", "Mummy cooking." But he suddenly stopped talking and would point to what he wanted and make a noise instead. I tried to encourage him to use words, but he would stare through me as though he hadn't a clue what I was talking about.'

'Had anything traumatic happened to Danny at that time?' Terri asked.

'I've wondered that, but I can't think of anything,' Reva said. 'Danny was with me all day and night. I would have known if something had happened. There was nothing.'

Terri nodded. 'OK. I just wondered.'

'Although Danny had stopped talking,' Reva continued, 'and was very quiet for long periods and all night, he'd started having tantrums. He would throw himself on the floor, screaming, and bang his head on the ground, the wall, a cupboard – any hard object within reach. It was frightening, and when I tried to pick him up he'd lash out, kick and punch me, pull my hair and bite and claw me as though I was attacking him and he had to fight me off. My beautiful baby boy. I was devastated. He's stopped the clawing, but he still does the other things when he's frustrated and upset.' Reva paused.

'At school we do all we can to encourage Danny to use language to express himself – if he wants something or is upset,' Sue said.

'So do I,' Reva said a little brusquely. 'But it's different at school. There are other children here and Danny has respect for you. At home it's just him and me, and he doesn't have respect for me. He does what he wants, and if he won't talk to me there is nothing I can do about it.'

'Does he talk to your husband?' Terri asked.

'Sometimes, a little. But he only sees him for a few minutes in the evening, and at the weekends, when Richard's not playing golf. Danny doesn't talk like other children his age do. He doesn't have a conversation; he repeats what you say or nods or comes out with half-sentences and words that don't make any sense. Then he gets frustrated because you don't understand what he wants, and that leads to a tantrum. Yet he can talk to George or himself. Danny would rather talk to himself or his rabbit than to me.'

'Does Danny smile or laugh or show his feelings?' Terri asked.

'Not often. His expression is usually blank. Sometimes he'll suddenly laugh but it's not at the right time or in the right context, if you know what I mean. He can laugh loudly – cackle – for no obvious reason. He does it in public. It's so embarrassing. It's impossible to know if Danny is happy or not, and he doesn't show physical affection normally. He'll let you touch him sometimes, but only on his terms. He let me hold him in the playground just now and carry him into school, but I can't remember the last time he let me cuddle him. It's as though he doesn't want or need anyone else. Not even his mother.'

'I'm sure he does need you,' I said. 'But he has difficulty showing it.'

Terri and Sue nodded in agreement.

'But other children kiss and hug their mothers,' Reva blurted, her eyes filling again. 'I've seen them in the playground kissing and hugging their parents goodbye when it's time to go into school. Danny just turns and walks away with his classroom assistant. She has to tell him to say goodbye to me. He shouldn't need telling. Other children don't, but Danny seems to have no empathy or feelings. If I cry in front of him, he just looks at me.' Reva was in tears again.

'I'm sure Danny does feel things,' Terri said seriously, looking at Reva, 'just as you and I do, but the difference is Danny can't express them. It's a trait of autism, if that is what Danny has.'

'And he does love you, just as other children love their parents,' I added, trying to console Reva.

'How can you be so sure?' she demanded, taking another tissue from her bag. 'You've only just met Danny. Wait until you know him better, you'll see. He'll be as cold to you as he is to me.'

I didn't reply. Reva was very upset and didn't mean to be rude.

'Sorry,' she said after a moment.

'It's OK,' I said. 'I can appreciate how upsetting Danny's behaviour is for you.'

'Have you fostered anyone like him before?' Reva now asked, wiping her eyes.

'No two children are the same,' I said. 'But I have seen some of Danny's behaviour in other children.'

'Do you think he is autistic?' she asked me.

'I don't know. And it would be wrong for me to guess.'

'The education psychologist is the person who should make the diagnosis,' Terri put in. 'I'll speak to your husband about it.' I saw Terri glance at her watch. She had to leave in fifteen minutes to go to her other meeting. 'We still need to talk about contact,' she said. 'But before we do, are there any strategies you've found particularly helpful in managing Danny's behaviour that you would like to pass on to Cathy?'

Reva shrugged. 'Not really. I just do what Danny wants to keep the peace, but that doesn't always work either.'

It won't, I thought but didn't say. Boundaries for good behaviour are essential for all children; as well as socializing the child they show them that the parent cares, whatever syndrome or condition the child may have. I knew Reva had developed some strategies for managing Danny's behaviour, although she probably didn't realize it.

'You taught Danny how to put on his clothes in the correct order,' I now said to her. 'That's important. Without it Danny would become frustrated, which could lead to a tantrum. So that's a useful strategy.'

Reva looked at me thoughtfully. 'I suppose you're right,' she said. 'I hadn't really thought of it that way.'

'And you've taught Danny a workable bedtime routine that includes him washing his face, brushing his teeth and getting ready for bed,' I said. 'These are all strategies that help him to cope with daily tasks that are simple to us but not to Danny. You taught him all of that.'

A faint smile crossed Reva's face. 'Have you noticed how methodical Danny is?' she said. 'He loves doing things in order. Patterns and order are his lifeline. Mealtimes used to be a nightmare, but then we discovered that as long as he can eat his food in order of colour he's fine. He always starts by eating the palest food first and then the darker. It takes him a while, but it works.'

I now realized that that was what Danny must have been doing at dinner the evening before when he'd arranged the components of the casserole around the edge of his plate. He'd eaten them a pile at a time, the lightest first: chicken, potatoes, carrots and then peas.

'So you've created quite a few strategies to help him without realizing it,' Terri said.

'I suppose I have,' Reva said, and her eyes filled again. But this time her emotion wasn't from despair; it was the realization that she had been doing some things right after all. 'Thank you,' she said, looking at me.

'There's no need to thank me. You're the one who's been helping Danny to cope all these years.'

And her look of gratitude made my own eyes fill.

'Well done, Reva,' Terri said, and Sue smiled. 'Now to contact,' Terri said. I took my diary and pen from my handbag and opened it on the table in front of me. 'You and your husband obviously want to see Danny regularly,' Terri said to Reva. 'So I suggest we set contact at two evenings a week, and one day at the weekend. The care plan is for Danny to return home as soon as possible, so we need to keep the bond between you strong. We can review the contact arrangements as we go and adjust them up once Danny is more settled.'

Reva nodded.

'I suggest Tuesday and Thursday evening after school, starting tomorrow,' Terri said. 'Reva, if you collect Danny from school on those nights and take him home and give him dinner, then return him to Cathy's at about six o'clock, then he'll have a little while to settle before he has to go to bed.'

'And time to feed George,' I put in, aware this was going to be part of Danny's evening routine.

'Yes, absolutely,' Reva agreed.

'Good,' Terri said, making a note. I also wrote the arrangements in my diary. 'I was going to suggest telephone contact on the nights Danny doesn't see you,' Terri said. 'But I'm not sure Danny would cope with it.'

'No, he doesn't use the telephone,' Reva said. 'It frightens him.'

'OK, so no telephone contact,' Terri confirmed as she wrote. 'Which day of the weekend would suit you and your husband best?' she now asked Reva. 'When does Richard play golf?'

'Sunday mainly.'

'So we'll make the weekend contact on Saturday. Cathy will bring Danny to you and you can return him.'

I wrote this in my diary.

'As routine is so important to Danny,' Terri said, 'it's essential we all keep to the contact agreements.'

Even for a child in care under a Section 20, where the parents retain full legal responsibility for the child, it is important to adhere to the timetable of contact, otherwise the child can become very unsettled (for example, if the parents keep changing contact arrangements, or suddenly turn up at the foster carer's home wanting to see the child or take them out).

'Is it for the whole day on Saturday?' Reva asked, concerned.

'Yes,' Terri said. 'I'm thinking ten o'clock till six. Why? Is there a problem?'

'I hope I can cope,' Reva said, her brow creasing.

'Your husband can help you with Danny,' Terri said, looking at her seriously.

'Yes,' Reva said uncertainly.

'If you feel you are not coping then telephone Cathy and she'll come and collect Danny, or you can return him early.'

Reva gave a small, unconvincing nod, and I thought that many of Reva's problems in coping with Danny seemed to come from her lack of self-confidence in her ability to meet his needs.

'I'm sure everything will be fine,' Terri said. 'Now, if there is nothing else, I need to be going. I'll leave the two of you to make the arrangements to collect George.' She glanced around the table, but no one had anything to add so she put away her notebook and pen. 'I'll need to visit you both,' she said to Reva and me as she stood. 'I'll phone to arrange the appointments. Reva, can you ask Richard when he is available. I need him to be present when I see you.'

'Yes,' Reva said in a small voice. 'He's very busy, though.'

'So am I,' Terri said. I could understand why she sounded terse. Danny's home life had deteriorated to the point where he'd had to come into care, so surely his father should be doing everything in his power to get him home again as soon as possible, including making time for the social worker.

'Can I see Danny to say goodbye before I go?' Reva now asked Terri.

'Yes, that's fine with me,' Terri said, and looked at Sue.

'Come down to the classroom when you've finished talking to Cathy,' Sue said. 'Yvonne will bring Danny out to you.'

'Thank you,' Reva said. 'I won't keep him long.'

Sue smiled, then she and Terri said goodbye to us and left the staff room.

I looked across the table at Reva. She seemed marginally more relaxed now there was just the two of us. 'Do you want to bring George to my house or shall I collect him?' I asked her.

'Can you collect him, please?' she said. 'I didn't like to say it in front of Terri but my car is a sports car and the hutch won't fit in the boot.'

'No worries,' I said. 'I'll come to you. My car is a hatchback, so I'm sure George and his hutch will fit in the back.'

'Thank you. Do you have my address?'

'Not yet. Jill, my support social worker, is bringing the placement forms this evening.'

Reva reached into her shoulder bag and took out a business card, which she passed to me. I read the smart black embossed lettering. Below her name was printed 'Corporate Hospitality' and then her contact details.

'I had some notion I would work freelance after I had Danny,' she said with a small, dismissive laugh. 'So I had the cards printed. But it's been impossible. I still have most of the cards.'

'Were you in the corporate hospitality business before?' I asked, making conversation.

'Yes, that's where I met Richard. He was one of my clients. I was good at my job. Far better than I am at being a mother. I should have known when I was well off.'

'You're doing fine,' I said encouragingly. 'You've got very tired and weighed down by all of Danny's needs. I've only had Danny for one night, but already I can see how much attention and patience he requires. Once you've had a break and time to recharge your batteries I'm sure you'll feel better and see things differently.'

'I hope so,' she said with a sigh. 'I'm in such a dark place right now. I'm no good to anyone – not Richard or Danny.'

'Give yourself time,' I said again.

'I'll try. Thank you, and thanks for having George. What time do you want to come to collect him tomorrow?'

'Shall we say about eleven?'

'That's fine. I'm in most days. I've little reason to go out. I'll give you some of Danny's toys and more of his clothes. I wasn't thinking straight yesterday. Have you got enough for now?'

'Yes. Plenty.'

'I'll go and see Danny now then. It'll be strange not having to come to school to collect him this afternoon.'

'Try not to worry,' I said. 'I'll take good care of him.'

'I know you will, and you'll do a better job of it than me.'

There was little more I could say right now to help Reva, for, as she'd admitted, she was in a 'dark place' and felt a failure as a mother, wife and, I suspected, as a person too. I assumed Terri would have advised Reva to see a doctor if she felt she needed help with depression. It wasn't for me to suggest it to her. We stood and left the staff room. At the end of the corridor we said goodbye to each other, and Reva went to Danny's classroom while I went towards reception and then out of the school.

Once home I made a cup of coffee and took it to the table, together with Reva's notes. I began reading as I sipped my coffee. There was so much detail. Too much detail. I flicked through. Every minute of every day was accounted for, with lengthy, painstaking instructions on what to do and what not to do in every situation. Mealtimes included how to position Danny's cutlery the way he liked it to avoid a tantrum, and the morning routine included what to say to Danny when I woke him, and then again at night when he went to bed. Reva had written how I should greet him at the end of the school day, and that I shouldn't ask what he'd done at school as he didn't like that and could become angry. I should say, 'We're going home in the car, Danny,' but then I had to remain silent as we walked to the car, because he didn't like to be talked to. I had to let him open the car door himself, and I wasn't to help him climb in, or touch his seatbelt, as it annoyed him. Reva had also noted that it took Danny a long time to fasten his seatbelt due to his lack of coordination, and consequently she always made sure she parked her car with the passenger door on the pavement side so she didn't have to stand in the road while she waited for him to fasten it. And so it continued, page after page …

While some of what Reva had written would be helpful – for example, Danny's bath-time routine, the toys he enjoyed playing with and the television programme that most engaged him – much of it was too regimented to be of use in my household. My family was very different to Reva's, and I couldn't expect my children to change their lives to revolve around Danny's routine. I also felt that so much regimentation was stifling. To have every minute of every hour accounted for meant there was no room for creativity or impulsive or impromptu actions. Yet I could see why Reva had run their lives like this. There's a feeling of safety in the familiar and predictable. She was in a fragile state and had desperately clung to what she knew worked as a coping mechanism. The downside was that she and Danny were hostages to his behaviour – prisoners locked in their routine.

Chapter Seven
Crisis Averted

*B*efore children were diagnosed with conditions such as autism, Asperger's, bipolar disorder, special needs, development delay, specific learning difficulties or many of the other syndromes we can now identify, they were referred to as backward, retarded or mentally defective. These are terms we wouldn't use now. They're considered derogatory. Yet in our ignorance was a certain freedom for the child and those involved with him or her. Without the diagnosis (or label) we have today, the child's parents, extended family, community and teachers acknowledged there was something 'wrong' with the child and then accommodated and modified their behaviour. True, some of these children ended up in institutions, but the majority remained with their families, where allowances for their different, unusual and sometimes bizarre behaviour were made by those who came into contact with them. I had an older cousin – he's dead now – who today would probably have been diagnosed with an autistic-spec-trum disorder and learning difficulties. But back then he was just Pete. He lived all his life with his mother – my aunt – and worked a few mornings a week sticking down envelopes. He never spoke much, made some very odd noises and often appeared to be in a world of his own. He seemed happy enough, though, and laughed – sometimes at the most inappropriate moments (once at a funeral). We all loved Pete and accepted him for what he was. I remember that as a child he seemed to me to be a big kid, who was always ready for a game. Would he have benefited from a diagnosis? We won't ever know. But I do wonder if we're over-diagnosing now, so that any child who doesn't fit neatly into the 'norm' must have something 'wrong' with them that needs a diagnosis so we can 'put it right'.

Obviously children have to learn socially acceptable behaviour, but there is a huge spectrum of conduct that could be described as unusual, eccentric or just odd. And after all it's our oddities and eccentricities that make us who we are – individuals. I'd just begun my journey with Danny, and Reva had coped as best she could for all of Danny's life, but by the time I'd read to the end of Reva's notes I'd made the decision that I wouldn't be using them much. As well as the rigidity of the routine being impractical in my household, I realized I'd be making a rod for my own back, as indeed Reva had. For, once in place, these routines had to be adhered to, because, as Reva had found, any changes were confusing and upsetting for Danny. I had the advantage of being able to start afresh, without the history and emotional baggage that had blighted Reva and Danny's relationship.

I put away the notes and then gave some thought to what I should make for dinner that evening. Jill was coming at 4 p.m. – I needed something quick and easy that we could have soon after she'd gone so we wouldn't be eating too late. I realized that the casserole I'd made the evening before hadn't been the best choice of meal for Danny (who liked his food

separate), but he'd coped. Reva had included in her notes that
Danny's diet was limited and that I should not give him meals
where the food was combined, for example, spaghetti
bolognese, cottage pie, porridge, rice pudding, etc. – many of
the dishes my family and I enjoyed. While I would be making
changes to Danny's diet to give him a better variety and therefore standard of nutrition, I knew I shouldn't make too many
changes too quickly, so I decided on fish fingers and chips,
which Reva had listed as one of Danny's favourites. I'd add
green beans for their vitamin content, and then for pudding
we could have yoghurt and fruit, which Danny also ate,
according to Reva's notes.

Later that afternoon as I drove to collect Danny from school I
thought again of Reva's notes. She'd written that I had to
stand in a particular place in the playground to wait for
Danny while Yvonne or one of the other classroom assistants
brought him out to me. The spot where I had to wait was at
the top end of the hopscotch design, which apparently was
painted in red on the playground, and which the children
presumably played on at break. I hadn't noticed the hopscotch
design that morning, but then I'd been preoccupied with
Danny and Reva.

I arrived ten minutes early and found the design easily. I
stood, as I'd been told, at the top of the number ten box and
waited for school to finish. As the playground filled with
other parents and carers arriving to collect their children, I
noticed that they waited some distance from where I was
standing, over to the right and in front of the main door
where the children would eventually come out. I began to feel
slightly isolated on my hopscotch island and wondered why

Crisis Averted

Reva hadn't arranged a more sociable pick-up point, closer to the other parents. I'm someone who likes a chat and I spend a lot of time waiting in school playgrounds to collect the children I foster, so I usually find it isn't long before I'm in conversation with another parent or carer. But there was no chance of that here. I'd need a loud-hailer to be heard by them.

The klaxon sounded from inside the school, and presently, the main door opened and the children started coming out. Danny was among the first, his coat zipped up and a large school bag over his shoulder that was nearly as big as him. He was holding the hand of a lady I took to be a classroom assistant. They looked in my direction and, seeing me, came across the playground. With his mop of blond hair, delicate features and slight build, Danny looked younger than six, especially compared to the other children, who appeared so robust as they ran shouting and laughing into the arms of their parents.

'Hello, I'm Yvonne, Danny's classroom assistant,' the woman accompanying him said with a cheerful smile as they arrived. 'You must be Cathy, Danny's carer?'

'Yes, hello. Lovely to meet you.'

'And you.'

'Sue asked me to give you this.' Yvonne handed me an envelope. 'It's a copy of Danny's education plan.'

'Thank you.'

'Danny has his reading book and the flash cards we're working on in his bag. We keep the same book and cards for a week, so there's no pressure to do the work every night. Just see how it goes.'

'That's great,' I said. 'We've got a social worker visiting this evening, so we may not have a lot of time.' Then, including Danny in the conversation, I said, 'Have you had a good day?' Which is what I asked all my children at the end of the school day.

I was expecting a nod or possibly a blank stare, but to my surprise Danny said, 'Yes, thank you very much.'

Yvonne smiled. 'It's the phrase of the day,' she said. 'Danny often has a pet phrase he uses all day, sometimes for a few days, and then it changes.'

'Well, it's a nice polite phrase, so that's good. How has he been after the trauma of yesterday?'

'All right, I think,' Yvonne said. 'Although it's sometimes difficult to tell what he's feeling. There's an exercise book in his bag that we use as a home school book. Record in it anything you think might be helpful to us and we'll do the same. Reva used to do it, but I suppose you will now.' I nodded. 'I've made a note of today's events in the book.'

'Thank you. That's useful.'

I'd immediately warmed to Yvonne. She was a middle-aged, mumsy type of lady who clearly had a very big heart, loved her job and, I guessed, had endless patience. I knew that children could become very close to their classroom assistants, or teaching assistants as they are also known. Danny clearly had; he was still holding her hand.

'I'll see you tomorrow then?' Yvonne said, with another cheerful smile.

'Yes, in the morning,' I said. 'Then Reva will collect Danny after school and take him home for contact. I'll explain the arrangements to Danny in the morning, but perhaps you could remind him at the end of school that his mother will be collecting him.'

'Yes, of course.'

'Yes, thank you very much,' Danny put in, having heard, and Yvonne threw me a knowing smile.

'Goodbye then, Danny, have a good evening,' she said, and went to pass his hand to me, but Danny snatched it away. 'Now, now,' she lightly cautioned him. 'There's a busy road out there. You know you need to hold Cathy's hand.' But Danny jabbed both his hands into his coat pockets. 'He can run off,' Yvonne said quietly to me, obviously concerned for Danny's safety.

'I know. Don't worry, I'm prepared.' Then more loudly, so Danny could hear, I said, 'I'm sure Danny will hold my hand once we are at the school gates. He's very sensible and will know how important it is to stay safe by the roads.'

'See you tomorrow then,' Yvonne smiled, and went over to see another parent who was waiting for her.

Danny and I turned, and began towards the school gates. My hand was by my side so he could take hold of it at any moment, but he chose not to. As we arrived at the school gates I moved out of the stream of parents, and bending towards Danny so I was in his line of vision, I said, 'Which hand would you like to hold, Danny? My left hand or my right hand? This is my left.' I showed him. 'And this is my right.' I offered him that hand too. 'Left or right?' I said, holding out both my hands. 'The choice is yours.' There was a moment's hesitation before he took my left hand, and we left the playground holding hands without a fuss.

This technique is called the 'closed choice' and is a useful little strategy for ensuring a child does what the parent or carer wants, while allowing the child to make the choice. I use it a lot and explain it more fully in my book *Happy Kids*.

Danny continued to hold my hand as we walked along the pavement to my car. I pressed the fob to unlock it and then opened the rear door for Danny to get in. He hesitated again. It was then I remembered that his mother had written that Danny always opened the car door himself. Nevertheless, he clambered into the child seat without protest and dropped his school bag on the seat beside him. He then began fiddling with his seatbelt, trying to do it up. I gave him a few moments and then reached in. 'It's different from the one in your mother's car,' I said. 'I'll do it and you can check it.'

There was another small hesitation, but the promise of being able to check the belt pacified him and he took his hands from the clasp, allowing me to fasten the seatbelt.

'OK, you can check it now,' I said, straightening.

Bless him, he looked down and his little face was a picture of concentration as he thoroughly checked the belt.

'All right?' I asked him.

'Yes, thank you very much,' he said sweetly, and my heart melted.

'Well done. We're going home now. To my house,' I clarified.

Before I closed the door he picked up his school bag and sat clutching it on his lap like a little old lady on a coach trip. He really was a quaint child.

I went round to the driver's door, got in and, dropping the envelope containing Danny's education plan on the passenger seat, started the engine. I didn't try to make conversation on the way home. Danny needed some time to adjust to the transition from school to home, and I was concentrating on driving. Danny was looking straight ahead, over the passenger seat in front of him and through the windscreen. Every so often I'd glance at him in the rear-view mirror, but he didn't meet my gaze. As Yvonne had said, it was difficult to know what he was feeling, for he said so little and his face was often expressionless.

'Are you all right, love?' I asked once as I drove.

'Yes, thank you very much,' he said. But given that this was his choice of phrase for the day it was impossible to know if he really was all right.

I pulled into the driveway at home, but before I'd parked and cut the engine Danny had moved his school bag from his lap and was tugging to undo his seatbelt.

'Don't undo your belt until I've stopped, please,' I said. This was a rule I had for all the children for their own safety.

His hands grew still but remained on the clasp. I parked, got out and went round to open his car door. He immediately began fiddling with the belt again, quickly growing impatient when the clasp wouldn't open. One of the reasons I'd chosen this particular car seat was that the fastener was very secure. I'd fostered children before who thought it was funny to take off their seatbelt and bounce around on the back seat while I was driving, when they knew I couldn't immediately do anything about it.

'It's different from the belt in your mum's car,' I said again. 'I'll unclip it and you can bring your school bag.'

He took his hands from the clasp and picked up his bag while I unfastened his seatbelt. 'We'll hold hands until we are inside the house,' I said – for, once out of the car, he could easily dash off up the street if he had a mind to. 'Left or right?' I offered.

He took my left hand and clambered off the seat and out of the car, dragging his bag behind him.

'Good boy,' I said. 'Well done.'

I locked the car and we crossed to the front door with Danny holding my hand. Now I'd put the ground rules in place for Danny getting in and out of the car it would be easier the next time, and each time after that, until it became second nature to him and part of his routine. *Start as you mean to go on* is a very good maxim for managing children's behaviour, but of course Reva hadn't had the luxury of that, as Danny's behaviour had built up gradually, over years.

I closed the front door and then let go of Danny's hand. 'George!' he shouted at the top of his voice, making me start. Dumping his school bag on the floor, he ran off down the hall, into the kitchen and to the back door. 'George! George!'

'George is coming tomorrow,' I said, arriving at his side. 'Did Mummy tell you when you saw her at school this morning?'

'George! I want George now,' Danny shouted, grabbing the door handle and rattling it.

'George is at your house,' I said. 'I'll be fetching him tomorrow and bringing him here.'

'George!' He screamed and kicked the door.

'No,' I said. I lightly took his arm to ease him from the door. 'Don't kick or scream.'

He pulled away and threw himself on the kitchen floor where he lay on his back, thrashing his arms and legs and shouting, 'George! George!'

At that moment I heard the front door open as Paula returned home from school. 'Mum, Jill's here,' she called from the hall. 'She said she's early.'

Perfect timing! I thought.

Crisis Averted

'I want George!' Danny yelled, now trying to kick me. 'George!'

'Can I come in?' Jill called. 'I take it you're in the kitchen?'

'Yes,' I returned over the noise. 'How did you guess?'

'George!' Danny screamed, drumming his fists and feet on the floor. 'I want George!'

Jill and Paula arrived in the kitchen.

'This is Danny,' I said, introducing him to Jill.

Jill looked at Danny, who was still in his coat, had his eyes screwed shut and was writhing on the floor. 'Hello, Danny,' she said evenly. 'You don't look very comfortable down there.' Jill had been a social worker long enough to have witnessed most types of behaviour and wasn't fazed.

'I want George!' Danny yelled.

'Who's George?' Jill asked.

'His pet rabbit,' I said. 'I'm collecting him tomorrow.'

'Are you all right, Mum?' Paula asked, concerned.

'Yes. Perhaps you'd both like to go into the living room? Then Danny and I will come in and join you in a few minutes when he's calmer.' I could see how worried Paula was, and I didn't think it would do Danny any good to have an audience.

Paula and Jill did as I suggested and went into the living room, and I heard Jill exclaim with exaggerated surprise, 'What a wonderful Lego pattern! I wonder who could have made this.' I'd left the Lego on the floor exactly as Danny had left it, and he'd heard Jill's remark. In an instant he'd stopped thrashing and was on his feet, running out of the kitchen and into the living room. Crisis averted, thanks to Jill.

Chapter Eight
A Work of Art

'It's mine!' Danny shouted protectively as he ran into the living room and then squatted on the floor in front of his Lego.

Jill and Paula were standing to one side of the pattern, admiring it. 'So you did it all by yourself?' Jill asked.

'Yes, thank you very much,' Danny said.

'He did,' I confirmed.

'It's very good. It must have taken you ages,' Jill said.

'Yes, thank you very much,' Danny said again.

'It's his phrase for the day,' I explained to Jill.

'Well, there are worse ones,' Jill said with a smile.

Jill had been my support social worker for many years and we enjoyed a comfortable working relationship. I'd come to view her as a friend as well as a colleague, and I knew she could be relied upon to give sound advice and offer support as necessary.

'If you don't need me, Mum, I'll go to my room,' Paula said.

'Of course, love. You do as you wish.' Sometimes I asked my children to look after the child we were fostering if I had to speak to the social worker in private. But that wasn't the case now. Jill had come to see Danny as much as she had me.

As Paula left the room I knelt down beside Danny so I was in his line of vision if he looked up. 'Do you want to play with the Lego again or something new?' I asked him. There were other boxes of toys and games within his reach and plenty more in the cupboard.

'Lego,' Danny said decisively.

'OK. That's fine. Tell me if you want a new game and I'll show you where they are kept.'

Jill and I sat on the sofa and for a few moments we watched Danny as he carefully removed one brick at a time from the lines of Lego and reinserted each one in a different place, creating a new sequence.

'Danny loves patterns and order,' I said to Jill. 'And he's very good at art.'

'So I understand,' Jill said. 'I spoke to Terri earlier and she briefly went over what was said at the meeting. It's good of you to have the rabbit. You know you don't have to.'

'I do now,' I said, glancing at Danny. 'I'm committed. I'm collecting George tomorrow morning, hutch as well.'

Jill nodded and, taking a note pad and pen from her large bag, which acted as a briefcase, turned to a clean page. Then she passed me a white envelope. 'The placement information,' she said. 'You can read it later.'

'Thank you.' I tucked the envelope into my fostering folder with the other paperwork I had on Danny.

'So, how's it going?' Jill asked. 'You've had an eventful twenty-four hours.'

'You could say that,' I said. 'But Danny's doing all right. He ate a good dinner and breakfast, and slept well.'

'I understood there were eating issues?' Jill said quietly so Danny, who had his back to us, couldn't hear.

'He's very particular about his food,' I said. 'And has had quite a limited diet. Hopefully I can make some changes and introduce some new foods.' Jill made a note. I'd be covering this and any other issues that came to light in more detail in my log and also the monthly report I sent to Terri and Jill.

'Perhaps I'll ask Terri to arrange a medical,' Jill suggested in the same lowered tone. 'He's quite small for his age. As he's accommodated under a Section 20 Terri will need the parents' permission for a medical. Or perhaps his mother could arrange one. I'll mention it to Terri.' If a child comes into care under a court order – where the local authority has parental rights – the social worker arranges a medical for the child quite quickly to identify any conditions that may need treating, but under a Section 20 the parents can arrange it themselves.

'Behavioural issues?' Jill asked, working her way through a mental check list. 'I believe that was the main reason Danny came into care.'

'There have been a lot of issues,' I said. 'Reva was at her wits' end. Danny can easily become frustrated and overloaded, which leads to a tantrum or meltdown. She clearly loves him, but she's very low. She told me she feels like a failure for not coping, and blames herself for the way he is. Autism has been mentioned, but the school are waiting to bring in the education psychologist for an assessment.'

Jill nodded. 'Terri is seeing Danny's parents next week and this is one of the issues she'll be discussing with them. Does he have an individual education plan?'

'Yes. His teacher has given me a copy, but I haven't had a chance to read it yet. He has a reading book and flash cards for homework and he's working towards reception level.'

'Specific learning difficulties?' Jill asked.

'It seems likely, but they haven't been identified yet.'

Jill nodded and wrote. 'Terri said his mother gave you notes on his routine?'

'Yes.' I hesitated. 'I'd like your advice, please.' Opening my folder, I took out the twenty-three-page document and passed it to Jill. While she read I took the opportunity to go over to Danny and praise him for playing nicely.

'That's a lovely new pattern,' I said. 'Well done.'

'Yes, thank you very much,' he said, without looking up at me.

'Do you want to continue playing with the Lego?' I asked. 'Or something different?' Given that he'd played with the Lego the previous evening I thought he'd be bored with it by now – most children would be, but not Danny.

'Lego, please. Yes, thank you very much,' he said.

'Good boy,' I said. He seemed happy enough. 'Tell me when you want to play with something new and I'll show you where the toy cupboard is,' I reminded him.

'Yes, thank you very much.'

I returned to sit beside Jill. She'd stopped reading every word of Reva's notes and was now scanning the pages. Coming to the end, she handed them back to me. 'Use what you can,' she said. 'I'll explain to Terri that a lot of it is unworkable here, and unnecessary. You would have to walk around with it in your hand to remember everything. Reva must have felt like she was balancing on a tightrope trying to keep to that; one false move and she'd fall off.'

'I don't think she had much support looking after Danny,' I said as I returned the notes to my folder.

'No,' Jill agreed. 'Terri said similar. Have you started your log?' Jill now asked.

'Yes.' I showed her the first page.

'I'll check it next time when Danny's been here longer.' As my support social worker Jill would be visiting us every month, and as part of her visit she would check and sign my log notes.

'And there's been no change in your household?' Jill asked, as she was obliged to.

'No,' I confirmed. 'There's still the four of us – five with Danny.'

'And what are the contact arrangements?'

I told Jill the agreed days for Danny to see his parents and she made a note.

'And on another matter, are you still willing and able to help with the training again next month?' Jill asked.

'Yes, I'm happy to.' Like many experienced foster carers, I helped run training for new carers. I enjoyed it, and it added another dimension to my role as foster carer.

'Thank you,' Jill said. 'Do you need anything to look after Danny?'

'No, I don't think so.'

'OK. Let's set the date for my next visit then.' We opened our diaries and arranged Jill's next visit for four weeks' time.

She returned her notepad and pen to her bag and, standing, crossed to Danny. She praised him for his wonderful Lego pattern and then said she was going and that she'd see him again in a few weeks. He didn't answer or even acknowledge he'd heard her. She said goodbye, and then again as we left the room, and this time a little voice called out, 'Yes, thank you very much.'

I went with Jill to see her out. I opened the front door and Lucy was coming down the garden path, returning home from school. 'Hi, how are you?' Jill asked her as she came in.

'Good. Thanks.'

'I hear your adoption application is going through quickly.'

'Yes!' Lucy cried, beaming. 'Can't wait. Then I won't be in care any longer!' Lucy planted a big kiss on my cheek and grinned happily at Jill.

Having spent most of her life in and out of care, Lucy had come to me as a foster child two years previously and I'd now applied to adopt her. I tell Lucy's story in *Will You Love Me?*

'See you soon then,' Jill said to us both with a smile, and left.

I closed the front door

'Have you had a good day?' I asked Lucy.

She pulled a face. Like many teenagers she resented some of the routine at school and would have liked more freedom.

'Where's the little fellow?' she asked, taking off her coat and shoes.

'In the living room, playing with the Lego bricks.'

We went into the living room. Danny was as I'd left him, sitting on the floor and concentrating hard on the Lego bricks as he reorganized them into another new pattern.

'Good work, Mister,' Lucy said.

'Yes, thank you very much,' Danny replied.

Lucy laughed kindly. 'That's very polite,' she said, impressed, having only heard the phrase for the first time. 'See you later, Mister.'

'Yes, thank you very much,' Danny said again.

Lucy disappeared up to her room to unwind and then start her homework before dinner. Danny was very settled creating his pattern, so I felt confident in leaving him alone briefly while I went into the kitchen to cook the meal.

'I'll be in the kitchen if you want me,' I said to him.

'Yes, thank you very much,' came his now predictable but endearing reply.

I left the living-room door open so I could hear him while I was in the kitchen. I placed the fish fingers and chips in the oven to cook. I fed Toscha, took the clean laundry from the dryer and then popped back into the living room to check on Danny. He was still in the same position on the floor, concentrating on reorganizing the Lego. 'Good boy,' I said, and came out to continue with what I had to do.

Danny seemed to have endless patience for quite small tasks and had been studying the Lego with such intensity that he appeared almost fixated. I wondered if he showed the same level of concentration in his school work. Sue had said he liked art and was good at it but was finding academic subjects very challenging. The sooner he was assessed by the education psychologist the better; then a learning plan would be drawn up to meet his needs.

Adrian arrived home later than normal from school, as he'd stayed behind to play rugby. He said hi to Danny and then went upstairs to shower before dinner. Once the food was ready I called everyone to the table and then went into the living room for Danny.

'Danny, it's time for dinner,' I said.

'Yes, thank you very much,' he replied, but made no move to stand and come with me.

'We're going to eat now,' I said. 'So leave the Lego and come with me to the table.'

I knew from Reva's notes, and from my own experience of looking after children with difficulties similar to Danny's, that he would need clear, precise instructions. I couldn't assume that he'd make a logical connection as other children the same age would. Telling Danny dinner was ready wouldn't necessarily equate, in his mind, with him needing to come to the table to eat it. Likewise, if I told him we were going out he wouldn't realize he had to put on his shoes and coat. Now I'd told him what he had to do, he left the Lego and came with me to the dining table, where he sat in his place at the table. 'Good boy,' I said.

Once everyone was seated I served the meal. I wouldn't have thought there was much you could do with fish fingers, chips and green beans; it was a very simple meal and surely simple to eat? But Danny spent some time surveying the contents of his plate without touching the food, while everyone else was busily passing around the tomato sauce and tucking in. Then he rotated his plate 180 degrees, picked up his knife and fork and with slow, measured cuts began slicing the fish fingers in half and half again so they were in quarters. He put them to one side of his plate, then set about cutting up the chips so that they were the same length as the fish-finger pieces. He put them to one side too, studied the green beans, which were all different lengths, and then began topping and tailing them so they were the same length as the chips and fish fingers. I could see Adrian, Lucy and Paula watching him curiously. During all our years of fostering we'd seen many different types of behaviour at the meal table, including bingeing, vomiting, loud burping and

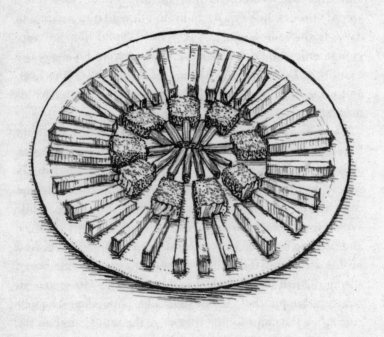

farting, throwing food and food refusal. Indeed, when Lucy had first arrived she'd had anorexia and had been too afraid to eat, although she was over the worst of it now. However, Danny's approach to food was unique. By the time he'd finished cutting and arranging his food it fanned out from the centre of his plate in an expanding swirling pattern, with the darkest in colour – the green beans – in the centre, then the lighter fish-finger pieces and the chips in the outer circle. It was truly a work of art.

'Do you want tomato sauce?' I asked him. He shook his head. 'I think you should eat your food now or it will be cold.' Indeed, I thought it must already be cold; the rest of us had nearly finished.

Danny nodded and finally began eating. Starting with the outer ring of chip pieces – the palest food on the plate – he ate them one at a time. Then he ate the fish fingers and lastly the green beans. The rest of us sat chatting as he ate, so the atmosphere was relaxed and he didn't feel we were waiting for him to finish. But while we had time to accommodate his behaviour this evening, I could see how frustrating it would be if we were in a hurry or eating with friends or at a restaurant. I wondered if Reva and her husband ever took Danny out for meals or to see friends. Certainly Sue, his teacher, had said that Danny was always the last to finish his school lunch, and I could see why. But he did finish – every last crumb – and for a child with so many other issues, trying to change his method of eating didn't seem a priority.

The yoghurt pudding could only be eaten with a spoon, and Danny ate it slowly and meticulously, as he approached most things. Once he'd finished he put down his spoon, wiped his mouth on the napkin and said, 'George.'

'I'm collecting George tomorrow,' I reminded him. 'He'll be here when you come back from seeing your mother.'

His brow furrowed as he processed this information. 'George coming here tomorrow?' he asked.

'Yes, love.'

'Tomorrow I am having dinner at my home. Then I come back here and feed George.'

'Exactly right!' I said, impressed. There was clearly a lot more to Danny than we realized.

Chapter Nine

Danny Drowning

I accepted that Danny would take much longer than the average six-year-old child to perform most tasks, and that patience was therefore a key element in managing his behaviour. However, I also thought that Danny needed to acquire more patience himself, for although, if an activity engaged him, he could stay involved in it for hours – the Lego, for example – he could also quickly explode with frustration if a task was challenging or didn't immediately go his way. One such time was after dinner. He and I were sitting on the sofa in the living room, ready for me to hear him read, when his school bag, which he'd fetched from the hall without being asked, wouldn't immediately open. He tugged the zipper a couple of times and then threw the bag angrily on the floor, stamped on it and began windmilling his arms like a giant insect stalled on take-off.

'Danny,' I said, searching for eye contact. 'Don't be upset. The zipper is stuck. I'll help you open the bag. It can be easily sorted.'

'Danny do it!' he shouted, gritting his teeth.

'Yes, you can undo it,' I said. 'I'll show you how, but you need to calm down first.'

'Danny do it!' he said again angrily.

'First, you need to sit down quietly,' I said more firmly.

'Danny do it,' he repeated again, as though he was beating himself up for not doing it and had to prove he could.

'You will do when I show you,' I said, taking his arm. 'Now sit down and calm down. It's a zip fastener, not the end of the world.' He let me draw him to the sofa and I sat him next to me. 'That's better,' I said. 'Now, take a few deep breaths and then we'll undo your bag. Breathe in,' I said, slowly drawing in a deep breath to show him. 'And out. In and out.' He began to copy me and gradually his breathing settled and he grew calmer. 'That's much better, good boy.'

I picked up his school bag from where he'd thrown it and set it on my lap. I could see straight away what was wrong. A small shred of paper had jammed in the teeth of the zipper, just as can happen with the material of a coat or jacket. Like most parents, I'd released many jammed zippers in my time and knew what to do.

'Danny, you see this?' I said, pointing to the shred of paper. 'That's the reason you couldn't undo the zipper. The paper stopped it.'

Danny peered closely at the zipper, his mop of blond hair falling over his forehead.

'This is how we fix it,' I said. 'Watch carefully and you'll know how to do it next time.' I gently eased the zipper up, scraped out the shred of paper, then drew it down again and the zipper ran freely, opening the bag. 'There,' I said, passing the bag to him. 'All done. There was nothing to worry about. You'll know how to fix it next time.'

He was quiet for a few moments as he surveyed the zipper and then said, 'Yes, thank you very much.'

'You're welcome,' I said.

'You're welcome,' he repeated.

I smiled. Another crisis averted, but as Jill had said, Reva must have felt as though she was balancing on a tightrope, never knowing when Danny was going to erupt. I knew from past experience and training that children like Danny could easily become frustrated and angry. They are awash in a world they don't understand or feel part of, and are therefore at the mercy of others' behaviour and unpredictable events. One of the reasons Danny was so independent and insisted on doing things for himself was that it felt safer to him that way, to have control. This is true for all of us to some extent, but more so for a child like Danny with communication difficulties, who couldn't easily voice his worries and fears.

Having calmed down, Danny took his book from his bag, confidently opened it and began reading the first page. He'd had the same book since Monday and it was very basic – a start to reading – but he read each of the six words that made up the short sentence correctly. There were four pages, each with a very short sentence and a colourful illustration. He loved the pictures and spent a long time studying them, both before and after reading the words. He stumbled on some of the sentences and I helped him, and he made it to the end of the book.

'Good boy,' I said. 'Very well read.'

'Yes, thank you very much,' he said. 'You're welcome.'

I smiled and could have kissed him, but he wasn't ready for that yet. Then, in his well-practised routine, he returned the book to his bag and took out the flash cards, which he placed face down on my lap.

'Thank you,' I said.

'You're welcome,' he returned.

Starting with the top card, I held it up for Danny to see. There was a long pause before he was able to recognize the word. 'Well done,' I said. I held up the next card and then the next, and so on. Each card showed a single word that had appeared in the book he'd just read, but taken out of context and without the picture for reference he struggled. He got about half of the eight cards right first time and I praised him. Those he got wrong we tried again and I helped him break down the word phonetically, but he quickly tired and grew agitated, windmilling his arms, so I knew it was time to stop.

'Good boy. You've done well,' I said. 'That's enough for this evening.'

'Yes, thank you very much,' he said. Whipping the cards out of my hand, he returned them to his bag and took out an exercise book, which he placed squarely on my lap. On the front was written 'Home School Book'.

'I have to write in this,' I said.

He nodded and then watched me carefully as I opened the book and turned the pages. I would read it thoroughly when I had more time, but I read some of the entries. His teacher had written: *Danny was able to sit with the other children while I took registration. He practised his numbers to ten. At morning break he stayed in the playground for the whole fifteen minutes.* His mother's comments included: *Danny was very tired and angry this evening so didn't do his reading. Danny tore up his homework sheet. Danny hid for most of the evening and had an early night. Danny says he hates school.* That morning Yvonne had written: *Danny took a long time to settle and we spent half an hour in the quiet room.* The afternoon had improved and

Danny Drowning

Yvonne had written: *Danny joined the other children in the class for art and story time*.

'So you had art today?' I said. 'You like that.'

'Yes, thank you very much,' he said.

I took my pen from the corner table and Danny watched me carefully as I wrote. I said out loud what I was writing. 'Danny had a very good evening,' I said slowly. 'He met my social worker Jill, played with Lego, ate a good meal and then read his book to me. We spent ten minutes working with the flash cards and Danny got half of them right first time. Well done, Danny.'

I closed the book and, smiling, handed it back to him, and he returned it to his bag.

'Time for your bath now,' I said. I stood and offered him my hand.

'Time for your bath,' he repeated.

He ignored my hand but came with me, and we went upstairs with Danny clambering up on all fours like a much younger child. I knew his bath-time routine from his mother's notes. First he went to the toilet while I waited outside. Then we went into his bedroom where he lifted soft-toy George from his pillow, took out his pyjamas and returned George to sit on top of the pillow.

'Time for your bath now,' he said again.

'Yes, that's right.'

We went out of his bedroom, round the landing and into the bathroom. I explained to him that I would run the water in his bath to make sure it was the right temperature, as I had done the night before with the water in the basin. I guessed he remembered this for he didn't object as he had done the previous evening. While the bath filled he took off his clothes and put them into the laundry basket.

'Good boy,' I said.

Once the bath was ready, I offered him my hand to help him in. 'You can get in now, Danny,' I said. 'It's the right temperature.'

He suddenly gasped and, turning, flung open the bathroom door and ran round the landing in his birthday suit. I went after him. Lucy came up the stairs at the exact moment Danny flashed by on the landing. 'Oh!' she cried in mock horror, covering her eyes. 'You haven't got any clothes on!' Lucy was joking, although in keeping with fostering guidelines we always wore clothes around the house and encouraged the children we fostered to do the same. While appearing naked in front of other family members is perfectly natural in many families, it can be very embarrassing, intimidating or even traumatic for a child who has been abused. But Danny was oblivious and continued into his bedroom, where he pulled open the bottom drawer of the chest and took out a plastic bag, which I now remembered contained his bath toys. 'Well remembered,' I said.

He closed the drawer, sped back round the landing to the bathroom and flung all the toys into the bath. Still refusing my help, he scrambled over the side of the bath, and then sat happily in the warm water playing with the toys. The brightly coloured plastic and rubber toys included a variety of fish, a small yacht and a dinghy that contained a little figure in diving gear. Danny chopped the water with his hands, creating waves, which made the fish appear to swim and the boats bob up and down as though they were on the ocean. While he was occupied playing, I washed his back with the sponge, and then gave it to him to wash his front and legs. Like with many boys his age, it was a very quick wash – he liked playing in the water but didn't like washing. I knelt beside the bath as he continued playing contentedly. A warm bath is comforting for children, as it is for adults. Danny took the little diving man from the dinghy and plunged him into the water. 'Drowning! Drowning!' he suddenly cried, holding the toy under the water. Then he pulled the figure out. 'Saved him!' he declared. 'Danny saved him!

I smiled.

He repeated this a number of times. He seemed to like the idea of the diver falling into deep water, nearly drowning and then being rescued by him. Perhaps it gave him a feeling of being in charge, I didn't know. But then suddenly, without warning, Danny threw himself under the water and lay submerged in the bath with his mouth and eyes shut and his blonde hair floating out. I was surprised he didn't mind the feeling of being completely covered by water – many children don't like it and keep their heads above water when learning to swim. But Danny stayed beneath the water with his face submerged until his breath ran out and he had to come up for air.

'Danny drowning,' he said, as he sat upright, with water running down his face. He looked at me carefully.

'No, you weren't drowning,' I reassured him. 'You were playing a game and having fun. You're safe.'

'Danny drowning,' he said again, more insistently, and taking a deep breath threw himself under the water again.

He stayed under for longer this time, and when he rose he looked at me, clearly expecting a reaction. 'Danny drowning,' he said adamantly.

I wasn't sure what game this was, but it didn't feel good to me. 'No, you're not drowning,' I said. 'You're playing.'

He went under again and when he resurfaced he almost shouted, 'Danny drowning!'

I thought it was time to end the game. 'You're safe,' I said. 'You've had your bath. Now it's time to get out and dry yourself.'

'Danny drowning,' he said, and was clearly about to take a breath and go under the water again.

I opened the plug and the water began to drain out. 'Danny will be on dry land very soon,' I said.

He looked at me oddly, clearly not knowing what to make of this.

'I like other games when Danny isn't drowning,' I said, and offered my hand to help him out.

He ignored my hand and with a lot of effort clambered over the side of the bath. I wrapped him in his bath towel and patted him dry as I knew from the notes his mother did. Reva hadn't mentioned the 'Danny drowning' game, yet I felt sure it wasn't something new, for it had seemed a well-practised routine to me.

Once Danny was dry I waited while he put on his pyjamas. He wanted to do it himself. I knew from the notes that he didn't like the noise of a hairdryer, so following Reva's advice I towel-dried his hair. I then waited as Danny meticulously brushed his teeth, wiped his mouth and spent some time folding and adjusting his towel on the rail beside ours. As we went round the landing I called to Adrian, Lucy and Paula that Danny was going to bed.

'Night, Danny,' Adrian called from his room.

Lucy and Paula came out of their rooms to say goodnight.

'Would you like a kiss, Mister?' Lucy asked, bending down to his height.

But he shook his head, so they just said goodnight.

In Danny's room I parted his curtains as he'd showed me he liked them the evening before – even so he went over and adjusted them – then he turned down the dimmer switch until the light was a faint glow, which would stay on all night. Finally, he climbed into bed. I knew from Reva's notes that she didn't read him a story in bed, but kissed him goodnight and came out.

'Would you like a kiss?' I asked him.

He shook his head. 'Mummy kiss Danny,' he said.

'That's all right. I understand. Goodnight, love.'

He looked at me, almost making eye contact, and I knew he had something to say and was searching for the words he needed. There was often a delay before he spoke. 'George come here tomorrow?' he asked eventually.

'Yes, that's right, love. I'm collecting George tomorrow while you're at school.'

He paused again before he said, 'Danny go home for dinner and then George here?'

'Yes. Exactly right,' I said. 'That will happen tomorrow.' There seemed to be little wrong with Danny's memory; it just took him longer to process and retrieve the information he needed and then find the words to express himself.

'Goodnight then, love,' I said again. 'Time to go to sleep. You must be very tired.'

He lay down, drew soft-toy George into bed beside him and then pulled the duvet right up over his head. 'Goodnight,' I said again as I came out, but there was no reply.

I closed his bedroom door as he liked it and then waited on the landing to see if he got out of bed, but it was all quiet. I'd check on him again later, and also ease the duvet from his face as I had the night before. I was pleased Danny was settling at night. Some children who come into care are so upset to begin with that it takes them hours to go to sleep – worries often seem worse at night – and I sit with them and comfort them until they eventually fall asleep. But despite Danny's difficulties, he seemed to be coping with all the changes and the loss of his parents in his own way, although of course I didn't know what he was really thinking or feeling.

It was now after 8.30 p.m. and the evening had disappeared, firstly with Jill's visit and then seeing to Danny. The foster child (or children) tend to have first claim on a carer's time, so it's essential we redress the balance and make time for our own children when we have the opportunity. Otherwise they can feel unappreciated and resent all the time their parents spend with the looked-after child. I now went to Paula, Lucy and Adrian in turn and spent some time chatting with each of them – about what they'd done during the day and any worries they had. There was always something to talk about. Satisfied they were all OK, I went downstairs to read the placement information forms Jill had brought, while they took turns in the bathroom, showering and then getting ready for bed.

I sat in the living room with Toscha curled up beside me on the sofa and read the paperwork, which included Danny's parents' names and contact details, a brief medical history of Danny and what was known of his behavioural and learning difficulties, much of which I already knew. I filed it in my folder and then took Danny's education plan from the envelope Yvonne had given to me. It was a single-page document headed with Danny's name, date of birth and the names of his teacher and classroom assistant. Below these were three vertical columns headed 'Target', 'Strategy' and 'Evaluation'. Danny's present learning targets, which would be revised as he met them, were to write his name; learn two new key words a week, which would be reinforced by the flash cards; and recognize which were the bigger numbers in one to five. These targets were obviously very basic for a six-year-old and would already have been achieved by most children that age. Danny and I had practised the key-word flash cards that evening, and the rest we'd do as and when we had time. Danny had a lot to cope with in life aside from school, and it was important he didn't feel under pressure and become overloaded. His emotional wellbeing was as important as his education, which I felt sure his teacher, mother and social worker would appreciate.

I filed the individual education plan in my fostering folder and then I looked up Danny's home address on a street map of my area in preparation for collecting George the following morning. Although I'd lived in the same area all my life, Danny's home was in a new development that I wasn't familiar with. I jotted down the house number and road and made some notes on how to get there. Before I wrote up my log notes I went upstairs to check on Danny and to say goodnight to Adrian, Paula and Lucy.

I slowly opened Danny's bedroom door and crept in. As the light was on low it was easy to see the lump in the bed that was Danny. I gently eased back the duvet and tucked it under his chin. He was fast asleep, flat on his back with soft-toy George snuggled on the pillow beside him and his mouth slightly open. He looked so angelic and vulnerable I felt a surge of love and protection. Clearly he must be missing his parents a great deal, but he lacked the ability to express his emotion. Perhaps he sensed my presence, for he stirred slightly in his sleep and very, very quietly said, 'George coming tomorrow. I love George.'

Chapter Ten
Don't Tell the Social Worker

The following morning I got the shock of my life when I went into Danny's room to wake him for school and found his bed empty. The duvet was on the bed, pushed back, but the pillow was missing. 'Danny!' I called, looking under the bed. 'Where are you?'

My heart immediately began racing with anxiety. Surely he couldn't have left his room in the night? I would have heard him, wouldn't I? But there was nowhere else in the room he could have hidden other than under the bed. I frantically looked around and with rising panic started towards the bedroom door. As I did I glanced at the small single wardrobe standing against the wall to my left. He couldn't be in there, could he? It wasn't big enough. I opened the wardrobe door and to my utter relief and surprise saw Danny at the bottom, curled on his pillow like a hamster in a nest. He was awake and looking at me.

'Danny, whatever are you doing in there?' I said, offering him my hand to help him out.

He looked at me blankly.

'Come on, out you get,' I said. 'You gave me a fright. How long have you been in there?'

Ignoring my hand and my question, he clambered out, dragging his pillow behind him. He silently returned the pillow to his bed and pulled up the duvet, making his bed.

'Danny, I don't want you hiding in the wardrobe again or in any cupboard,' I said. 'It's dangerous. You could have got trapped inside.' Although all the doors in my house, including cupboard doors, could be opened from the inside, Danny didn't know that, and one day he might find himself in a house that didn't have this safety precaution and accidentally lock himself in. There'd been tragic accidents reported in the news of children hiding in cupboards and disused freezers, and suffocating. 'Do you understand? No hiding in cupboards,' I said, emphasizing the point.

He didn't look at me but gave a small nod.

'Good. Now it's time for you to get dressed.'

I waited while he laid out his clothes in order on the bed, and then I left him to start dressing while I woke Adrian, Lucy and Paula. When I returned to his room there hadn't been much progress, but I'd allowed plenty of time for him to dress and get ready in the morning. When he was finally dressed and we were going downstairs he said, 'For breakfast I have cornflakes in a bowl, with milk and half a teaspoon of sugar.'

'Yes, you can have that,' I said with a smile. 'It's what you had yesterday for breakfast. Or you could have something different.'

'For breakfast I have cornflakes in a bowl, with milk and half a teaspoon of sugar,' he said again, concentrating hard as if he might forget it,

'That's fine. You will have that,' I confirmed.

Adrian, Lucy and Paula were just finishing their breakfasts as we arrived.

'Hi, Danny,' Paula said as she left the table to finish getting ready.

Danny didn't reply.

'Good morning,' Adrian said to him as Danny sat at the table.

Danny looked blank.

'Are you going to say hi, Mister?' Lucy asked him, affectionately ruffling his hair.

He pulled away.

'Suit yourself,' she said, a little put out.

'Not everyone likes having their hair ruffled,' I said to Lucy. Adrian did it to the girls and they thought it was funny.

'Are we allowed to talk to him?' Lucy asked a tad sarcastically, not at her best first thing in the morning.

I threw her a warning look.

'Just asking,' she said with attitude, and flounced upstairs to finish getting ready. I knew she'd be fine later. We all have our moments.

Although I'd left plenty of time for Danny to dress, eat his breakfast and then wash and brush his teeth, there was no time to spare and we arrived in the playground five minutes before the start of school. I waited with Danny at the end of the hopscotch as the other children played around us. When the whistle blew, Yvonne appeared from the main doors and came over to us.

'Good morning,' she said with a cheery smile. 'Did you have a nice evening?'

Danny managed a small nod. I said, 'Yes, thank you. Danny met Jill. He played with the Lego and we also had time to read his book and work on the flash cards. I've written it in the home school book.'

'Excellent,' Yvonne said, looking at Danny. 'So you had a good evening at Cathy's.' Our rather overstated conversation was to help Danny develop language; the more he heard language being used the more he would hopefully learn what to say and when.

'Yes, thank you very much,' he said at last.

'Good. And Mummy is collecting you tonight from school?' Yvonne said to him.

'Yes,' I said when Danny didn't answer.

'And I think something important is happening this morning,' Yvonne said with a twinkle in her eye, encouraging Danny to make conversation. 'I think it's about George?'

We both looked at Danny for a response, but his expression remained neutral. 'That's right,' I said. 'I'm collecting George this morning.'

'It'll be nice having George stay with you,' Yvonne said. 'Now say goodbye to Cathy and we'll line up with the other children, ready to go into school.'

'Goodbye, Danny,' I said. 'Have a good day. See you this evening.'

Danny didn't reply.

'Say goodbye to Cathy,' Yvonne encouraged. But he kept his eyes down.

'It's OK, don't worry,' I said to Yvonne. 'There's a lot going on for him, and he's been a bit quiet this morning.'

She smiled, we said goodbye and they crossed the playground to line up with Danny's class. While it didn't really affect me that Danny refused to say goodbye, I could see how upsetting it must have been for his mother, when all the other children were calling goodbye and hugging and kissing their parents. Why Danny had refused to say goodbye to me or talk to Yvonne about George I didn't know, but it seemed to be part of his difficulties that he couldn't always understand how to communicate appropriately or respond to the emotional expectations of others. An assessment from the educational psychologist should offer some explanation.

I went home, had a coffee, loaded the laundry into the washing machine and then set off in my car to Danny's house to pick up George, with my written directions on the passenger seat beside me. I'd seen some of the houses in the development where Danny lived advertised for sale in the local newspaper. The estate agents had used terms like 'select', 'luxurious', 'magnificent', 'spacious' and 'bespoke living' to describe them, so I assumed they were rather nice. But it wasn't until I drove into the road marked 'Private' that led to the new estate that I realized just how magnificent they were.

Huge detached houses stood majestically in their own grounds on both sides of the road, many behind security gates. Each house was unique and different from its neighbours, but they all had double or treble brick-built garages with sweeping carriage driveways, mature shrubs and neatly trimmed front lawns. Clearly a lot of thought had gone into the planning of the estate, for although it was relatively new it looked well established and had character and charm. I briefly wondered what the houses cost – the advertisements had stated 'price on application' – and who could afford to buy them. Certainly no one I knew.

I slowed the car to glance at my notes, then continued to the end of the road and turned left towards Number 11, where

Danny lived. I stopped outside his house and hesitated, unsure if I should pull to the end of the drive and approach the security gates or leave my car in the road. There were no other cars parked in the road, presumably because the owners' and visitors' cars could be accommodated in the garages and on the massive expanse of driveways. Reva must have been looking out for me, for as I hesitated the security gates began to swing open. I pulled over and drove between the two stone pillars either side of the entry gate and then along and round the drive. There were no other cars on the drive, so I parked close to the vast mock-Tudor house. Cutting the engine, I got out and crossed the brick driveway to the front door. Although Reva knew I was there she didn't open the door until I'd pressed the chimes. When she did I could see she was far more composed than when I'd met her the previous day at school.

'Good morning, Cathy, do come in,' she said politely.

'Thank you. How are you?' I stepped in.

'Well, thank you. This way. Follow me.'

There was a formality in Reva's manner, and she was dressed quite formally too, in a navy skirt and blouse, stockings and low-heeled navy shoes. Perhaps she was going out straight after I'd collected George. In my casual trousers and jersey top I felt underdressed. I tried not to appear overawed by the splendour of the house as I followed Reva through the reception hall, which was about the same size as most of the downstairs of my house. It was decorated a pale cream and was furnished in a minimalist style, but splendidly, with a large palm tree in a huge stone pot beside a luxurious hand-crafted grey leather chaise longue.

'You've got a lovely home,' I said.

'Thank you,' Reva said. We continued into a sitting room.

If the outside of the house and the hall were grand, the sitting room took my breath away: expansive glass sliding patio doors extended the entire width of the room, giving a panoramic view over the countryside and rolling hills beyond. The plain décor continued in this room, with pale walls, two long cream leather sofas, matching coffee tables and a mature fig tree in a cream marble pot, which matched the magnificent marble fireplace.

Reva hesitated. 'Let me show you George first and then I'll make us a drink,' she said.

I nodded and followed her out of the sitting room and into the bespoke modern kitchen, where an expanse of polished silver-grey granite work surface glittered in the concealed lighting. A six-hob double oven was built into the oak units, as was a towering American-style fridge freezer. Reva opened a door at the end of the kitchen and I followed her through the utility and laundry room, which was about the same size as my living room. Given that my house was so very different from Danny's, I thought he was doing well in the way he was settling with me.

Round the back of the house, against the rear wall, was a very large rabbit hutch on a wooden stand. It was covered with a heavy-duty blue plastic sheet to protect its occupant from the wind, for though the house was beautifully situated with views across the countryside, it was also exposed.

'Meet George,' Reva said, lifting the plastic sheeting.

I stared in amazement as the image I'd previously entertained of a cute little bunny was replaced by George. 'He's huge,' I said.

'Yes. He's a British Giant. The hutch will fit in your car, won't it?' Reva turned to me, worried.

'Yes, it should with the back seat down,' I said. 'But I've never seen a rabbit that big.'

'Neither had we,' Reva said. 'But once Danny saw him he wouldn't settle for any other.'

George had stopped nibbling a carrot and was looking at me suspiciously. He was bigger than many small dogs, but had a kindly face. He'd obviously been well looked after; his black fur shone healthily and his inquisitive blue eyes sparkled.

'How old is he?' I asked, interested.

'Nearly two,' Reva said. 'He's fully grown now. When he stretches out he's about two feet long, and he weighs six kilos. Don't worry, I'll give you plenty of food. Let me know when you need more. You shouldn't have to buy it.' Which was thoughtful of her. 'Danny takes him out each day, but he hasn't been out since he left.'

'Can he lift him?' I asked, thinking how small Danny was compared to George.

'He doesn't have to,' Reva said. 'Danny opens the hutch door and George jumps out. He follows Danny around just like a puppy. Then, when it's time to go back into his hutch, Danny opens the door and he jumps in.'

'That's clever,' I said. 'I wonder what our cat Toscha will make of him. He's twice her size.'

'They'll be OK,' Reva said. 'It's dogs you have to be careful of. Their instinct is to chase rabbits and eat them.'

It was actually Toscha's welfare I was concerned about, given the difference in size, but I didn't say anything.

'You won't have to do much,' Reva assured me. 'Danny does most of it. The help cleaned the hutch out yesterday, so it won't need doing again for a few days.'

'I'm sure it'll be fine,' I said.

'Let's go inside then,' Reva said, giving a shiver. 'It's cold out here.'

She lowered the plastic sheeting over the front of the cage and we returned indoors to the living room, where she took my coat.

'Would you like a drink?' she asked. 'I'm not a great one for tea or coffee in the morning, but I can make you one.'

'No, I'm fine, thank you,' I said.

I sat on one sofa and Reva sat on the other. The sofas were so big I felt like one of the little people from *The Borrowers*. 'You've certainly got a lovely home,' I said again, looking around and trying not to appear star-struck. 'I don't know how you keep it so tidy with a child.' For there were no toys or books in sight. Indeed, there were no real signs that anyone lived here, apart from the three magazines fanned out on the coffee table, and they looked more for display purposes than reading material. It was like a set from an ideal home exhibition.

'Danny has his own playroom upstairs,' Reva said, waving a hand towards the ceiling. 'It's next to his bedroom. You can see it later, if you like. Terri wanted to see it.'

'So Terri has been here already then?' I asked.

'The week before Danny came to you. She's going to see us again soon. Richard is supposed to be finding some dates when he's free and can be at home.'

'I expect he's very busy,' I said, making conversation.

'Yes, he is,' she said stiffly, and there was an uncomfortable silence.

'Danny slept well,' I said.

'Good. And did you get to school on time?'

113

'Yes. We stood in the playground by the hopscotch, as you said in your notes. What made you choose that spot?' I asked out of interest.

'Danny insists we stand there,' Reva said. 'He doesn't like me talking to the other mothers.'

'Why not?'

Riva shrugged. 'I think because he doesn't talk to the children he doesn't want me talking to their mothers. I tried once, but he made such a fuss it wasn't worth it. It's easier to go along with what he wants.'

This seemed to be the model for most of Reva's parenting: do as Danny says to avoid him making a fuss or having a tantrum. Danny was a child and shouldn't be dictating to his mother. 'You don't think that if you set an example by being sociable and talking to the parents it might help him to interact with their children?' I asked. Children learn by example, even children with difficulties like Danny, and by doing as Danny wanted Reva was unwittingly reinforcing his isolation.

'I hadn't thought of it like that,' she said. 'But I couldn't risk another tantrum. I know everything is on Danny's terms, but it's easier that way.'

'Do you meet other mothers socially?' I asked.

'No. Richard goes out – he has lots of functions to attend connected with work – but he goes alone now. Or I assume he does,' she said with a small embarrassed laugh. 'Danny can't cope with change, and I'd feel guilty if I left him screaming with a babysitter so I could go with Richard.'

'What about going out as a family?' I asked, for it seemed that Reva was as isolated as Danny.

She shook her head. 'We stopped that when Danny was a toddler and began having tantrums. Richard found it too embarrassing. He won't even let his two children from his first marriage see Danny. He visits them by himself each month. I don't think Danny even knows he has a step-brother and sister.'

'That's sad,' I said. 'It's nice to do things together as a family.'

'Wait until you've taken Danny out a few times and you'll see what I mean,' Reva said a little sharply. 'Danny's all right going to school now, because he's familiar with it. But try anything new and it isn't worth the stress. I don't think he gets much from going out either, apart from a telling-off.'

I gave a half-hearted nod. I couldn't agree. 'He likes his bath,' I said. 'Have you ever tried taking him swimming?'

Reva looked at me, shocked. 'Good gracious, no! We don't even allow him to go swimming with his class at school. Although Yvonne offered to go in the water with him.'

'Why not?' I asked, puzzled.

'He'd drown,' she said emphatically. 'He tries to drown himself in his bath. He goes right under the water and doesn't come up for ages.'

'He did that last night when I bathed him,' I said. 'I thought it was a game.'

'It is to him,' Reva said, frowning. 'But not to me. Weren't you frightened he'd drown?'

'No. I didn't think it was a particularly good game and I told Danny that, but I knew he couldn't drown. I knew he'd have to come up for air at some point, which is what he did.'

'Oh, I see. I thought he could drown,' she said.

I saw her gaze flicker to the ornate clock on the marble mantelpiece and thought I should offer to leave. 'Shall we get George and the hutch into the car?' I said.

'No, stay for a bit longer, please, if you can. I don't have many visitors. I was just thinking I'd pour us a drink. It's nearly midday. What would you like? I have most things.'

'A glass of water please.'

'Are you sure you won't join me in a glass of wine? Oh, but you're driving. You don't mind if I do?'

'No.'

She stood and went into the kitchen, and a minute or so later returned with an open bottle of wine, a large wine glass and my glass of water on a silver tray. She set the glass of water on the occasional table within my reach and the tray with the wine on the table beside her.

'If you ever meet Richard don't tell him I've been drinking in the middle of the day,' she said as she poured the wine. 'I'm not supposed to. And you'd better not tell that social worker either.'

Chapter Eleven
'Carrot Before the Donkey's Nose'

While one glass of wine in the middle of the day wasn't likely to raise the concerns of a social worker, a whole bottle might. Reva had finished her first glass and was on her second before I'd taken a sip of my water. As the alcohol relaxed her it loosened her tongue, and her fears and worries spilled out – not only in respect of Danny, but also her husband, Richard.

'He has no patience with Danny,' Reva complained. 'None at all. He thinks Danny behaves as he does on purpose, to provoke him and wind him up. And of course it's always my fault. He cites the example of his other two children – from his first marriage – who are not only normal but doing very well at school. So it must be my fault; I've either mothered Danny incorrectly or not mothered him enough. I'm fed up with having to make excuses for Danny and apologize for his existence. It's difficult enough trying to look after him without Richard going on and on at me.' She stopped, drained her glass and poured another. 'Are you sure you won't join me?'

'No, thank you.'

She took a large swig of wine and continued. 'Richard comes home less and less now. I know some of it's due to him working away, but I doubt it all is. And who can blame him? What is there for him to come home to? A screaming child and a wife who's so stressed out all she can do is moan about what Danny has been doing or not doing. We used to have so much in common. We used to talk and enjoy each other's company. We're different people now – or rather I am,' she added bitterly. 'I can't remember the last time we had sex or even a cuddle. Richard has lost interest in me in all ways. He's so cold to me now.'

Reva's face crumpled and her tears began to fall. I was about to go over and comfort her, but she suddenly stood and went into the kitchen, returning with a box of tissues. She wiped her eyes and blew her nose. 'Sorry,' she said. 'Richard's right, I shouldn't drink. It makes me feel even worse.' She set her empty wine glass on the silver tray and pushed it slightly away. 'Don't worry, I'll have plenty of coffee before I collect Danny from school this afternoon. There's three hours yet. I'd never do anything to jeopardize his safety.'

I gave a small nod and hoped three hours was long enough for the alcohol to process out of her body.

'I've packed some more of Danny's clothes and also some of his toys,' Reva said. 'I'll help you into the car with them.'

'And George and his hutch,' I reminded her.

'Oh yes,' she said with a small, embarrassed laugh. 'The reason you're here. I forgot.'

'Will Danny's father be home this evening when Danny is here?' I asked.

'I doubt it,' Reva said. 'He's not usually home from work until after seven, even on a good day. Danny won't expect to see him. Hopefully he'll be here on Saturday.' She paused and then said, 'Anyway, I'm sure you've got better things to do than listen to all my problems.' So I thought it was time for me to leave.

'I'll have to put the back seats down in my car first,' I said, making a move to go.

'I'll help you,' Reva said, and stood.

Despite drinking three large glasses of wine in quick succession (two-thirds of a bottle) Reva appeared steady on her feet and not in the least drunk or even light-headed. We went into the hall where she helped me on with my coat and then slipped on her jacket. She pulled out a suitcase and toy box that had been tucked ready under the winding balustrade staircase, and opened the front door. 'Let me know if Danny needs more,' she said. 'He has lots of clothes – and toys, although he only uses a few of them.'

'It'll be nice for him to have his own things with him,' I said.

I picked up the toy box and Reva took the suitcase and we went out the front door to my car. I opened the boot and spent some moments lowering the back seats so they were completely flat, and then we lifted in the suitcase and toy box, pushing them to one side so there was room for George's hutch.

'We'll use the side entrance to bring out the hutch,' Reva said. 'Rather than carry it through the house.'

I left the boot open ready to receive the hutch and followed Reva back across the drive towards the right of the house, where she opened a side gate marked 'Private'. The wind nipped down the sideway from the rear of the house and open countryside beyond. I drew my coat closer.

'We'll leave the plastic sheet down so he won't be so scared,' Reva said as we arrived at the hutch.

She took one end of the hutch and I took the other and together we lifted it off the wooden stand and carried it down the sideway. George scampered in his hutch, destabilizing it and causing it to tilt.

'It's all right, George,' Reva soothed. 'You're going on a little holiday to be with Danny.'

I smiled.

We slowly turned the corner of the house and began across the driveway. 'The stand for the hutch won't fit in as well,' I said as we walked.

'It will probably fit in my car,' Reva said. 'The legs unscrew. I'll bring it with me tonight, otherwise Richard will have to bring it at the weekend. The hutch will be all right on the ground until then.'

Arriving at the car, I lowered my end of the hutch into the boot first, and then the two of us manoeuvred it in fully. With the backseats down the boot was just long enough.

'I'll fetch his food and bedding,' Reva said.

I waited by the car as she returned down the side of the house. I lifted the corner of the plastic sheet to check on George. 'Are you OK?' I asked him.

Two blue eyes looked back at me a little surprised, and his nose twitched. 'Good boy,' I said. 'We won't be long.' I lowered the plastic sheet.

Reva returned with a bag of compressed hay for George's bedding and a large packet of food. There was just enough room for it beside the hutch.

'Danny can feed George when he returns to you this evening,' Reva said. 'He knows what to do. And he usually lets him out for some exercise when he gets home from school. In the garden if the weather is good, or if it's raining he brings him indoors.'

'It'll be dark by the time you bring Danny back this evening. Shall I let George have a run in the garden this afternoon?' We'd had a rabbit when the children were little and I knew they needed daily exercise.

'Yes, that would be good. And thanks again for having George,' Reva said gratefully. 'You are a gem. Sorry for going on about all my problems. Forget what I said, will you?'

I gently closed the boot lid. 'You take care of yourself and enjoy your evening with Danny. I'll see you later.'

'Thank you,' Reva said again. We said goodbye. 'The gates will open automatically as you approach them,' she added.

I climbed into my car and started the engine as Reva returned indoors. I set off round the driveway and as I approached the gates they parted. I left the drive with the image of the house receding in my rear-view mirror. I felt sorry for Reva and my heart was heavy. *Forget what I said, will you?* she'd asked me, but as a foster carer I couldn't simply forget what I'd seen and heard if it related to the child's well-being. If Reva was a heavy drinker, as her tolerance of alcohol and her reliance on it in times of stress might suggest, it could have an effect on when, or even if, Danny returned to live with her. All that luxury, I thought; everything she could possibly need in material terms, yet her marriage was falling apart and she was unable to look after her only child.

* * *

To give George as comfortable a ride as possible I drove more slowly than usual and took corners and roundabouts very gently. Even so, every so often I could hear him frantically scampering around his hutch. I talked to him reassuringly: 'It's all right, George. We'll soon be there and then you can have a run in the garden.' Unsurprisingly, he didn't reply.

I realized I'd need help lifting George in his hutch out of the car and then carrying it round to the back of my house, and I anticipated asking a neighbour. I didn't want to leave George in the car until Adrian or the girls were home from school and could help me. As luck would have it, as I drew onto my driveway and parked, my good neighbour Sue came out of her house and was about to get in her car. 'Sue!' I called, going over. 'Could you possibly give me a hand for a couple of minutes?' And I explained what I needed.

'So, you're fostering a rabbit now as well,' she laughed.

But she was happy to help. She came over and together we lifted the hutch out of the car and carried it down the sideway that led to my back garden. We set it on the patio against the wall in a similar position to where it had stood at Danny's house and where Danny had expected to find it when he'd first arrived.

'Thank you so much,' I said to Sue. 'This is George.' I lifted the plastic sheet so she could have her first view of him.

'Oh my stars!' she exclaimed. 'He's enormous. I've never seen a rabbit that big before.'

'He's a British Giant,' I said.

'You're not kidding!' She bent down to the hutch for a closer look.

'He's a pedigree,' I said. 'He's supposed to be that size. He's not fat, just big. I think he's rather handsome in a rabbity sort of way, don't you?'

She laughed. 'Yes, I suppose he is.'

'I'm going to let him out for a run in the garden once I've unloaded the car. You're welcome to stay and join me.' For I could see that Sue was as fascinated by George as I was.

'Another time,' she said. 'I was just on my way out.'

I thanked her again for her help and, leaving the plastic sheet up so George could familiarize himself with his new surroundings, I returned down the sideway with Sue and we said goodbye. I unloaded George's hay and food, and Danny's suitcase and toy box, and carried them into the house. I left the suitcase in the hall to take upstairs later, and carried Danny's toy box through to the living room where Toscha lay curled up asleep on the sofa. I then stowed the bags of hay and rabbit food in the cupboard under the stairs and went through the kitchen and out the back. It was nearly one o'clock and I was ready for some lunch, but I wanted to give George a run first. I didn't like the idea of him being shut in his cage without having had any exercise. The day was bright and cold, but because my house and garden was in a street of houses and not exposed there wasn't the same piercing wind there had been in Reva's back garden. George was at the front of his hutch now, with his nose pressed against the wire mesh, looking out. There were two sections to the hutch, both with their own doors: a wire-mesh one to his living area and a solid wooden one to his sleeping quarters.

'Hello, George,' I said gently, bending down to look at him. 'Do you want to come out for a run?' I opened the door to his living quarters and he looked at me, his nose twitching as he sniffed the air. 'Come on, out you come,' I encouraged.

He sat very still, sideways on, his long ears erect and his nose twitching continuously as he listened and smelt for any sign of danger. He was truly a magnificent creature. Our rabbit had been a standard bunny-sized rabbit, nowhere near as grand as George. He was majestic and had a real presence. I knew Adrian, Lucy and Paula would be taken with him too.

George was a bit reluctant to come out, possibly because it was all new to him. I slowly reached into the hutch so I didn't startle him and began stroking the top of his head, between his ears. I remembered our rabbit had liked that. George's fur was very soft and silky, like velvet. His head lowered a little as he relaxed and then he began sniffing along the front edge of the cage where it met the patio outside, tentatively exploring it.

'Come on, out you come,' I said again.

George raised his head and sniffed the air, clearly trying to decide if it was safe to venture out. And who could blame him? Not only were his surroundings different, but so too was the voice of the woman talking to him. Animals don't like being moved any more than children do.

'Good boy, George, come on,' I said, tapping the ground a little way in front of the hutch, hoping to entice him out. 'There's lots of nice grass for you to eat down the garden.' I remembered how our rabbit had liked to eat grass, and plants and flowers!

George went very still for a moment, possibly summoning up his courage, and then with one gigantic hop he leapt out of his cage and landed beside me on the patio, making me start a little.

'Well done, George,' I said.

Squatting on my haunches, I stroked his back, running my hand lightly from behind his ears to just above his bobble tail. He stayed very quiet and still, all his senses alert. Then, deciding it was safe, he hopped off across the patio and onto the lawn. I followed him. His 'bunny hops' were more like leaps as his strong back legs propelled him upwards and forwards. Now he was out of his cage and moving I could see his full size. He certainly was two feet in length as Reva had said, if not longer. I watched him, fascinated, as he went up and down the lawn, stopping every so often to sniff at something that caught his attention or nibble a patch of grass. He began leaving a trail of pellets in his wake, which doubtless would be good manure for the grass. Then he started circling the tree that grew to the right of the lawn and I followed him round. After a couple of laps he stopped, turned and came to me. I stood still as he sniffed my legs and then tried to nibble my shoes.

'Oh no you don't,' I said, stepping out of reach.

I was in the garden with George for nearly half an hour, playing with him. He was truly a delightful creature who had real character. When he finally flopped out on the grass exhausted and panting, with his legs stretched out in front and behind like a small dog, I guessed he'd had enough exercise for now.

'Time to go back into your hutch,' I said. I wasn't going to leave him unattended in the garden in case he came to harm.

He looked at me, but didn't move.

'Bedtime,' I said.

That same dismissive look and he stayed where he was, stretched out, content and enjoying the space. But I had things to do: apart from lunch, I had Danny's case to unpack, some housework to do, paperwork, and I needed to start planning the training I was due to give. I couldn't wait on George all afternoon, much as I'd have liked to. I tried moving away from him while calling his name. 'Come on, George. Come here. Good boy, time for bed.' But he stayed firmly where he was.

I went over to the hutch and called him from there, for Reva had said that when it was time for George to go back into his hutch Danny opened the hutch door and he jumped in, but George stayed where he was. I tried opening and closing the hutch door a few times, thinking this might be a trigger, but George stayed put. I decided on a different approach. As far as I knew, all rabbits liked carrots, and George had been nibbling one at Reva's, so I went into the kitchen, selected a nice big juicy carrot from the bunch and returned outside. George was where I'd left him, stretched out in the middle of the lawn, but when he saw me coming he stood, alert, ready to flee if necessary.

'It's OK,' I said gently as I gradually approached him. I held the carrot out in front of me. 'Would you like a nice juicy carrot? I bet you would. Yummy.'

George looked at me, as well he might, but his nose twitched. Then he must have picked up the scent of the carrot, because with two big hops he was at my side and taking a bite. I took a step back in the direction of the house, holding out the carrot to him so he had to take another hop towards me for another bite. It was literally the carrot before the donkey's nose, or rather the rabbit's nose. So gradually, with me slowly walking backwards and George hopping towards the receding carrot, we went up the lawn and then crossed the patio. There was a little stub of carrot left as we arrived at the hutch and I placed it just inside his living quarters. George obligingly hopped in and I closed the door.

'Carrot Before the Donkey's Nose'

'Thank you, George,' I said. It wasn't how Danny got him into his hutch, but it had worked.

Leaving the sheet up so he could see out, I went inside for a hot soup lunch. No two days are ever the same in fostering – it's one of the reasons I enjoyed it so much.

Chapter Twelve

Forever?

The afternoon disappeared in the jobs I had to do, and very soon Adrian, Lucy and Paula were returning home from school. As I greeted each of them, I asked if they'd had a good day, and then took them through to meet George. They were all as impressed as I was with George and stroked and petted him in his cage, and gave him tufts of grass to eat and then another carrot. Paula was keen to take him out for a run as I had done, but I said it would be dark soon and I was worried that he might disappear among the shrubbery and we'd have trouble finding him, so we agreed to wait until Danny was home when he would look after him.

The four of us sat down to dinner – Danny was having dinner with his mother – and as we talked I mentioned to Adrian, Lucy and Paula that Danny lived in a very nice house and I described some of it. Often the children we fostered came from badly deprived and impoverished backgrounds, so hearing of Danny's circumstances gave my children a more balanced view: that children from many different backgrounds could come into foster care if a crisis in the family necessitated it.

'Why didn't Danny's mother hire a full-time nanny to look after Danny if she couldn't cope? She could afford it,' Lucy said, which was a fair point. Lucy herself had experienced poverty and neglect before coming into care but still loved her mother, whom she saw a couple of times a year.

'I don't know. I suppose Reva wanted to look after Danny herself,' I said. 'She gave up her job to do so. It's the level of care that Danny requires that's caused difficulties.'

'Will he be going home eventually?' Paula asked.

'I hope so,' I said. 'That's the care plan.'

'And his mother knows where we live?' Lucy asked.

'Yes, she's bringing him here tonight. I shall be working with his parents.'

It was normal practice for the parents of a child in care under a Section 20 to know the foster carer's address, whereas if a child comes into care under a court order there may be reasons why the carer's address is withheld from the parents. Contact then takes place in a family centre with a supervisor present.

At six o'clock we'd finished eating and were clearing away the dishes when the doorbell rang. 'That'll be Reva with Danny,' I said.

As soon I opened the front door Danny shot in with a cry of 'George!' Discarding his school bag in the hall, he ran through to the kitchen.

'He couldn't wait to get back to see George,' Reva said.

I smiled. 'Come in.'

'Can we bring in the stand for the hutch first?' she said. 'It's sticking out of my car window. It was the only way I could get it in.'

'Sure,' I said, and was about to go out when I heard Danny shouting.

'George! George!' Then I heard him kick the back door.

Reva heard it too and looked at me anxiously.

'I'll ask Adrian to help you with the stand while I see to Danny,' I said to her.

I left Reva at the front door and went through to the kitchen. Danny was pulling on the door handle and rattling it hard. As I approached he gave the door another kick. Adrian, Lucy and Paula, who were still at the table, were looking very worried, not knowing what to do for the best.

'Danny, don't kick that door, please,' I said firmly, going up to him. 'George is outside in his cage, safe, and you'll see him very soon.' Then to Adrian I said, 'Could you help Reva bring in the stand for the hutch, please?'

'Sure, Mum,' he said, and went out of the room.

'George needs stand!' Danny yelled, and kicked the back door again.

'Danny,' I said firmly, touching his arm to get his attention. 'Do not kick the door. As soon as you're calm I'll open the door and show you where George is. He is fine.'

'George!' Danny yelled again and raised his foot ready to kick the door.

'No, Danny,' I said, touching his raised foot. 'You must not kick the door.' I sought to make eye contact.

There was a moment's pause, then, without meeting my gaze, he lowered his foot. 'Good boy,' I said.

'Why did you tell him he was good when he kicked your door?' I heard Reva say behind me. I turned and saw her standing at the end of the kitchen, with Adrian a little behind her. She must have followed me straight in.

'Because Danny did as I asked and stopped kicking the door,' I said.

'What would you have done if he hadn't stopped?' Reva asked.

'Warn him again, and then tell him that if he didn't stop he'd lose a privilege.'

'Like what?' Reva asked.

I opened the back door and Danny went out. 'I would have stopped something Danny enjoys doing,' I said to Reva. 'Just for a few minutes. It's called a sanction. I sanction negative behaviour if it can't be ignored, and reward good behaviour.'

'What would *you* have done?' Lucy asked Reva a little bluntly, although Reva didn't seem to mind.

'I'd have probably opened the door straightaway and let Danny out,' she admitted.

'But that's giving in to his negative behaviour,' Lucy said. 'It's rewarding it.'

I stifled a smile, although of course Lucy was right. Child care was a career Lucy was considering when she left school, and we sometimes discussed managing difficult behaviour in the children we were fostering as well as managing hers!

Reva didn't reply and I thought that Lucy had probably said enough. Also the front door was wide open – I could feel the draft – and Danny was alone in the garden, hopefully on the patio.

'Adrian, will you help Reva bring the stand in now, please? And I'll help Danny with George.'

'I'll help with George too, Mum,' Paula said.

'So will I,' Lucy added.

George was clearly already very popular.

'Danny just needs to feed George now,' Reva said.

'I know,' I said. 'I gave him a run earlier.'

Adrian and Reva went to fetch the stand for the hutch from Reva's car as Danny appeared at the back door, looking very anxious.

'What's the matter?' I asked him.

He looked down and began banging the heels of his hands together agitatedly, his face grimacing as he tried to find the words he needed.

'George went in the garden this afternoon,' I said, wondering if this was the problem. 'He just needs feeding now.'

This wasn't the problem, and Danny continued pumping the heels of his hands.

'Do you want the toilet?' Lucy asked him.

I didn't think this was the reason. He'd been very good at going to the toilet and just took himself upstairs when he needed it.

Danny shook his head rigorously. 'Food!' he eventually blurted.

'You're hungry?' Lucy asked.

'No. Food!' he cried, his voice rising.

'George's food?' Paula asked.

Danny nodded. 'George's food,' he repeated. 'George's food.'

Well done, Paula.

'I'll show you where it is,' I said to Danny and offered him my hand, which surprisingly he took.

I led him to the cupboard under the stairs where I'd stored the bags of food and hay. Paula and Lucy joined us. 'This is where we will keep George's food and hay,' I said to Danny.

Danny stepped forward and tried to lift the bag of food, but it was too heavy for him. 'I think it would be best if you brought George's food bowl in here to fill,' I said. But the sentence was too long and not directive enough for Danny to follow. 'Bring George's bowl here,' I said.

Danny turned and ran through the kitchen and out of the back door. Lucy and Paula followed to see if he needed any help, but he didn't. They returned quickly with Danny carrying the empty food bowl. He clearly knew what to do and wanted to do it all by himself. The girls and I watched as he set the bowl carefully on the floor, opened the resealable bag of food and, taking out a small plastic scooper, began filling the bowl.

'One. Two. Three.' He counted out the measured helpings and then replaced the plastic scooper in the bag and carefully sealed the top. He was as meticulous in this as he was in other things and it was touching to watch.

'Well done,' I said once he'd finished. I closed the cupboard door.

Adrian and Reva were now coming in carrying the stand, so I left Danny with Lucy and Paula and went to see if I could be of assistance. The stand wasn't heavy, as the hutch had been, but it was cumbersome and I guided them around the corner in the hall, through the kitchen and out of the back door. It would have been easier to take it down the sideway as I had the hutch, but it was dark and the gate was locked. Lucy, Paula and Danny were already outside, Danny with the bowl of food in his hand, waiting by the hutch. There was enough light coming from the kitchen to see what we were doing. Adrian and Reva set down the stand, then I helped them lift the hutch onto it and shift it into position against the wall. Now the hutch was on the stand it was a much better height, especially for Danny, who hardly had to bend at all to see George at eye level. George seemed a little bemused as he looked through the wire mesh of his living quarters at the gathering outside.

'It's past his dinner time,' Reva said to Danny. 'You can give George his dinner now and say goodnight.' Then to me she said, 'Danny always feeds George after he's had his own dinner, but of course it's been different tonight because he had dinner with me and then we came here.'

'Shall I open the hutch door?' Lucy asked.

'Danny likes to do it,' Reva said.

Danny took his time doing this, as he did with most of his routines. First he set the bowl of food on the floor, then slowly opened the door as far as it would go. He didn't immediately pick up the bowl and put it into the hutch, and George didn't seem to expect it but sat waiting patiently.

'Danny checks he has water and hay before he says goodnight and feeds him,' Reva explained. 'And he always gives him fresh water and hay in the morning.'

Once Danny had done this Reva said, 'Say goodnight now, Danny, and give George his food.'

We watched as Danny leant into the hutch and pursed his lips to kiss George goodnight. As he did, George tilted his head as though offering his cheek for kissing.

'Look at that!' Adrian said, amazed. 'George was waiting for a goodnight kiss!'

And even more amazing was that, when Danny offered his cheek for kissing, George nuzzled his nose against it.

'He kissed him!' Paula exclaimed.

'They always kiss each other goodnight,' Reva said.

'Did Danny teach him to do that?' Lucy asked.

'Not really,' Reva said. 'It was just something that seemed

to develop between them. They're very close. It's as though George senses what Danny wants. You'll see what I mean when he takes George out in the garden. He follows Danny everywhere.'

'Can he come out now?' Lucy asked.

Reva hesitated but clearly didn't like to say no.

'I think it's too late,' I said.

'Yes, it's night time,' Reva said.

'Night time,' Danny repeated, having heard our conversation.

'Danny has George in a routine,' Reva explained to Lucy. 'He lets him out when he gets home from school, and then feeds him and says goodnight after he's had his dinner. Danny will be coming here tomorrow straight from school, so you'll see him out then.'

'Does he just have the one meal a day?' I asked.

'Yes, but if you have any raw vegetables to spare he can have some of those too. Danny knows.'

We continued watching Danny and George. Danny hadn't given George his food bowl yet, but was lightly stroking George's head and face, and petting him gently. The special bond between them was obvious. Then Danny rested his cheek gently against George's and rubbed it a little, obviously enjoying the feel of his soft warm fur. I wasn't sure about the hygiene of all of this, but it was incredible to watch, and Danny obviously took much comfort from the physical contact – the touch and the warmth of George's fur. George appeared to be enjoying it too. I'd never seen a rabbit keep so still and be so accommodating – ours certainly hadn't behaved like this. Finally Danny said, 'Goodnight, George,' and stood back.

He picked up George's food bowl and placed it in the hutch, then closed and bolted the door. 'Goodnight, George,' he said again. 'You're safe with me. Call me if you need me. I'm up there.' He pointed up to his bedroom. Then he drew the plastic sheet over the front of the hutch so George was protected from the cold of the night.

My children and I stood motionless, transfixed by the glimpse of Danny and George's world and their bond of love, understanding and affection. Perhaps George sensed that Danny needed extra care. I'd heard before of children with special needs who'd formed a strong bond with their pet; it was therapeutic for children who often struggled with life and relationships. But what struck me most was the ease with which Danny had talked to George: *Goodnight, George*, he'd said. *You're safe with me. Call me if you need me. I'm up there.* It was the most I'd heard him say to anyone, even his mother, and the words had formed sentences that made sense. Reva must have been aware of this too, and I now understood her comment about Danny loving his rabbit more than he loved her.

We returned indoors and I asked Reva if she'd like a tea or coffee. I didn't say drink as that could have suggested alcohol, which wasn't on offer. She didn't want a drink, so I offered to show her around the house, which she accepted. It's usual to show parents where their child is staying if it's appropriate. Danny had gone straight into the living room, as had the girls, so we began our tour in there. Danny was squatting on the floor, still in his coat and shoes, again playing with the Lego bricks. Paula and Lucy were sitting on the floor, watching him.

'Danny's been making some lovely patterns out of the Lego,' I said to Reva. We went over for a closer look.

'It's good,' Reva said a little flatly. 'But he won't take his coat and shoes off, will he? He does that at home. Sometimes he has dinner with his coat and shoes on. It infuriates Richard.'

It was a pity Reva had said this in front of Danny. Doubtless he'd heard, and it would reinforce his negative behaviour, which wouldn't help her or me in managing it, so I felt I had to do something.

'Danny,' I said, 'it's warm in the house so we take off our coats and shoes when we come in. Do you remember where you hang your coat and put your shoes?'

There was no reply. He continued playing with the Lego. Reva glanced at me.

'Danny,' I said again, now going up to him. 'Would you like to show your mother where you hang your coat and put your shoes, or shall I show her?'

Still no response; his gaze was down as he concentrated on the Lego. So I took a step away and said to Reva, 'I'll show you where Danny hangs his coat and puts his shoes. This way.'

Danny was immediately on his feet, scampering past me and down the hall to the coat stand. It wasn't rocket science, just a variation on the 'closed choice' and a bit of child psychology. Reva and I went down the hall, where Danny sat on the floor, took off his shoes, paired them and set them neatly beside ours.

'Good boy,' I said.

He undid the zipper on his coat and struggled out of it. He raised his arms up to his mother, wanting her to lift him up so he could reach to hang up his coat, as he had done with me the evening before. 'He needs your help to reach the hook,' I said to her.

Saving Danny

A smile crossed her face and she took Danny in her arms and lifted him up. My heart went out to her. Danny wanted so little in the way of physical contact from her, and he gave even less, so this little passing closeness meant a lot to her. She made the most of it, holding him after he'd hung up his coat until he struggled to be put down.

'Good boy,' I said again, praising him, and he went back to the living room.

'Could you watch Danny while I show Reva around the rest of the house?' I called to the girls, who were in the living room. Adrian was in his bedroom.

'Yes, Mum,' they returned.

We were standing by the door to the front room so I showed Reva in there first, and then we went upstairs into Danny's bedroom. I was conscious that my house must seem very small and basic compared to Reva's, although I was happy with it. It was my home. Reva didn't say anything as we entered Danny's room, and given that Danny had a bedroom and an adjoining playroom I wasn't surprised. She hadn't shown me his rooms as she'd said she would when I'd collected George that morning, but I could imagine that they were very spacious and palatial. She spent some minutes looking around Danny's room, at the posters and pictures I'd put on the walls, at the duvet and matching pillowcase depicting Disney cartoon characters. Then she picked up soft-toy George who was sitting on Danny's pillow, absently stroked his head and then returned him to the pillow.

'Thank you for showing me Danny's room,' she said. 'I'll be able to picture him at night now. You've got a lovely home. It's very warm and welcoming; so are you and your children.'

Which was the biggest compliment anyone could pay me. 'I know Danny will be happy here,' she added.

We went downstairs and I suggested we sat in the living room for a while, but Reva said she would just say goodbye to Danny and go.

'Are you sure you don't want to stay for a while?' I asked. Most parents of the children I fostered would have done so, and often had to be persuaded to leave.

'No, thank you,' Reva said a little stiffly. 'Not today. Richard will be home soon and I should be there.' From which I understood that her husband hadn't been at home when Danny had been there earlier, which was a pity.

We went through to the living room so that Reva could say goodbye to Danny. He was still poring over the Lego, rearranging the bricks into a different pattern as Paula and Lucy watched.

'I'm going now,' Reva said to Danny. 'I'll see you on Saturday.'

Danny had his back to us and didn't move or acknowledge he'd heard his mother.

'Danny, your mother is going,' I said, going round to face him. 'Do you want to come to the front door to say goodbye to her, or say goodbye to her here?'

Silence.

'Say goodbye to your mummy,' Lucy encouraged.

'Say goodbye to your mummy,' Danny echoed without turning to look at her.

Reva apparently saw nothing strange in accepting this as Danny's goodbye. 'Goodbye, Danny,' she said. 'Bye, girls.'

'Bye,' Paula and Lucy said.

Saving Danny

I went with Reva to the front door where she thanked me again for all I was doing for Danny and then left. Her parting from Danny had been completely emotionless and barren. Often parents of the children I foster leave in tears, distraught at the thought of being separated from their child until the next contact. But Reva had appeared as detached as Danny, unlike at school when she'd been very upset. Also Reva had shown a complete lack of urgency about having Danny home again. Usually parents question me endlessly about when I think their child is likely to be able to go home. True, Danny was in care under a Section 20, so theoretically Reva could remove him at any time, but she'd given no indication that she was hoping to have Danny home again – either in the short or long term. Perhaps she wasn't? There'd been an unsettling finality when she'd said, *I know Danny will be happy here.* Had she meant forever?

Chapter Thirteen

Cooped Up

I returned to the living room where Danny was still sitting on the floor redesigning his Lego pattern, while the girls sat close by chatting between themselves. They would have played with Danny if he'd wanted them to, but he didn't. Outwardly self-sufficient and in his own personal bubble, Danny appeared unaffected by going home and then having to return to me and part from his mother, which would have unsettled and upset most children. Although, of course, what Danny was thinking and feeling might well be another matter, unless he really was incredibly resilient, which I doubted.

It was nearly seven o'clock and I needed to start Danny's bedtime routine. I'd already decided we'd miss his bath on the nights he had contact so that he didn't become overtired, which could easily develop into a tantrum. Most children become crotchety if overtired, and special needs children like Danny are more prone to this. I was just thinking that maybe we should give his homework a miss too, when he suddenly stood and, leaving the Lego, went down the hall. I thought he was going to the toilet, so I followed him out, ready to go upstairs and begin his bedtime routine. But instead he went to his school bag, picked it up and came towards me with it clutched to his chest. 'Do you want to do your reading?' I asked him.

'Yes, thank you very much,' he said.

'Good boy. Come on then.'

I guessed Danny must have sensed it was that time in the evening when he normally did his homework, for he couldn't tell the time. We returned to the living room and sat side by side on the sofa. The girls said they were going to make themselves a drink and asked Danny if he'd like one, but he shook his head. He carefully opened his bag, took out his reading book, turned to the first page and began reading. But two pages later, when his progress had become agonizingly slow and he struggled to recognize even the simplest of words, it was obvious he was too tired or unsettled by the changes that evening to concentrate, and he lost his patience. His fists tightened around the book as he let out a low, guttural noise of anger.

'That's enough reading for this evening,' I said. 'You did well. Put your book away.'

There was the usual delay as Danny processed what I'd said, and then he repeated, 'Put your book away.' He often repeated or echoed what someone said, as if it helped him process the information.

'Yes, put your book away,' I confirmed. 'We won't do the flash cards tonight. It's too late and we're both tired.'

'No flash cards?' he asked.

'No. Not tonight.'

Another pause and then he did as I asked. Then he passed me his home school book for me to write in. I spoke the words out loud as I wrote them so that he knew what I was writing.

Cooped Up

The record book was as much for his benefit as it was for his teacher's and mine. 'Danny read two pages tonight. He had contact with his mother and settled well on return, but it was too late to do any more homework. We will do some more tomorrow.' I signed and dated my entry, closed the book and passed it to Danny, who carefully tucked it into his school bag. Then he took his bag down the hall and set it precisely beside his shoes ready for morning.

'Good boy,' I said.

On the way upstairs I explained to Danny that he would wash his face and hands and brush his teeth, but because it was late he wouldn't have a bath. Advising a child in advance of changes in routine causes them less disruption, especially children like Danny who thrive on routine. I also knew from Reva's notes that she sometimes skipped Danny's bath if he was tired or was being especially difficult. Danny didn't say anything but began his bedtime routine as I waited on hand in case I was needed – first outside the toilet, then in his bedroom, and finally in the bathroom, where he began by once again repositioning the step stool in front of the wash basin until he was satisfied it was perfectly square. I helped him run the water to the right temperature and then I perched on the edge of the bath as he slowly and meticulously washed and dried his face, brushed his teeth in the rhythm he'd perfected and then spent some time patting his mouth dry, before hanging his towel on the rail beside ours and adjusting it.

'That's perfect,' I said eventually. We'd been in the bathroom for nearly half an hour.

'That's perfect,' Danny repeated.

'Time to get into bed,' I said.

'Time to get into bed,' Danny repeated. Then added, 'Yes, thank you very much.' I couldn't help but smile, bless him.

In his bedroom Danny spent a long time checking everything was in its correct place and that his clothes were ready for morning, precisely folded on the foot of his bed as he liked them. Then he adjusted the dimmer switch and went to the slightly parted curtains and adjusted those too, but now he added a new element to his bedtime routine. Pressing his nose against the glass, he said softly, 'Night, George. I love you so very much.'

A lump immediately rose to my throat. How much his mother would have liked to hear those words instead of being ignored when she left. How easily he'd said them to George. Danny clearly did have feelings; it was the expression of those feelings he struggled with. I doubted this was from any conscious refusal to show them but part of his condition – he didn't know how to express himself. And it wasn't chance that it was an animal he'd told, for an animal wouldn't show or demand any emotion in return, as people – especially his mother – would, which Danny wouldn't be able to handle.

He came away from the window, climbed into bed and, drawing soft-toy George in beside him, pulled the duvet over his head.

'Goodnight, love,' I said.

There was no reply.

'Night, Danny. See you in the morning.'

I came out and closed his door behind me, the brief window into his emotions closed too.

'Did you see his mother's car?' Adrian said, coming out of his bedroom and clearly impressed.

'Reva's car? No, I didn't.'

'It's a BMW convertible! My dream car!'

I smiled. 'You'd better start saving your pocket money then. You've got two years before you're old enough to learn to drive.'

'Very funny,' he said. 'They cost a packet. I'll need a big raise in my allowance.'

'Or a very good job,' I said. 'That's how Reva afforded her car. Have you finished your homework yet?'

'Yes.'

'Good boy.' I stood on tiptoes to kiss his cheek. At fifteen, Adrian was six inches taller than me, although of course he'd always be my little boy.

Downstairs the girls, having completed their homework, were in the living room watching a soap on television before going to bed. I went into the kitchen to make a cup of tea – just as Toscha shot in through the cat flap with an indignant look on her face. If she could have spoken I am sure she would have said, 'What's that hutch doing in my garden?'

'That's George,' I said. 'You'll meet him properly tomorrow when Danny takes him out for a walk.'

She wasn't impressed, so I gave her a cat-treat biscuit and stroked her to make up for having to share her territory. Danny hadn't shown much interest in Toscha, and Toscha had largely ignored him. I think some of Danny's loud noises and sudden movements frightened her, for she was usually quite a sociable cat.

Later that night, when all the children were in bed, I sat in the living room thinking about Reva, and Danny, and his father who seemed to be largely absent from his life. Lucy had never known her father, and while Adrian and Paula saw their father every month they weren't as close to him as they had been when he'd lived with us, which was a pity. Deep in thought, I started as a noise came from the kitchen. It wasn't the cat flap closing – Toscha was asleep by the radiator. I was sure I'd locked and bolted the back door; as a female and the only adult in the house I was conscientious about security. As I listened I heard the noise again. It was at moments like this I wished I had a big strong man in the house, but Adrian, as big as he was, was my son, and I still protected him.

Summoning my courage I went into the kitchen and looked around. All was quiet. Nothing appeared to have fallen or been moved, and the back door was shut and bolted and the windows closed. Everything was as I'd left it, so what had made that noise? I began towards the back door to look outside. As I did so, the noise sounded again, and with relief I recognized it – George was thumping the floor of his cage. If a rabbit senses danger its instinct is to thump its hind legs, and George's legs were big and gave a powerful thump. I thought I'd better check he was all right. Very occasionally a fox came into the garden. I raised the blind on the rear window, so the light from the kitchen fell onto the hutch, and I went out. The night was cold but the air still, and there was no sound of a predator fleeing. Perhaps George was just reacting to his new surroundings. I raised the plastic sheet and looked in. George looked back. 'Are you OK?' I asked him.

His nose twitched.

He seemed fine, so I lowered the sheet and returned indoors. I hoped his thumping wouldn't wake Danny or Adrian, whose bedrooms were at the rear of the house. If it did I'd have to consider moving the hutch, although I was reluctant to do that as it was in a similar position to where it had been at Danny's house, and would mean another change for Danny to accommodate.

The following morning when I woke Danny for school I said, 'Last night I heard George thumping. Did he wake you?'

Danny looked down as he struggled to find the right words to answer, and eventually replied, 'George thumping goodnight.'

'I see,' I said, pleased by the clarity of his reply. 'George was saying goodnight to you?'

Danny nodded.

'Did he wake you?'

He shook his head and again searched for the right words. 'Mummy hear George. Danny sleep. George thumps. It's OK.'

I smiled. 'Thank you for telling me. I won't worry now.'

It was the best conversation I'd had with Danny, and it wasn't a coincidence that it was about his beloved George.

At breakfast I asked Adrian if he'd been woken by George's thumping and he said he hadn't, so George's hutch stayed where it was. Despite waking Danny ten minutes earlier to allow time for him to tend to George, he was so meticulous and precise that the process took longer than I'd anticipated, and we arrived in the school playground just as the whistle was blowing for the start of school. Yvonne was already waiting and I apologized, saying we'd have to start getting up earlier to incorporate George's routine into ours.

'So how is George?' Yvonne asked Danny.

Danny didn't reply.

'He's fine,' I said. 'Settling in.' Then, trying to encourage Danny into the conversation, I said to him, 'You're going to give George a walk in the garden after school, aren't you?'

Danny looked away.

The other children were lining up ready to go into school, so I said goodbye to him and reminded him that I'd meet him at the end of school. He remained silent.

'Bye,' Yvonne said.

'Bye. Have a good day,' I said to them both.

'We will,' Yvonne replied cheerfully.

Danny slipped his hand into Yvonne's as they walked away. Again I could see how hurtful his gesture would have been to his mother when he'd been unable to even say goodbye to her, but Danny wouldn't be aware of this.

That morning Terri telephoned for an update on Danny, and as I told her I concentrated on all the positives. She said she needed to visit us, so we made an appointment for Monday at 4.30 p.m. Terri also said she would be arranging Danny's first review soon and was anticipating holding it at my house. Children in care have regular reviews, where their parents, social worker, foster carer, the foster carer's support social worker, their teacher and any other adults closely connected with the child meet together to ensure that everything is being done to help the child. The care plan (drawn up by the social worker) is also updated. The reviews are chaired by an independent reviewing officer (IRO), who minutes the meeting. Very young children don't usually attend their reviews, but older children can do. There was no reason why Danny's review shouldn't be held in my house, and Terri said she would send out the invitations once she had set a date and time. We said goodbye and hung up. Fifteen minutes later Jill telephoned to see how the week had gone and I gave her a similar update to the one I'd given Terri, although I included my concerns about Reva's drinking. As my support social worker she could offer advice on how to approach the matter.

'You must tell Terri on Monday in case there is a problem,' Jill said.

'All right, I will.'

'Any plans for the weekend?' Jill then asked. She wasn't just being polite; it was part of her job to know what I had planned for Danny.

'Danny has contact all day Saturday,' I said. 'And I've invited my parents to dinner on Sunday. I thought we'd keep the weekend reasonably quiet to allow Danny the chance to settle in. I'll take him out next Sunday when he's feeling more at home.'

'It'll be nice for Danny to meet your parents.'

'Yes, and they're looking forward to meeting him.'

My parents had always been supportive of my fostering and treated the child or children we were looking after as another grandchild while they were with us.

That afternoon, as I busied myself with housework and then paperwork, I occasionally heard George thumping in his cage and I went out to check on him. He always seemed all right and came up to the wire mesh to greet me, but I was concerned he was spending too much time cooped up in his cage. When we'd had a rabbit we'd bought an enclosed run, which had sat on the lawn. On a fine day he'd been in it for most of the day, nibbling the grass and with room to exercise. I'd given the run and the hutch away when our rabbit had died, but now I was wondering if I should mention buying one to Reva. Or would she see it as a criticism? Half an hour later, when I heard George thump again, I decided to let him out for some exercise. I slipped on my coat, tucked a carrot into my pocket and went outside. As soon as I opened the hutch door he jumped out, pleased to be free, and with a few long bunny hops had crossed the patio and was on the grass. He raced up and down the lawn and then around the tree, really appreciating his freedom. At one point I glanced up and saw my neighbour, Sue, watching from her upstairs window. She smiled and waved, and I waved back. I heard the cat flap open and Toscha appeared, probably having seen George from the living-room window.

'Come and meet George,' I called to Toscha from the lawn.

She took a couple of steps towards us as George sat nibbling the grass, but as soon as he moved, Toscha's back arched and her hackles rose. Turning, she fled back inside through the cat flap. I guessed it would take time for them to be friends.

When George finally collapsed exhausted on the grass with his legs spread out in front and behind him I assumed he'd had enough exercise, so I enticed him back into his hutch with the carrot. It was only a couple of hours before Danny would be home from school, and then George would have another run.

Fifteen minutes before I had to leave to collect Danny from school, the telephone rang. I answered it and a familiar but unsteady female voice said, 'Cathy?'

'Yes. Is that you, Reva?'

'It is … I hope you don't mind me phoning,' she said, slurring her words, 'but I need to talk … and you're a good listener. Cathy … my husband is having an affair … and I think I'm going to divorce him … What do you think of that … Cathy?'

Not a lot, and even less that Reva was blind stinking drunk.

Chapter Fourteen

Traumatic

'I've suspected he's been up to something for a while ...' Reva continued haltingly. 'But now I have proof. You'll never guess what I found ... A receipt, tucked in the pocket of his best jacket ... a receipt from a jeweller for a very expensive necklace ... He hasn't given me a necklace, so who the hell has he given it to?'

While I could sympathize with Reva – I'd also discovered a jeweller's receipt when my husband had been having an affair – she wouldn't be interested in what I had to say. Having tried to anaesthetize her pain with alcohol, she was now wallowing in self-pity and just wanted to talk and unburden herself.

'What have I done to deserve this?' she said with a small sob. 'I've always been faithful to him, honestly I have ... I've had my chances ... I used to be attractive. I gave up a good career to have his child. I've always put myself second, and this is how he rewards me! The bastard. I hate him!' There now followed a diatribe against Richard and all he'd done to hurt her and not done to help her, culminating in his rejection of Danny. 'It's his fault as much as mine that Danny is like he is ... He's never been a father to Danny ... At least I tried to be his mother.'

While I appreciated Reva was upset and needed to talk, I was mindful of the time. 'Reva, I'm sorry,' I said. 'I'm going to have to phone you back. I have to leave soon to collect Danny from school.'

'Oh, silly me, of course,' she slurred. 'Time has become a bit meaningless with nothing to do all day. You go … No need to call me back though … I'm going to bed to sleep this lot off before Richard gets in.' She hung up and the line went dead.

I left the house with my concerns for Reva mounting. She was obviously upset at discovering her husband's infidelity, but it had also sounded as though she resented having to give up work to parent Danny. Her comment about being attractive once showed just how low her self-esteem had sunk. But drinking herself into a stupor wasn't going to help, and she'd now placed me in the unenviable position of having to tell Terri of this incident as well.

Thankfully, in contrast to his mother, Danny had had a good day.

'I'm so pleased with Danny,' Yvonne said. 'He's done a lovely piece of writing on our topic, The Great Fire of London. He also joined the other children for story time.'

'Well done, Danny,' I said, smiling at him.

'George,' Danny replied, flapping his arms in excitement.

Yvonne laughed kindly. 'He's been so looking forward to seeing George when he gets home.'

'I'm sure George is looking forward to seeing you too,' I said to Danny.

Yvonne and I wished each other a nice weekend and said goodbye. Danny held my hand nicely as we walked to the car.

Traumatic

George wasn't the only one looking forward to Danny's arrival. When we got in, Adrian, Lucy and Paula had their coats on ready to go with Danny when he took George for a walk in the garden. They appreciated George was more than a pet to Danny and he was Danny's responsibility, so they wouldn't take the initiative in looking after George but would follow Danny's lead. Danny was immediately at the back door, and as soon as I opened it he rushed out. However, just at that moment a large raindrop fell, quickly followed by another and another.

'House,' Danny said as he opened the hutch door.

'Can we take George in the house?' Paula asked me excitedly.

'Yes, that's what Danny does at home,' I replied.

'Oh, great!' Paula said.

'But we'll have to make sure Toscha is all right,' I added. 'She's a bit unsure of George at present.'

'I'll look out for Toscha,' Lucy said.

'House,' Danny said again, this time to George.

Danny turned and headed in through the back door with George at his heels like a well-trained puppy.

'Look at the size of him!' Lucy exclaimed, seeing George out of his hutch for the first time.

'I bet he does massive poops,' Adrian declared.

'Hopefully not too many,' I said.

But there was a feeling of light-heartedness and gaiety as we followed Danny through the kitchen with George hopping beside him. When it comes to cute animals and adorable pets we're all children at heart, and George was truly in a category of his own. Even Danny, whose movements were often slow and cumbersome and who had difficulty expressing emotion, had a lightness about him, now clearly far more at ease with George beside him. In the living room Danny went to the Lego still on the floor and, squatting down, began telling George about it in some detail.

'I change my Lego pattern every day,' Danny said clearly. 'This is a yellow brick and this is a green brick. This is a red brick. I have made a yellow, green and red pattern.'

George put his nose to the bricks and sniffed them as though understanding Danny's narrative.

'I've done well,' Danny told George. 'I've done a good job. I've made an interesting pattern.' I was amazed. These were some of the phrases I'd used to praise Danny, yet he'd given no indication at the time that he'd even heard them – let alone remembered them.

Adrian, Paula, Lucy and I stood watching Danny in awe as he continued telling George about the sequence of colours while stroking and petting him. The improvement in Danny's language skills while talking to George compared to people was remarkable. Danny was using phrases to converse and was interacting with George, so why didn't he talk to children at school and try to make friends? What had made him so fearful of interacting with his peer group? George, for his part, sat still with his head cocked slightly to one side as though listening to what Danny was telling him.

After some minutes Danny stood and said to George, 'It's warm in the house. In the house I take my coat off. I hang my coat on the coat stand.'

'Yes, well done, Danny,' I said, completely bemused.

Danny went out of the living room, with George at his heels and us following, to the coat stand where he told George, 'I undo the zip on my coat like this.'

Danny began drawing down the zip, as usual finding it difficult but wanting to do it himself. 'It's a zip fastener, not the end of the world,' he told George, using the exact phrase I'd used when his zip had stuck. I hid a smile.

He took off his coat and then told George, 'I can't reach to hang up my coat. I have help.'

I went forward ready to lift him up so he could reach, but he turned and held up his arms to Adrian, wanting him to lift him up. We watched, touched, as Adrian lifted Danny high into the air, higher than I did and making it into a game. Danny looped his coat over the stand and actually smiled. When Adrian set Danny on the floor again he said to George, 'Shall I show you around the house now?'

I was speechless. When I'd asked Danny previously if he'd like to see the other rooms in the house, which I'd done quite a few times, he had always shaken his head. Until now he had followed the same route from the front door to the living room and kitchen-cum-diner, and upstairs to the toilet, the bathroom and his bedroom. Now with George beside him he was braver and more inquisitive.

'Shall we go in the front room first?' I asked Danny.

He nodded.

Lucy opened the door to the front room and we all went in. 'This is the front room where the computer is,' Danny told George, which is what I'd said to Reva when I'd showed her around. Although Danny hadn't been with us, he must have heard.

George paused, sniffed the air and then hopped up and down the room, depositing some pellets behind him.

'Oh, gross!' Lucy exclaimed. Adrian and Paula laughed loudly.

Saving Danny

Danny looked worried, as though he'd done something wrong.

'It's all right' I said. 'They'll easily sweep up.'

I thought it best to clear up the pellets straight away before George or one of us trod in them, so I fetched the dustpan and brush from the kitchen. The droppings were firm and were swept up easily, but not before Lucy had uttered another 'Gross!'

'It's all right,' I reassured Danny. 'Do you want to show George upstairs now?' For this seemed a good opportunity to show Danny around.

'Would you like to go upstairs?' Danny asked George.

I guessed George said yes, for Danny began leading us out of the front room and upstairs.

'Look! George can climb stairs!' Paula declared.

'And poop at the same time!' Adrian said, dissolving into more laughter.

'Arghh!' Lucy cried dramatically. 'I nearly trod it in!'

'It's one pellet,' I said, brushing it into the dustpan. 'Stop making such a fuss, and be grateful George isn't an elephant.' Which made Adrian laugh even more.

Upstairs we followed Danny and George into Danny's bedroom.

'This is my room,' Danny said to George. 'This is my bed. This is toy George. You know him.' He took soft-toy George from his pillow and held it to George to sniff and then set it on his pillow again.

George spent some time hopping around Danny's room, sniffing various items, without leaving any more droppings.

'Would you and George like to see the other bedrooms?' I now asked Danny.

'Yes, come and see my room,' Lucy said. 'But don't let him poop.'

'He hasn't got control over it, you muppet,' Adrian said affectionately to Lucy. 'He isn't human.' Although from the way George was behaving with Danny you could almost believe he was.

'This way,' Lucy said to Danny. 'Tell your rabbit to follow.'

'He's George,' Danny said indignantly. 'Not rabbit.'

'That told you,' Adrian said.

With George beside him Danny was clearly far more confident in expressing himself. We were seeing a very different side to him, and it was good.

The novelty of having a large rabbit hopping around her bedroom overrode any thought of it pooping – Lucy was like a little child as George explored, sniffing the objects he came across, sticking his head into corners and then under the bed.

'I think George likes my room,' Lucy said, pleased.

Then George began trying to nibble a flower off the pattern on the duvet and Danny gently pulled him away. 'Naughty boy!' he said firmly. 'Don't do that. You'll go to your room if you do it again.' I wondered where he'd heard that, as I didn't use those words.

'Come and see my room now,' Paula said.

We filed out of Lucy's room and into Paula's. George went straight to her school bag, left on the floor, and began scratching at it, trying to get into it. Danny rushed to stop him.

'He can smell my apple,' Paula said.

'Is that the apple you were supposed to eat with your lunch?' I asked. I was always trying to encourage the children to eat more fruit and vegetables.

'Yesterday's,' Paula said. 'It's bruised. Can I give it to George?'

157

Danny looked worried and then said, 'George makes a mess. George eat in his hutch.' Which I guessed was a rule in his house.

'We won't feed him in the house,' I said to Paula. 'But if it's all right with Danny, you could give George the apple when he goes back in his hutch.'

Danny nodded and Paula took the apple from her bag while George had a good sniff around the rest of her room. Then we all went to Adrian's room. Danny looked around with interest; it was very much a boy's room, with model aircraft and large posters showing scenes from *The Lord of the Rings* and various action movies. George had a good look too, and under the bed he discovered a pair of Adrian's socks that hadn't found their way into the laundry basket. He sniffed and then tried to nibble them.

'Oh no! Gross!' Lucy cried as Paula held her nose. The girls often teased Adrian about having sweaty feet. He didn't mind and gave as good as he got.

My bedroom was next and George showed his appreciation by depositing half a dozen pellets in quick succession on my carpet. My children found it hilarious – 'He likes you, Mum,' Paula giggled – but Danny was looking worried. I quickly swept up the pellets but thought that in future when George came into the house we'd limit his run to downstairs, for hygiene's sake.

'Does your mum let you have George in your bedroom?' Paula asked Danny, almost reading my thoughts.

Danny shook his head.

Good, I thought, that helps. 'George is upstairs this once,' I clarified. 'So Danny can show him the rooms. But in future, if it rains and he has to come into the house, we'll keep him downstairs. He can have plenty of exercise running up and down the hall.'

Danny didn't object, but Lucy did. 'It's fun having him up here,' she grumbled.

'So perhaps you'd like to clear up his mess?' I said, offering her the dustpan and brush. She took my point.

After my bedroom Danny showed George the bathroom. 'This is my towel,' he said, taking the opportunity to straighten it. 'This is the bath. This is the tap. The water is hot. Hot water can burn.' So Danny had been listening when I'd told him that.

Once George had seen the bathroom we went round the landing ready to return downstairs.

'You haven't shown George the toilet,' Paula said.

Danny stopped and his face grew serious. He was quiet as he struggled to find the words he needed. I knew the signs now: the furrowed brow, the element of panic as his body tensed and he tried to think of what to say. Sometimes he flapped his arms in agitation. Eventually he said, 'George scared of that room.'

'Why?' Adrian asked.

Danny turned away and made no attempt to answer, then he began downstairs. And I knew, possibly from years of fostering or having seen something in Danny's body language, that whatever had happened to make George scared had been very traumatic for Danny.

Chapter Fifteen

Danny's World

George stayed in the house, downstairs, running up and down the hall with the children in attendance, while I began the preparations for dinner. After about fifteen minutes Danny came to me and said quietly, 'George go in hutch now.'

'All right, love.' I went into the hall and explained to Adrian, Paula and Lucy that it was time for Danny to put George away.

'Oh, can't he stay out a bit longer?' Lucy asked.

Danny shook his head.

'It's Danny's routine for George and we need to keep to it,' I explained.

George seemed to know his routine too, as he was already heading for the back door. We went outside with Danny and George and onto the patio. It had stopped raining now. Adrian, Paula, Lucy and I watched as Danny opened the hutch door and George immediately jumped in, far more compliant than he had been with me when I'd had to entice him up the garden and into his hutch with a carrot.

'See you after dinner,' Danny said easily. 'Bye, George.'

'Bye, George,' the rest of us chorused, for he really was like a little person.

Danny's World

We returned indoors; Adrian and Danny to the living room and the girls to their bedrooms. It was Friday evening, so we could be more relaxed in our routine without the pressure of having to be up early for school the following morning. I suggested again to Danny that he might like to play with something different as a change from Lego. His toy box from home was in the living room but had been left untouched. Danny didn't reply and went to the Lego. 'I'll stay with him for a while if you like,' Adrian said, sitting on the floor beside him.

'Thanks, love. I'll be in the kitchen.'

When I called everyone to dinner Danny was still playing with the Lego and I wondered if he would ever tire of it. Adrian had, and was sitting on the sofa reading a book. I thought that Danny's interest in the Lego was starting to seem a little obsessive.

He was quiet at dinner. Without George beside him he'd retracted into his shell again and couldn't – or wouldn't – talk, despite our encouragement. As we ate we said things like, 'You must be very proud of George.' And Paula asked Danny if he'd taught George to do little tricks, like jumping over a low fence as our rabbit had done. But Danny kept his head down and concentrated on his food – as usual arranging and eating it in colour-graded order. Danny was the last to finish and the rest of us sat with him and talked while he ate. As soon as he'd finished he said, 'George,' then slid from his chair and went to the back door.

It was now time for George's bedtime routine, and Lucy and Paula, still intrigued by George, went with Danny to fetch George's food bowl from the hutch and then waited as Danny carefully measured three scoops from the bag of rabbit food stored in the cupboard under the stairs. As George's water bottle needed topping up, I positioned the kitchen stool in front of the sink so Danny could reach the taps. Then we filed outside and stood in silent awe as George and Danny kissed each other goodnight, their special relationship so very touching to see.

That night as I bathed Danny he again threw himself back in the bath and lay submerged under the water, pretending he was drowning, as I now knew he did with his mother at home.

'Danny drowning,' he said as he resurfaced, furtively glancing at me to see my reaction.

'No, you're not,' I said lightly. 'You're safe. You're playing.'

'Danny drowning,' he said more firmly, jettisoning himself back and under the water.

'Danny playing,' I said as he came up. 'You're safe. I wouldn't let you drown.'

He did it twice more, each time glancing at me as he rose from the water to see if he'd managed to provoke a reaction. I smiled and said it was nearly time for him to get out of the bath and dry himself, but I was wondering how much of his negative behaviour at home was about trying to elicit a response from his parents. Some of Danny's conduct was beyond his control, but not all of it.

It was nearly 8.30 p.m. by the time Danny was in bed and I said goodnight to the lump in the duvet. I came out and went downstairs. Adrian, Paula and Lucy were in the living room playing whist and I joined in on the next round. Then we had a game of Scrabble, which Adrian won. Before they went to bed I reminded them that I'd be taking Danny home for contact in the morning and asked if anyone wanted to come with me, but there were no takers understandably, as they preferred to have a lie-in on a Saturday morning.

Danny was awake at his usual time the next morning and I again explained to him the arrangements for the day: that I would take him home and he would spend the day with his parents. Then they would bring him back to me at six o'clock.

'Six o'clock,' Danny repeated, and opening his wardrobe door he began choosing some clothes to wear.

After some time he eventually selected a pair of shorts and a T-shirt, so I gently explained that they weren't suitable, as it was cold outside, and he needed to choose something warmer – suitable for winter. I wasn't sure why Reva had packed shorts and T-shirts – there were quite a few in the case – unless she'd decided that Danny would definitely be staying with me for summer, which was a possibility. Danny didn't like being told what to wear and rejected all the trousers and jerseys I took from his wardrobe and placed on his bed, pushing them aside. He then threw himself on the floor, his body tense and his eyes screwed shut ready for a tantrum, which would certainly wake Adrian, Lucy and Paula. Thank goodness for school uniforms, I thought.

'Get dressed, please, Danny,' I said, firmly. 'George is waiting to see you.'

Danny lay still, his eyes closed, but clearly having heard what I'd said.

'Come on, quickly, or there won't be time to see George before we have to leave,' I added for good measure.

Danny opened his eyes, hauled himself from the floor, then took one of the jerseys and pairs of trousers I'd put on the bed and arranged them with his vest, pants and socks in order, ready to dress.

'Good boy,' I said. 'George will be pleased.'

Paula, Lucy and Adrian were up and in their dressing gowns when it was time for Danny and me to leave, and they called, 'Goodbye, Danny. See you later. Have a nice day,' as we went out.

Danny didn't reply and looked confused, so I explained once more that he would be spending the day at home with his parents and then they would bring him back to me at six o'clock. I avoided calling my house 'home', which might have added to his confusion.

'Six o'clock,' he repeated, looking no less confused.

From past experience I knew it took children coming into care many weeks to adjust to the changes that contact brought, and much longer for special needs children, who relied heavily on familiarity and routine and had limited understanding of their situation. Danny was silent in the car as I drove and whenever I glanced at him in the mirror he was staring blankly through his side window. Twenty minutes later I pulled into the end of the drive that led to his house and stopped. The security gates were shut. Danny leant forward in his seat and tapped me on the shoulder to gain my attention.

'Yes, love?' I asked, turning.

'Danny going home?' he asked anxiously.

'For today, yes. Then you will come back to me at six o'clock.'

'Six o'clock,' he repeated. He couldn't tell the time but at least this gave him some reference point and was marginally better than me saying 'later' or 'this evening', which were vague terms and not very helpful.

The security gates didn't open so I lowered my window and pressed the call button. After a few moments Reva's voice came through: 'Sorry, Cathy. I'll open the gates now.'

'Mummy?' Danny asked, hearing her voice. Perhaps he'd never heard his mother through the intercom before.

'Yes. Mummy is in your house waiting for you,' I explained.

The gates opened. I drove through and they closed automatically behind me. There were no other cars on the drive, so I parked where I had done before, close to the house.

'Six o'clock,' Danny said as I cut the engine.

Unfastening my belt I turned to face him. He was pale and anxious and I could see the uncertainty in his eyes as he stared through the windows trying to make sense of what was happening.

'Danny, love,' I said. 'You remember you came home for tea on Thursday, and then came back to my house? Well, now you are staying for the whole day. Then Mummy and Daddy will bring you back to me at six o'clock.' I didn't know how else I could explain it. I'd tried everything.

'Mummy!' he suddenly cried, his face brightening.

I turned to see Reva coming out of the front door. I got out of the car and called, 'Good morning,' then went round and opened Danny's door. He scrambled out and ran into his mother's arms, much as he had done on that first morning in the school playground, very pleased to see her. She picked him up and smothered him in kisses as he clung to her, his arms and legs wrapped tightly around her.

'He's missed me,' Reva said, as though this was a revelation.

'Of course he has,' I said. 'Far more than he can say.'

'Would you like to come in?' she asked.

'No, this is your time with Danny.'

'All right, thanks. I'll bring him back later.'

'Bye, Danny,' I said, but he didn't answer.

As I returned to my car Reva was carrying Danny indoors, with him still clinging tightly to her. It was such a pity he couldn't tell her how much he loved and missed her, for Reva certainly needed to hear it. I hoped she understood it from his actions.

When I arrived home Paula, Lucy and Adrian were still in their dressing gowns but at the table, tucking into a cooked breakfast of eggs, bacon, sausages, baked beans and hash browns, which they proudly told me they'd cooked together. I was impressed – even more so when Adrian took a plate from the oven for me. 'Thank you very much,' I said, sounding like Danny, and I joined them at the table. I love a cooked breakfast at the weekend when we have time to enjoy it, and it's especially nice when it's cooked for you!

With Danny at his parents' all day it allowed me the opportunity to give Adrian, Lucy and Paula my full attention. Although we all thought the world of Danny, he was hard work and took up most of my time. We had a leisurely breakfast and then the kids finished their homework while I cleared away. In the afternoon, as they were in the mood for cooking, we baked some cupcakes and also made an apple crumble for my parents' visit the following day. As Danny wouldn't be home while it was light, we let George out in the garden for about half an hour and were very vigilant. Paula, Lucy and Adrian had great fun, but then had to spend a long time enticing George back into his hutch with a carrot and then some cabbage leaves.

'Why doesn't he do what we want?' Paula moaned. 'He does what Danny wants straight away.'

'They have a special bond,' I said. 'They're very close.'

'Danny seems to like George more than he does us,' Lucy commented, much as Reva had done.

'I think Danny finds it easier being with his pet, because he doesn't make any demands of him,' I said. 'I'm hoping the educational psychologist will be able to help Danny express himself and lose some of his distrust of adults.'

'Why doesn't he trust us?' Paula asked. 'We haven't done anything to him.'

'No, but we're part of a world Danny doesn't understand and it scares him. He's the same with his parents and the other children at school.' Although I'd talked to my children about Danny's difficulties, and we'd fostered other children before who'd been on the autistic spectrum, it was still hard for them to fully appreciate how differently Danny perceived the world around us, as indeed it was for his parents and me. While Danny hadn't been diagnosed with autism (we were waiting for the educational psychologist's assessment), he displayed many of the traits of autism.

I wondered if Danny's father, Richard, would bring Danny home – I still hadn't met him. But when I answered the door shortly after six o'clock it was just Reva and Danny. They came into the hall, Danny holding a new toy: a maze game where the aim was to pot silver balls into holes by tilting the box.

'That's very nice,' I said, admiring the game. 'Lucky boy.'

Reva gave a small sigh. 'He doesn't deserve it, really, but he made such a fuss in the shop I had to buy him something to keep him quiet.'

I thought it was just as well Lucy hadn't heard this, as clearly Reva had rewarded Danny's negative behaviour.

'So you all went shopping?' I said to Danny. 'Did you have a nice day?'

Danny didn't answer but put down the toy and began undoing his coat. 'It wasn't good,' Reva said quietly to me. 'We were going to buy him some new shoes, but he made such a fuss we had to leave the shop. Can you get him some new shoes? I'll give you the money.' She began opening her shoulder bag.

'I can buy Danny some new shoes if he needs them,' I said. 'But I can't take your money. I'm given an allowance from the council, so I'll use that.'

'But I want you to buy the best,' Reva said, taking her purse from her bag. 'I take him to –' And she named a children's boutique in the city that sold designer clothes and shoes for kids and was exorbitantly expensive.

'I'm afraid my allowance doesn't stretch that far,' I said. 'But I really can't take your money. If Danny needs new shoes either you can buy them or I'll buy him some good ones, although they won't be designer.' I also had a moral objection to buying designer wear for children when they would outgrow them very quickly and there were so many families with so little. It just didn't seem right to me.

'He doesn't really need new shoes,' Reva admitted, looking at the nearly new leather trainers Danny was now taking off. 'But I wanted to buy him some stuff, I guess to make it up to him for not being with me.'

I hesitated and then said, 'Reva, can I give you some advice?'
She gave a small nod.

'Many parents with children in care feel guilty and over-compensate by showering them with gifts. The child comes to expect them and it causes problems, especially when they return home and it can't be sustained. The best present you can give Danny is your time – play with him and do things together that he enjoys.'

Reva looked at me thoughtfully. 'Yes,' she said. 'Although I do play with him when he lets me, which isn't often.' She put away her purse. 'Oh, and by the way,' she added, 'Richard was impressed that you managed to get Danny to wear his winter clothes. He usually refuses and insists on wearing shorts and T-shirt, which makes going out in winter with him a no-no.'

I nodded, but didn't say anything; I thought I'd given enough advice for one day, but here was another example of the child being in charge of the parents and making decisions without the knowledge or maturity to make the correct one. From the sound of it, Reva and Richard's life had been ridiculously controlled by Danny's behaviour, but I'd tackle that another time.

Having taken off his shoes and coat, Danny turned to his mother and raised his arms, ready for her to lift him so he could hang up his coat.

'He's remembered from last time,' she said, surprised and delighted.

'Yes, Danny remembers far more than he is able to say,' I said.

She lifted Danny up and he looped his coat over the stand, then she set him down again. As soon as his feet touched the floor he cried, 'George!' and headed for the back door.

'Would you like to stay a while?' I asked Reva.

'No. Danny's had enough of me for one day.'

'I'm sure he hasn't,' I said. 'He just struggles to show his feelings. He's a lovely boy underneath, very caring.'

Reva's eyes immediately misted. 'I know, I just wish he could love us.'

'Danny does love you,' I said, astonished that Reva could believe otherwise. 'But he can't show it. I'm sure once the educational psychologist is involved she'll be able to help Danny.'

'That's not going to happen,' Reva said decisively. 'Richard is still opposed to the assessment.'

'Why?'

She shrugged. 'All sorts of reasons, but it's not going to happen. I've told Terri. Say goodbye to Danny for me, please.' She turned and left.

'Reva,' I called after her. She was clearly upset, but she continued down the path and onto the pavement towards her car.

I closed the front door, aware that Richard's attitude wouldn't go down well with social services. He needed to cooperate with them, not block measures that would help Danny, and I didn't understand why he wouldn't want the best for his son.

Chapter Sixteen

Making Friends

$\mathcal{S}$unday was a disaster, although it started well enough. We'd enjoyed a leisurely cooked breakfast, when Danny had contentedly separated the white of the egg from the yolk so he could eat it (palest first) before the bacon, tomatoes and baked beans, but he had eaten it all. He'd also dressed in the clothes I'd suggested were suitable for winter without too much fuss and had then begun playing with something other than Lego: some cars from his toy box. But when my parents arrived he hid behind the sofa and no amount of encouragement would persuade him to come out. To begin with we treated it as a game, making comments loud enough for Danny to hear, like, 'I wonder where Danny is?' and 'Where can he be hiding?' Mum said, 'I'm looking forward to meeting Danny,' with Adrian adding, 'He'll want to show you George.' But Danny stayed behind the sofa and didn't make a sound.

I thought he needed time to adjust to new company, so I left him there a while longer as the rest of us chatted and caught up on our news, as families do. But it was disconcerting to know Danny was there, wedged behind the sofa, silent and not part of our group. So after about twenty minutes I looked behind the sofa and said, 'Danny, come out and sit with us. My parents would like to meet you.' But he kept his head down, mute and unyielding. I tried again ten minutes later but with the same result. Then I had to keep popping into the kitchen to check on dinner, so I left the others talking between themselves and also trying to encourage Danny out. If Danny thought that by hiding he was going to make himself invisible, he was wrong. It had the opposite effect, as our concern for him highlighted his presence and made him the centre of attention.

When I called everyone for dinner Danny was still behind the sofa, and no amount of cajoling or encouraging would persuade him out. I didn't want their dinner to spoil. I also thought that having so many people involved might be over-whelming for Danny and keeping him behind the sofa, so I suggested they began dinner while I saw to him. With the living room empty and quiet, I slowly eased the sofa forward. Danny put his head in his hands so he didn't have to look at me. I knelt on the floor in front of him.

'Danny, what's the matter?' I asked gently, touching his arm. 'Can you tell me?'

He shook his head.

'My parents have come to see us all. They're staying for dinner and then they will go home later.' Perhaps he thought they were staying for good – I didn't know what his expecta-tion of having visitors was, and Reva had said they'd stopped inviting people to their house. 'Danny, I want you to come with me for dinner now,' I said gently but firmly. 'I know dinner is earlier today than it is on a school day, but you can sit in the same place at the table, just as you always do.'

There was no response.

'Danny, would you feel happier if you saw George?'

He gave the slightest nod.

'All right. Once you've had dinner you can take George in the garden, but I want you to come and eat with us first.'

I stood and offered him my hand. He refused it but did stand and then followed me out of the living room and to the dining table. Everyone else had begun eating, but without their usual light-hearted chatter. Danny's behaviour had created an atmosphere, which was having an effect on us all. He slid silently into his chair. 'Well done,' I said quietly as I sat next to him. Mum threw me a look of relief. I smiled and hoped that now Danny had joined us he would start to relax and enjoy my parents' visit. But as we began chatting and the noise level rose, as it often does at family mealtimes, Danny suddenly put down his cutlery, shut his eyes and clamped his hands over his ears. My father looked at him, clearly thinking his behaviour was rude, and I motioned to him not to say anything.

'Let's just carry on as normal,' I said. 'I'm sure Danny will start eating again soon.'

He didn't. He sat at the table with his hands pressed to his ears and his eyes screwed shut as though trying to block us out. I touched his arm a couple of times and spoke to him reassuringly, but it didn't help. I was becoming torn between catering for Danny's needs and those of my guests and children. Then suddenly Danny let out an ear-piercing scream, making us all jump, and shot from the table and ran upstairs. I stood. 'Please carry on,' I said. 'I'll go to him.'

I could see my parents were shocked and worried, as were my children, but I left the now silent meal table and went upstairs to Danny's bedroom. He was about to climb into the wardrobe.

'No more hiding, Danny,' I said, lightly taking his arm. 'I want you to calm down and tell me what's wrong.'

He spun round and lashed out. 'No!' he screamed at the top of his voice, trying to hit me and grab my hair. I took his hands and he threw himself onto the floor, screaming, shouting and drumming his legs. I knew he was going into meltdown. I knelt on the floor beside him, scooped him into my arms and then held him on my lap as he continued screaming and thrashing. I was conscious of how distressing all this would sound downstairs and how worried my parents and children would be, but I hoped no one came up to try to help, for I suspected that part of Danny's distress was that he'd become overwhelmed and now needed some space and time out. I held him close and then began gently rocking him, which he seemed to find soothing. When he finally stopped shouting and screaming and could hear me, I talked to him gently, reassuring him that he was safe. Eventually he relaxed against me, quiet, still and exhausted. Footsteps sounded on the stairs and my mother appeared at the bedroom door. 'Are you all right, love?' she asked anxiously. 'We're all worried about you.'

'We'll be with you in a minute,' I said. 'You go down and we'll join you soon.'

Mum looked at Danny, now lying limp in my arms, and then reluctantly went downstairs. I continued to soothe Danny for a while longer. Time slipped by and when we finally returned downstairs I realized I'd been upstairs with Danny for nearly an hour. My family had finished eating the main course, had cleared away the dishes, stacked the dishwasher and were now in the living room trying to make the best of what had become a very difficult day. They were clearly worried about Danny and the strain his behaviour was putting on me. My father, not understanding Danny's disabilities, said, 'Is he always this naughty?'

'Yes,' Lucy replied, annoyed Danny's behaviour was ruining the day. 'Can we have pudding now, Mum, please, before he has another tantrum?'

'There's no need for that, love,' I said. 'But, yes, if everyone is ready we can have pudding.'

They were ready, and I held Danny's hand as we returned to the dining table. I served the pudding and Danny ate a very small amount, but he remained sitting quietly at the table with his eyes down while we finished. Then he slid silently from his chair and went to the back door.

'He wants to see George,' Adrian explained to my parents.

'Doesn't he talk at all?' my mother asked.

'When he wants to,' Lucy said, still disgruntled with his behaviour.

'He has communication difficulties,' I explained.

'As well as other things,' Lucy put in.

I could see why she was out of patience with Danny. She'd been looking forward to Nana and Grandpa's visit just as Adrian, Paula and I had, and the day was being spoilt.

I thought that, as Danny was clearly struggling with having visitors and the changes this had brought to his routine, it would be better if just he and I went into the garden with George so he wasn't overloaded further. I suggested that everyone else watch through the living-room window.

'Suits me,' Dad said. 'It's cold out there.'

'I wasn't coming out anyway,' Lucy said tetchily.

They went into the living room as I fetched Danny's and my coat and shoes. He put them on in silence, and outside he didn't say anything to George as he opened the hutch door. George was pleased to see him and be let out, and he hopped off down the lawn. Danny walked up and down the garden with George beside him, lost in his own little world, which was doubtless more familiar and secure than the one he'd left indoors. I saw my parents and Paula watching from the living-room window, and when Danny turned to face the house Mum waved to him, but Danny looked away. Adrian and Lucy appeared briefly at the window and then they all disappeared from view, probably sitting and chatting as we usually did after Sunday dinner. I stayed in the garden with Danny and George for half an hour and Danny didn't say one word. The temperature began to drop, and I was conscious that I'd hardly seen anything of my parents, so presently I said to Danny, 'It's time for George to go into his hutch now, love.'

Danny ignored me and walked away. I went round to face him. 'Danny, it's time for George to go into his hutch now,' I repeated. 'Do you want to put him in or shall I?'

He didn't reply but took another couple of steps away from me. Not knowing any better, George followed him.

'I'll put George away then,' I said. I went into the kitchen and returned with a stick of broccoli. 'Time to go into your hutch, George,' I said, and dangled the broccoli in front of George's nose. It twitched with delight and he hopped towards me. I saw the look of surprise on Danny's face.

'I do it!' he cried, quickly coming between us. They were the first words he'd spoken all afternoon. 'Bedtime, George,' he said quietly. George hopped after him without any entice-ment, and I followed them up the lawn and onto the patio. Once George was in his hutch I gave him the broccoli and Danny closed the door.

'Good boy. Now we can go indoors and join the others.'

Danny came with me into the house and we took off our coats and shoes. I led the way into the living room, but he stopped at the door, took one look at the room full of people talking and laughing and fled to his room.

'Not again!' Lucy sighed.

'Stay downstairs with us, Mum,' Paula pleaded.

'We've hardly seen anything of you,' my father added.

'I'm sorry, but I can't sit here knowing Danny is upset.' And feeling bad at deserting my family again, I went upstairs to Danny. He was lying on his side on his bed with his arm around soft-toy George. He wasn't crying, but looked lost and afraid. I perched on the edge of the bed.

'Come downstairs and show me where you'd like to sit to play with your toys,' I suggested. 'We can put your toy box wherever you like. But it would be nice if you could sit in the same room as us. It's friendly and we'd all like it if you could.' He didn't move or acknowledge he'd heard me but stared blankly ahead. I continued to talk to him, trying to persuade him to come down. Then Paula came up. 'Nana says they have to go soon. It's after five and it's nearly dark.'

I hadn't realized the time, and I knew my father didn't like driving in the dark now he was older. 'I'm coming down,' I said, sad that they were leaving. Then to Danny, 'Can you come and say goodbye?'

He shook his head and buried his face in soft-toy George.

'I won't be long,' I said, and left him on his bed.

Downstairs, I apologized to my parents. 'It's all been too much for Danny,' I explained. 'I should have realized. He's not used to visitors – they don't have many at his house.

Saving Danny

'I'm not surprised,' Lucy said dryly, and my father stifled a smile.

'He'll slowly get used to it and become more sociable,' I said. 'But it will take time.'

'So what about you coming to us?' Mum asked, concerned. My parents lived about an hour's drive away and we tended to take it in turns visiting each other.

'I wouldn't try it yet,' I said. 'Not until Danny is more used to being with different people. But he does have contact with his parents on Saturdays, so we could visit you then, until he's able to join us.' Normally the children I fostered joined in all family occasions, but I had to be practical and realistic.

Mum nodded and kissed my cheek. 'You take care then, love,' she said, subdued.

'The meal was delicious,' my father said, hugging me. 'It's just a pity you didn't have a chance to enjoy it.'

'Don't worry,' I said. 'You had Paula, Adrian and Lucy to keep you company.'

'And they did a fantastic job,' Mum said positively.

We stood on the doorstep and waved them off. I was sorry to see them go, but also slightly relieved. Danny's behaviour had put me under a lot of pressure, and I'd been torn between spending time with him and my parents. I'd telephone them later and try to explain the reasons Danny behaved as he did. I knew they'd understand. They appreciated the difficulties many of the children we fostered faced. However, Lucy, Paula and Adrian weren't so forgiving.

'He's ruined our day,' Lucy declared.

'Nana was so worried about you,' Paula said.

'So was Grandpa,' Adrian added, which made me feel guilty.

Making Friends

I understood my children were upset at having their day spoilt, and I also – more than ever – understood why Reva had stopped socializing and now led an isolated life. But that wouldn't help Danny. He needed socializing, by gradually meeting new people and experiencing new situations. Perhaps if I'd explained to him in more detail beforehand what a visit from my parents actually meant he might have found the experience less difficult. Next time I would prepare him better – and there would certainly be a next time, for Danny's sake.

After my parents had gone Danny came downstairs and, without speaking, went to the back door. He seemed instinctively to know that it was time to feed George and settle him for the night. Only Paula and I went outside with him – Adrian was on the telephone and Lucy, still unhappy with Danny, said she had 'things to do'.

As the three of us went out and round the back of the house we stopped dead. Toscha, who until now had been afraid of George and had kept clear of him, was now at the hutch, standing on her back legs with her front paws resting against the wire mesh, sniffing through the small gaps. George, unafraid, was on the other side with his nose up to hers. 'Look, they're making friends,' I said.

Paula smiled.

'They're making friends,' Danny repeated, and took a step towards the hutch. Toscha, intent on sniffing George, didn't run off as she often did when Danny was close, worried by his loud noises and unpredictable behaviour. 'Making friends,' Danny said, and took another tentative step closer to Toscha.

I felt the atmosphere shift, as though something new and exciting was about to happen. Danny took the final step that brought him to Toscha and he slowly extended his hand and began lightly stroking her back. It was the first time he'd shown any interest in her or touched her. Then he looked up at me and, making eye contact, said, 'Danny making friends.'

I felt my eyes filling. 'Yes, Danny is making friends with Toscha,' I said. 'Well done, Danny.'

'Danny making friends,' he said again later as we went upstairs to begin his bedtime routine.

'Yes, you have made friends with Toscha,' I said. 'And Toscha and George have made friends too. That's very good.'

As Danny began his meticulous and protracted bath and bedtime routine I took the opportunity to talk to him about the importance of friendship and how we went about making friends. Although this comes naturally to most children – through example and by socializing with similar-aged children – it doesn't come naturally to a child with difficulties like Danny, who didn't understand the world around him and had never been encouraged to socialize. It was impossible to know how much of what I said he understood, as he often echoed my words and phrases, sometimes later using them in the correct context, but other times not. On this occasion, though, an incident followed that showed he *had* understood. As we left the bathroom and went round the landing to his bedroom, Lucy came out of her room.

'Danny's going to bed now,' I said. 'Would you like to say goodnight to him.' I liked the children to say goodnight to each other. It was a pleasant way to end the day and drew a line under any harsh words or arguments that had taken place so they could start afresh in the morning.

'Goodnight,' Lucy said not too enthusiastically, and began downstairs.

'Goodnight,' Danny repeated. There was a pause and then his little voice called out, 'Is Danny Lucy's friend?'

Lucy stopped, turned and began back upstairs. Kneeling on the top stair so she was at Danny's height, she said, 'Yes, you are my friend, Danny. But the next time Nana and Grandpa come you must be good. Do you understand?'

Danny nodded, although I doubted he understood what was required 'to be good', as it was such a loose and ill-defined phrase.

'Danny Lucy's friend?' he asked her again.

'Yes, you are my friend,' Lucy confirmed.

'And Lucy is Danny's friend,' I said, trying to show him that friendship was a two-way process. 'You've made friends with Lucy.'

It was one of those moments that stay with you. His face lost its usually blank, sometimes angry, expression and broke into a smile. 'Danny's made friends,' he said. 'Danny's made friends. Danny's made friends with Lucy.' I could see Lucy was as moved as I was.

'Yes, you're all friends,' I said. What better way to end the day!

Chapter Seventeen
Terri's Visit

'Danny's made friends,' he told Paula, Lucy and Adrian as they arrived at breakfast the following morning, dressed for school.

They agreed with nods and grunts befitting a Monday morning.

'Danny's made friends,' he told Yvonne when we met her in the playground for the start of school.

'Fantastic!' she said, clasping her hands together. 'So you've had a good weekend, Danny.'

Danny nodded.

'It began and ended well,' I said, throwing her a knowing look. I didn't have to say more. Yvonne had been working with Danny and other special needs children long enough to know that their behaviour was often volatile and unpredictable.

'Danny's made friends,' he said again, now tugging Yvonne's arm to regain her attention.

'That's great,' Yvonne said. 'Is this with a child who lives near Cathy?'

Danny looked lost, so I explained about the friendships that had been cemented at my house.

'I see,' Yvonne said. 'So, Toscha and George are friends, and you are friends with all of Cathy's children. That's wonderful. I'm sure lots of children in the class want to be friends with you too.'

The whistle blew for the start of school, so I said goodbye and watched Danny go with Yvonne to join his class. The day passed as Mondays often do with clearing up after the weekend, and then paperwork for the training I would be helping to run. When I collected Danny that afternoon at the end of school the first thing he said was, 'Danny making friends.'

'Excellent,' I said.

'He's had a good day,' Yvonne confirmed. 'I've written in his home school book.'

I thanked her, praised Danny, and then on the way home I told him that his social worker, Terri, was coming to visit us at four o'clock. I hadn't told him that morning as it would have been something else for him to accommodate and worry about during the day, and he was easily overloaded with information. I also emphasized that Terri was a very nice lady who was helping him and his parents, for the last time he'd seen her it had been traumatic and he'd run off and hidden in the school fields. I explained to him carefully what he could expect from her visit: that she'd spend time talking to him and me to make sure he was all right, and then she'd leave and we'd have our dinner.

'George,' he said.

'Yes, you'll be able to take George for his walk too,' I said. 'Just as you always do.'

* * *

On arriving home, and following his usual routine, Danny went into the garden to give George a walk. He was still there fifteen minutes later when the doorbell rang, signalling Terri's arrival. Paula was with us and I asked her to stay with Danny while I went to let in Terri.

Having exchanged a good afternoon with Terri, I told her that Danny was in the garden giving George some exercise and that I'd bring him in.

'Leave him for now if he's happy,' Terri said. 'It'll give us a chance to talk first.'

She went through to the living room and I went outside to check that Paula could stay with Danny while I spoke to Terri; she was happy to. I also told Danny that Terri was here but he could stay in the garden for a little while longer, and then I would call him in. He didn't reply.

I went indoors and into the living room. Terri was standing at the patio windows watching Danny with George. 'He loves that rabbit,' she said. 'It was in their house when I visited Danny, before he came into care. I was surprised that Reva allowed it inside – her house is immaculate. But she said a little mess was worth it to keep Danny happy.'

I nodded. 'They're inseparable, and I'm sure having George here has helped Danny to settle here.'

Terri left the window and sat in one of the armchairs. I offered her a tea or coffee, but she said she'd just had one. I sat in the chair that gave me the best view of the garden so I could keep an eye on Danny. Terri took a large notepad and a pen from her bag-style briefcase. 'So, how has Danny been?' she asked, pen poised. 'Is he still eating and sleeping well?'

'He's sleeping very well,' I said. 'He has a soft toy, also called George, which he cuddles up to in bed. He sleeps with his bedroom door closed, the curtains slightly parted and the light on low.' Terri wrote as I spoke. 'Danny goes right down under the duvet to sleep, so I usually go in and move it down once he's asleep, so he doesn't get too hot.'

'Any nightmares?' she asked as she wrote.

'No, not so far. He's been sleeping well.'

'And eating?' Terri asked. 'Reva said Danny is a very fussy eater; that's why he's so small. I've written to his doctor asking for a report.'

'Danny eats very slowly, but then he's slow and meticulous in most of the things he does. He spends a lot of time cutting up his food and arranging it on the plate before he starts eating. He loves design and patterns and sees them everywhere. He creates patterns out of his food and likes to eat the palest first.'

'So he is a fussy eater?' Terri said, looking up.

'Not really. He takes his time, but he usually finishes his meal. I tend to think of fussy eaters as those who will only eat certain foods.'

'And he eats with you and your family?' Terri asked.

'Yes.'

'He doesn't at home,' Terri said bluntly. 'Reva gives Danny his meal first and then he's in bed before she and Richard have theirs.'

It wasn't for me to criticize Reva, although I felt family mealtimes were important, as I'm sure Terri did.

'And how is Danny's behaviour generally?' Terri now asked. 'I phoned Reva this morning and she told me he was uncontrollable on Saturday when they went shopping.'

'We had a mixed day too yesterday,' I said, and I briefly explained Danny's behaviour during my parents' visit while Terri made notes.

'But his behaviour is manageable?' Terri asked.

'Yes. It's tiring. You have to reinforce the boundaries and keep a watchful eye on him. Everything needs to be carefully explained beforehand and then repeated, but he usually gets there in the end.'

'So if you can manage Danny's behaviour, why can't Reva?' Terri said abruptly.

I met her gaze. 'I've had a lot more experience of looking after children than Reva, including those with special needs. I've also attended training and have a degree in Education and Psychology. Reva hasn't had the benefit of any of that, and from what I've seen she's very vulnerable right now and feels Danny has rejected her. She considers Danny's negative behaviour as a failure on her part, and takes it personally. I don't think she gets a lot of support either.'

'No. Richard is never there and Reva's parents live a long way away. She has a sister, whom she used to be close to and who doesn't live far away. But she hasn't seen her for nearly two years. Reva said her sister's three kids are angels and her sister could never understand why Danny behaved as he did. The inference being it was Reva's and Richard's parenting skills that were at fault.'

'That wouldn't have helped Reva,' I said. 'And Reva has no support from Richard's family either?' I asked.

Terri shook her head. 'Richard's parents are alive and well, and don't live far away, but Richard never takes Danny to see them. Reva doesn't see them now either, although they still see Richard's children from his first marriage sometimes.'

'It's a pity Danny can't see them. Grandparents are so important,' I said, thinking of my own dear parents.

'It's one of the issues I shall be discussing with Richard when I finally meet him,' Terri said. 'And unless there's a good reason why Danny shouldn't be in contact with his grandparents, then I will want visits to start when and if Danny returns home.'

I heard the word 'if' and went cold. 'Is there doubt that Danny will return home?' I asked. 'I thought Danny was in care voluntarily under a Section 20, at the request of his parents.'

'He is at present,' Terri said. 'But I can change that if necessary and apply for a court order. I've had a discussion with my manager and we have concerns. Reva's drinking, for one, and that she believes Danny doesn't have any feelings. Danny's isolation. And Richard's refusal to cooperate. There are a lot of unknowns, and Richard is not acting in Danny's best interest by refusing to allow the educational psychologist to assess him or to meet with me.'

Although I was slightly relieved that Terri already knew of Reva's drinking and I wouldn't have to tell her, I was very concerned that the social services were considering applying for a court order. If that happened, Reva and Richard would have limited contact with Danny and it would be supervised. They would have to mount a court case to show why Danny should be returned to their care.

'Reva says Richard can't accept there's anything wrong with Danny,' I said, feeling I needed to say something in their defence.

'Then he has to discuss his worries with me,' Terri said curtly. 'I haven't been able to see him yet. He's always working. We're all busy, but I would have thought that having your child in care should be pretty near the top of your priorities.'

Saving Danny

I could see Terri was annoyed, and I knew that Richard had done his wife and child a great disservice by not making time to meet with her to discuss Danny.

'Danny talks and communicates with you and your family?' Terri now asked.

'Yes, a little, in his way,' I said. 'It sometimes takes us a while to understand what he is saying, but we can usually work out what he wants. He's far more fluent with George,' I added with a smile.

Terri nodded. 'I know. Reva said. Danny had some speech therapy before he went to school, but it was stopped. I think because Danny wouldn't engage. His teacher thinks some more now he's older would be helpful, and I'm inclined to agree. What do you think?'

'Yes, I'm sure it would help,' I said.

Terri made a note. 'Does Danny have tantrums and meltdowns with you like he does at home and at school?'

'Yes. Sometimes. I think it's largely a result of frustration – not being able to express himself or understand what is required of him. He can easily become overloaded and panic. And possibly he's scared. He's had so many changes recently. He's coping as best he can.'

'I can tell you like him,' Terri said, glancing up. 'You're making excuses for him.'

I was slightly surprised by her comment. 'I don't think Danny sets out to be naughty, he just can't cope,' I said. 'He needs boundaries, as all children do. Of course we like Danny, we're all growing very fond of him. And George,' I added, for I could see Paula running up and down the garden happily with George and Danny.

Terri's Visit

'And Danny is doing his homework – the targets from his education plan that Sue mentioned?' Terri asked.

'Yes, I have a copy of the plan and we have a home school book too. I'll fetch his school bag.' I knew that the child's social worker usually liked to check on their school work when they visited. As I went down the hall to fetch Danny's school bag the front door opened and Lucy let herself in.

'Hello, love, have you had a good day?' I asked her.

'Not bad.'

'Danny's social worker is in the living room, and Danny and Paula are in the garden giving George a walk.'

'I'll join them,' she said. She dropped her school bag in the hall and went out through the kitchen, calling hi to Terri as she went.

I returned to the living room and gave Terri Danny's school bag, and then sat in the chair with the view of the garden. As Terri looked through Danny's reading book, flash cards and the home school book, I watched Danny, Lucy, Paula and George in the garden. Although Danny couldn't express his emotions, he was nevertheless, in his own way, bonding with my family, as we were with him. Words are not the only way we tell others how we feel; body language plays an important part too, and I could see that Danny was as relaxed and happy as he could be.

'Have you seen what Danny's teacher has written today?' Terri asked, glancing up from the home school book.

'No. Not yet.'

'I'll read it out,' she said with a smile. *'Danny has been very enthusiastic in making friends today. He sat on a big table with other children for lunch, but he became a bit upset when they finished their meals first and went into the playground. Yvonne explained to Danny that friends don't always do as we want them to, but they are still our friends.'*

I also smiled. 'That's nice. Yvonne is very good with Danny. She has endless patience and knows how to calm him.'

'And her sense of humour must help,' Terri said.

'Absolutely,' I agreed.

'Here's a copy of Danny's care plan,' Terri now said, passing the papers to me. 'And I've set the date for Danny's review. Two weeks on Wednesday at ten-thirty in the morning, so Danny can go to school as normal.' I opened my diary and entered the date and time of Danny's review. 'I've informed Jill,' Terri said. 'I'll send out the invitations tomorrow. Is it still all right to hold it here in your house? It seems appropriate.'

'Yes,' I said. 'That's fine. Hopefully I'll meet Danny's father then.'

'Hopefully I'll have met him by then,' Terri said pointedly. 'He's a bit elusive. I think that's everything then. So unless there is anything you want to say we'll bring Danny in now so I can have a chat with him.'

We stood and went out through the kitchen. Terri waited on the patio and called, 'Hello, Danny! Nice to see you again. How are you doing?'

I saw Danny start slightly at hearing her voice, but he didn't turn or look at her. He squatted down and stroked George. The girls were close by. Terri shivered, having left her coat indoors. 'Let's go inside, Danny,' she called to him. 'It's cold out here. I want to talk to you. Nice rabbit.'

Danny concentrated on George and ignored her.

'I think we have to go in now,' I heard Lucy say to Danny, but he shook his head.

George, who'd had a good run, was now sitting contentedly nibbling grass.

'Come and tell me all about your rabbit!' Terri tried again from the patio. 'I spoke to your mother this morning, Danny, and you're seeing her again tomorrow. That's nice, isn't it?' Although Terri was well meaning and trying to engage with Danny, I thought she was giving him too much information to process all at once, so it was easier for him to do nothing. But I could also see that there was a touch of obstinacy in his refusal to come in or even acknowledge her.

'Come on, Danny, let's go in, it's cold,' Lucy said, and she and Paula began up the lawn towards us.

Danny stayed where he was, head down and stroking George. Clearly we couldn't stay out here forever and Danny needed to do as he'd been asked, so leaving Terri on the patio I went down the lawn to Danny. Although he had his head down I stood in front of him so I was in his peripheral vision where he could at least see my feet and legs. 'Danny, we are going indoors now. It's time to put George in his hutch. Do you want to put George in his hutch or shall I?'

'Me,' he said without hesitation. Straightening, he began up the lawn towards the house, with George following.

'Mum's very good with children,' Lucy said to Terri.

'I can see that,' Terri said. I didn't explain to her the magic of the closed choice.

Inside, we took off our shoes, which were wet from the grass, but Danny kept his coat firmly on. I decided not to make an issue of it; he'd done as I'd asked in putting George away, so he could stay in his coat for now if he wished. Guiding children's behaviour is always a balancing act between what they have to do and what can be reasonably let go and accommodated. Lucy and Paula disappeared upstairs, and Danny came with me and Terri into the living room. Adrian would be home later, having stayed for chess club after school. I took some toys out of Danny's toy box, including the cars he'd been playing with previously, and arranged them on the floor. He sat by them and began playing with a lorry, silently pushing it round in circles. Social workers usually spend some time alone with the child when they visit, so that the child has the opportunity to talk about issues they may not feel comfortable voicing in front of their carer. Now Danny was settled and playing, I asked Terri, 'Do you want to speak to Danny alone?'

'Yes, please,' she said.

'Danny, Terri is going to talk to you for a while,' I said. 'I will be in the kitchen making dinner.'

He didn't look up but concentrated on pushing the toy lorry in the same circle. He didn't appear distressed, so telling him again that I would be in the kitchen, I went out of the living room, pulling the door to behind me but not completely closing it. I fed Toscha and then began peeling vegetables, but two minutes later I heard Terri call from the living room: 'Cathy! Can you come? There's been an accident.'

I immediately went in to find Danny standing in a puddle of urine.

Chapter Eighteen
Footprints in the Snow

I cleaned Danny, reassured him that he'd done nothing
wrong and then left him in his bedroom to change into
clean clothes while I took his wet clothes downstairs and put
them in the washing machine. I filled a bucket with warm
water, added disinfectant and went into the lounge where
Terri was writing up her notes.

'Does Danny wet himself often?' she asked as I scrubbed
the carpet.

'No. This is the first time since he's been with me,' I said.

'I guess he was worried by my visit,' she said.

'I guess he was,' I agreed.

Terri left soon after, calling goodbye to Danny from the hall
as she went. Usually the child's social worker looked at the
child's bedroom when they visited, but I think Terri realized
that wasn't appropriate now and might upset Danny further.
He came downstairs once she'd gone and played silently in
the living room with his toys while Paula watched television.
He didn't seem very interested in television and often ignored
it if it was on. After dinner I talked to him again about Terri's
role, but he looked sad and, at one point, close to tears. It

would take time for him to trust her and appreciate she was trying to help him and his parents – for now, though, Terri was the reason he couldn't be at home.

The following day, Tuesday, Danny was very quiet after contact, and the same was true after contact on Thursday. I asked him both times if there was anything worrying him, but he shook his head, either unable or not wanting to tell me. His behaviour at school deteriorated during the week too, and the social start he'd made on Monday – where he'd wanted to make friends with everyone – disappeared. He didn't join in any class activities and kept his distance from the other children. He spent most of his time with Yvonne or the other classroom assistant, drawing and painting patterns or creating them out of anything that came to hand. As I'd told Terri, Danny could see patterns everywhere and appeared to depend on them for comfort. I suppose there is something comforting in a pattern, where their repetition is reliable and guaranteed. Much safer to know which shape or colour comes next, compared to the unpredictability and randomness of life's events.

At home with us Danny spent nearly all his time (when he wasn't with George) making patterns. He arranged his toy cars in an increasing circle, with over thirty vehicles spiralling out from the centre, the smallest in the middle and the largest – the buses, lorries and road diggers – nose to tail on the outer ring. He took out the Lego again but now created a pattern of squares within squares instead of parallel lines. There were three boxes of coloured dominoes in his toy box and he emptied out the tiles and laid them end to end to create a giant triangle of colour and number sequences. The children and I often offered to play with him but he wasn't interested, preferring to play by himself. I also noticed that when Danny was in the garden with George he walked in patterns: a circle, a figure of eight and a large square, which he dissected by crossing from corner to corner. Possibly he'd always done this, but it couldn't have been as pronounced as it was that week or I would have noticed it before.

I made a note of Danny's behaviour in my fostering log and also that he was very quiet and withdrawn. When I mentioned to Reva that Danny seemed rather quiet she said he'd been like that during contact, and also compliant – doing exactly what he'd been told – which she'd taken as a positive sign. I didn't want to worry Reva, but I knew from years of fostering that children in care often believe that if they're very 'good' they will be allowed to go home. Was this what Danny was thinking? That if he was quiet and obedient he could return home? If a child believes he or she is responsible for being in care, they carry a huge burden of guilt, not only about their own fate but that of their parents too. When the opportunity arose I had a chat with Danny. 'Love, lots of children live with foster carers like me,' I said. 'It is to help their mummies and daddies. The children haven't done anything wrong. It's not their fault they are in foster care.'

He didn't reply – I hadn't expected him to – but I would repeat the message from time to time as I had with other children I'd fostered.

Late Friday morning Reva telephoned and she was angry. 'That bloody social worker!' she stormed. 'She's threatening us with a court order if we don't have Danny assessed by the educational psychologist! Richard is furious and I agree with him. How dare she! We placed Danny in care voluntarily. I needn't have done so. I could have carried on as I was and no one would have been any the wiser.'

That wasn't actually true, for Danny's teacher had raised concerns, so it would only have been a matter of time before Reva and Richard had been asked to attend a meeting with a social worker. But I could understand why Reva was angry; she was frightened at the prospect of losing Danny for good.

I was about to say something conciliatory when she said, 'Richard agrees that we should remove Danny from foster care while we still can. I don't want you to collect him from school this afternoon. I'll go and bring him home. I'll collect his belongings from you another time. If necessary we'll move out of the area.'

'That won't help, Reva,' I said.

'Why not?' she demanded. 'He's our child. We can do what we like.'

You can't, I thought, but didn't say. 'Reva, calm down and listen to me, please. If you take Danny out of care now, without the agreement of his social worker, the social services will go straight to court and apply for an Interim Care Order. He'll be back in care immediately and you will have little say in the matter.'

'They can't do that!' she snapped.

'They can if they have concerns for the child,' I said.

'Why? Because Richard refused to meet with Terri and doesn't want his child seeing a shrink!'

'Well …' I hesitated, 'there are other concerns as well, aren't there?'

'Like what?'

'Your drinking, Danny's social isolation. Also, you weren't coping before, which is why you put Danny into care.' It sounded harsh, but Reva needed to understand the gravity of the situation if she removed Danny from care.

'I'm going to speak to my solicitor,' she said, and hung up.

Two hours later Reva telephoned again. This time she was subdued and, I guessed, had had a good cry, for she sounded fragile.

'Sorry for speaking to you like that,' she began quietly. 'It's not like me. I was upset.'

'It's all right. I understand.'

'Our solicitor has spoken to Terri,' she said. 'And I've agreed to leave Danny in care for now, but I'm having extra contact next week. It's half-term holiday, so he won't be in school. I'm going to have him Tuesday and Thursday afternoon from twelve till six. Terri said to tell you.'

I thought it would have been nice to be asked – either by Terri or Reva – if this fitted in with my arrangements, but as a foster carer I'd become used to having arrangements changed, sometimes at the last moment, and then having to fit in with them.

'Richard doesn't know that I've agreed to this yet,' Reva said. 'He's in a meeting, so I've left a message on his voice-mail. He won't be pleased Danny is still in care and we have to answer to Terri. He'll probably blame me, but I'm used to that. The solicitor said it was the best he could do for now.' I guessed that somewhere in the discussion the solicitor had 'done a deal' with Terri: extra contact in exchange for Danny staying in voluntary care under a Section 20. The social services wouldn't want to apply for a court order unless there was no alternative. It's costly, time-consuming and leaves the parents feeling impotent and embittered. Care Orders are only used as a last resort.

Reva apologized again for her rudeness earlier and then said she'd see me at ten o'clock the following morning for Saturday contact. Before she said goodbye she added, 'And I've agreed to see my doctor about my drinking.' So I guessed that had also been raised by Terri.

That evening I served chicken nuggets, chips and baked beans for dinner. It was the end of the week and having processed food occasionally doesn't do anyone any harm. Everyone enjoyed it and it was a relatively easy meal for Danny to eat – he cut the chips and chicken nuggets in half, arranged the pieces around his plate and then ate them in colour order, chicken first, chips and then the baked beans. After dinner we did a little of his homework and then I began his bath and bedtime routine, which still took about an hour and a half. I tipped his bath toys into the water as I usually did, but he took them all out again except for the dinghy and the diving man, which he played with continuously while I washed his hair, throwing the diver into the water, holding him under and then saving him. The time the toy diver spent under the water grew longer and longer, and as Danny held him under he chanted, 'Drowning, drowning, drowning.' His face was creased in anguish, as though empathizing with someone drowning. What with this and the way he often threw himself back in the bath and stayed under the water, he seemed rather obsessed with drowning. It crossed my mind that possibly this was how Danny felt – as though he was drowning. We often refer to drowning metaphorically when were are unable to cope – drowning in sorrow, regret, too much work. Was Danny drowning in everyday life?

'Save the diver,' I encouraged Danny, which he did. Only to hold him under the water again.

On Saturday morning I dropped Danny off at his house for the day and then returned home to collect Adrian, Lucy and Paula, who had forgone their lie-in and were dressed, ready to visit Nana and Grandpa. I'd suggested the visit to them the evening before and they'd jumped at the chance. It was only a short visit as I had to be home in plenty of time for when Danny was returned, but we had a very pleasant and relaxing few hours with my parents, although I think we all felt someone was missing. Mum said a few times she hoped it wouldn't be long before Danny could visit her and Grandpa too, as our other foster children had done.

When Reva returned Danny that evening she seemed reserved and a little standoffish with me. She didn't want to come in, although the night was cold, and called a quick goodbye to Danny from the doorstep. He went straight through the house to see George. I asked Reva if she'd had a good day, and she replied, 'Pleasant enough, thank you.'

'And how was Danny?' I asked.

'Fine,' she said. 'I'll see you on Tuesday. I'll collect him and bring him back to you.'

'Thank you,' I said.

She said a rather curt goodbye, turned and left. I had the feeling I'd just been assigned to 'them' in a 'them and us' situation, putting me on the side of the social services. It was a pity when this happened, as it made working with the parents more difficult, when we should have all been working together for the good of the child.

As soon as I woke on Sunday morning, even before I'd opened the curtains, I knew we'd had some snow in the night. That glow, the unusual stillness, the muted sound, all suggesting nature had cast its magical white cloak. There wasn't much snow – about an inch – but any snow is exciting when it's a relatively rare occurrence. When the children woke, Adrian, Lucy and Paula were as enchanted by it as I was, but Danny seemed bemused, not only by the snow but our excited reaction to it. Toscha was unsure and gingerly tiptoed around the edge of the patio, past the patio doors where Danny and I were looking out. I explained to Danny very simply what snow was – frozen rain.

'Frozen rain,' he repeated.

'I wonder what George will make of the snow when you take him for a walk later,' I said. But the sentence was too complicated and Danny looked blank. 'You can take George in the snow later,' I said.

'George in the snow later,' he echoed, no less bemused.

As there wasn't enough snow to make a snowman I suggested we walk to our local park where we could feed the ducks, who were always hungry in winter, and make footprints in the snow while it was fresh. We'd done this in previous winters and it was fun, especially seeing the ducks trying to walk on the icy pond. Adrian, Lucy and Paula readily agreed to the outing, and Danny nodded, although I wasn't sure he had much idea of what he was nodding to. We had a quick breakfast: porridge for us, and Danny wanted his usual – 'Cornflakes in a bowl, with milk and half a teaspoon of sugar, please.' After breakfast we wrapped up warm in our coats, scarves and gloves. Reva hadn't packed any boots for Danny, so I found some in my spares that fitted him.

'Not mine,' Danny said, at first refusing to put them on.

'I know they're not yours,' I said. 'But you are going to wear them to walk in the snow.'

Danny looked at the boots and made no move to put them on.

'You can't wear your shoes,' Lucy said. 'Your feet will get wet and cold.' We were all in the hall by then, at the front door, waiting for Danny to put on the boots.

'Do you want to put the right boot on first or the left one?' I asked him, resorting to the 'closed choice' again. 'Right or left?' I repeated, touching each boot.

'Right,' Danny said quietly and began putting on the boot.

'Good boy,' I said.

Once Danny had his boots and gloves on, Adrian opened the front door. I went out last with Danny and locked the door. Danny took one step into the snow on the front path, stopped dead and screamed.

'Whatever's the matter?' Lucy asked, spinning round.

'Sshh, you'll wake the whole street,' I said. 'It's early.'

Danny, rooted to the spot, stared horrified at his boots.

'He's scared of the snow,' Paula said, and offered him her hand.

Danny didn't take it but, still staring at his feet, screamed again.

'Oh no! Be quiet,' Lucy said, embarrassed.

A bedroom window opened above us and my neighbour, Sue, poked her head out. 'Everything OK, Cath?' she asked.

'Yes, sorry,' I said. 'I hope we didn't wake you.'

'No, my family are up. Beautiful, isn't it?'

'Absolutely,' I agreed.

'Well, enjoy your day,' she called, and with a small wave to us all she closed her bedroom window.

'Danny, you need to be quieter,' I said. 'It's early on Sunday morning and people stay in bed.'

'Come on, Danny, we're going to the park,' Lucy encouraged, eager to get him away to avoid further embarrassment.

Danny remained where he was, as though his feet were set in concrete. I could see we weren't going anywhere fast, and I didn't want Danny's refusal to spoil Adrian's, Lucy's and Paula's enjoyment of our outing or to embarrass them more. 'You three go on to the park,' I said. 'Danny and I will join you shortly.' The park was only a ten-minute walk away and I knew I could trust them to be sensible.

'I'll stay with you, Mum,' Paula offered.

'You don't have to, love,' I said. 'Danny will be fine soon.'

But Paula wanted to stay, so Adrian and Lucy went ahead while Paula and I talked calmly to Danny, trying to reassure him that the snow wouldn't hurt him and to encourage him to take another step. There was so little snow it would have been comical, had he not been so afraid of it.

'Watch me, Danny,' Paula said. She walked to the end of the path and back again.

Danny stared, horror-struck, at her footprints as though she'd performed witchcraft.

'Put it back,' he said, pointing to the indents she'd left.

'You can't put the snow back,' I said. 'It's not missing. Paula has squashed the snow down. It's nothing to worry about.'

Footprints in the Snow

I assumed Danny hadn't experienced snow before, although we'd had some in recent years. I tried to think of something I could compare it to that might make him less afraid. 'You like making patterns, Danny,' I said. 'You can make patterns out of snow.'

I squatted and drew some circles in the snow with my finger. Danny watched carefully. Then Paula drew two eyes, a nose and an upturned mouth in each of the circles, creating three smiling faces.

Danny's expression lost some of its anxiety.

'You can make all sorts of patterns in the snow,' I said. I drew a zig-zag line, a triangle and then a house.

Finally Danny raised his hand and tentatively poked a gloved finger at the snow. He watched the impression it made and then gradually moved his finger around, drawing some wavy lines.

'Wonderful, well done,' I said. 'That's a nice pattern. Footprints are patterns too. Let's see if we can make some footprint patterns, shall we?'

Danny let me hold his hand and we took a step along the path, then another and another. 'Patterns,' he said, pointing to the footprints we'd made.

'Yes, that's right,' I said. 'We are making patterns, and we are going to make them all the way to the park.' Which is what we did.

Chapter Nineteen

Love

By the time we were in the park Danny had lost much of his fearfulness of the snow and actually began enjoying it by hopping and jumping to create different footprint patterns. Paula and I praised him enormously. He'd just needed encouragement to gain the confidence to experience something new. We spotted Lucy and Adrian laughing and running around as they threw snow at each other. Paula ran over to join them while Danny stayed with me and we concentrated on making more footprints in the snow. There were other people in the park, but much of the snow was still untouched.

'Danny's footprint,' he said in wonder each time he created a fresh imprint.

'Yes, that's your footprint,' I said. 'And here is mine.'

He was mesmerized and in wonder at it all. I was so pleased I'd made the effort to bring him, for it would have been far easier to return indoors. But the more Danny broke out of his comfort zone and tried what the world had to offer, the more his confidence would grow.

I'd brought some slices of bread with us to feed the ducks, so Danny and I made our way towards the pond. Adrian,

Lucy and Paula joined us there, but Danny was frightened of the ducks and it took a lot of persuading before he would break off a piece of bread and throw it to them, as we were doing. Most of the ducks were standing on the bank, and Danny jumped back with a start if one of them came too close. He watched in awe as Adrian extended his arm trying to encourage the ducks to take the bread from his hand, but laughed, as we did, when one adventurous mallard came slipping and sliding across the icy pond towards us to take some.

'People should never walk on ice,' I took the opportunity to caution Danny. 'It's not safe.' Although I didn't think it was likely he'd ever try – he wasn't a child who was tempted by adventure.

Once we'd thrown all the bread to the ducks, Adrian, Lucy and Paula went off across the park in search of some fresh snow to throw at each other. I asked Danny if he wanted to go with them or play in the children's area and have a swing or a slide, but he shook his head.

'We'll go on the swings another time then,' I said.

Danny was content to keep making footprints in the snow. As with most of his pursuits and activities, when he found something that interested him he wanted to do it over and over again, long after most children would have grown bored and wanted to play something else.

Eventually, with our faces glowing from the cold and ready for a hot chocolate, we made our way home. The snow was melting and Danny became agitated when he saw that the footprints we'd made on the front path had distorted and were disappearing. I tried to explain that the snow was melting, but he scowled and told it to 'Stop!'

Lucy and Paula smiled indulgently, but I could see that Danny was becoming very agitated. I diverted his attention by pointing out the large pigeon that was sitting puffed out against the cold on the neighbour's fence as I opened the front door and let us in.

The green light of the answerphone on the hall table was flashing, signalling a message. I thought it might be John, Adrian and Paula's father, who sometimes telephoned on a Sunday if he wasn't seeing them. But when I pressed play Reva's voice came through, tight and anxious: 'Whatever you do, Cathy, don't take Danny out in the snow! It will freak him out, he's petrified of it.'

'Mummy?' Danny asked, puzzled.

'Yes. It's all right, love. There's nothing for you to worry about. I'll telephone your mummy later and tell her you've had a good time in the snow.' Which Danny accepted. He was now more interested in letting George out in what was left of the snow.

Adrian went into the garden with Danny while I made the hot chocolate and a snack. Lucy and Paula had had enough of the cold for one day and stayed indoors. I watched Adrian and Danny through the kitchen window as the milk warmed in the pan. George was on the lawn and Danny had squatted down to examine the footprints he'd left, which were clearly very different to ours. I could see he was intrigued, and Adrian was beside him, doubtless talking to him about the footprints. Adrian read a lot and had good general knowledge, which, like my father, he was happy to share with others.

When everyone was at the table with their hot drinks and snacks I took the opportunity to telephone Reva – from the living room, so Danny couldn't hear. I explained that I'd only got her message after we'd returned home and that Danny – after some persuasion – had been fine in the snow.'

'As long as he's all right,' Reva said a little stiffly. 'I'll see you Tuesday then.' And with a rather curt goodbye she hung up, so I guessed I was still in her bad books, although I wasn't sure why.

Danny desperately needed new experiences, even if it stretched him to his limit, otherwise he would miss out on so much. By Monday morning all the snow had melted and I needed to do a small shop at our local supermarket, about a fifteen-minute walk away, so as it was half-term holiday I decided to take Danny. Adrian, Lucy and Paula didn't want to come, preferring to stay at home. I explained to Danny where we were going and why. He didn't say anything but did put on his coat and shoes when I asked him to without a fuss. We passed the supermarket on our way to school, so it wasn't completely unfamiliar to him, although I'd never taken him inside before.

Outside Danny held my hand, as he knew he had to in the street, and as we walked I talked to him about some of the things we passed – the crocuses and other plants in the front gardens, the house numbers on the gates, the birds looking for food, as well as the shop we were going to. Danny didn't say much, but I knew from the look of concentration on his face that he was taking it all in. Talking to him would also widen his vocabulary as well as his general knowledge.

I've found before that if children are involved in shopping they are less likely to become bored and disruptive, so I enlisted Danny's help from the start, explaining that I needed a big boy to help me. I took a wire basket, showed him my shopping list, read out the first item – a can of tomatoes – and asked him to help me find it. I knew where it was, but we had the time and it was an interesting challenge for him to search it out.

'Well done,' I said, as he proudly took the can from the shelf and placed it carefully in the basket.

I showed him the list again and read out the next item – bananas – and we went off in search of the fruit and vegetables. It took a long time before we had the dozen or so items on my shopping list and were at the checkout. The assistant was very patient as Danny, in his slow methodical way, insisted on taking each item from the basket and handing them to her one at a time for scanning. As we left the store I praised him and thanked him for his help. Although shopping was a comparatively small achievement, it had been another positive experience for Danny that would help boost his confidence and self-esteem.

Unfortunately, as we headed back an ambulance sped past, its siren suddenly switching on and wailing. It made me start, but Danny was petrified. He threw himself on the ground and, clamping his hands over his ears, curled into a ball as he tried to protect himself from the noise. I knelt beside him and talked to him calmly as passers-by looked at us. Eventually I persuaded him to his feet, but it was some minutes before he felt able to take his hands away from his ears and was ready to continue home, even though the siren had long gone. I'd noticed before that Danny covered his ears if there was a loud or sudden noise, as though it was painful for him, and I was aware that some special needs children have very sensitive hearing. It was something I would mention to Terri.

* * *

Love

On Tuesday morning Danny returned to using the phrase 'Yes, thank you very much', which was to prove useful later that morning when the questionnaire for his review (due to take place the following week) arrived in the post. As usual with a child's review there were two sets of forms: one for me as his carer to fill in, which I would do later when I had a quiet moment, and one for the child. It was a small booklet designed to encourage the child to give their views on being in care. As a foster carer I had a duty to ensure the child received the booklet and help them to fill it in if necessary. Although it was child-friendly – with coloured sketches and simple questions – given that Danny could barely write his name and had communication difficulties, I knew it was beyond him, even with my help. Nevertheless, I sat him down quietly at the table with the booklet in front of us and told him that Terri had sent the booklet for his review. I explained in simple language what a review was, and that the booklet gave him the chance to tell everyone what he thought about being in foster care. By the time I'd finished he was agitated and drumming his clenched fists on the table.

'Don't worry,' I said. 'I'll read out each question. You say what comes into your head and I'll write it down.' I'd done this with other special needs children I'd fostered who couldn't read or write. I began with the first question, which asked if he knew why he was in care. 'Yes, thank you very much,' Danny replied.

It was his response, so I wrote it down and read out the second question, which asked how often he saw his social worker. 'Yes, thank you very much,' he said, which I also wrote. The next question asked what he liked about living with his foster carer and what he didn't like. 'Yes, thank you very much,' Danny replied to both. And so on and so on until we'd completed the ten questions, all with the same response. Some questions included drawings of little faces with various expressions ranging from happy to sad to angry, and the child had to tick the one that best applied to them. Danny ticked them all, which I thought was probably a fair appraisal of the mixture of feelings he often had.

On the back of the booklet was a line where the child had to sign their name, and Danny carefully wrote 'Danny'. Beneath that was another line where the name of any person who had helped the child complete the form had to be entered. I wrote my name and added a note that 'Yes, thank you very much' was Danny's favourite expression. I told Danny he'd done well, but I wondered how much he'd gained from the experience other than a degree of patience. While it's important children in care are given the opportunity to express their views and have a say in planning their future, I sometimes feel that correct procedure can override common sense when it comes to form-filling. The review would learn more from me about Danny's views on being in care than it would from the form.

At twelve noon Reva arrived to collect Danny for the extra contact. She thanked me for having him ready with his coat and shoes on and said that she would return him at six o'clock. I used the time to catch up on the housework, which had fallen into second place due to the high level of Danny's needs, as well as taking the opportunity to spend time with Paula, Lucy and Adrian. I was planning on taking Danny out again the following day. Like many parents and foster carers I liked to make the most of the school holidays, with a mixture of outings and activities at home. Normally I would have taken us all out on at least one day trip, but I knew Danny couldn't cope with a full day in a strange place with new sights and sounds, so I was considering taking him to the cinema. Because it was half-term there was a good selection of films on suitable for children of most ages. Whether Danny could cope with a trip to the cinema was another matter, but I wanted to try.

When Reva returned Danny she didn't come in but said goodbye to him on the doorstep. Danny went through to see George and I asked her if he had ever been to the cinema.

'Good grief, no!' she exclaimed, astounded. 'He couldn't cope with that.'

'Have you ever tried?' I asked. I hoped it didn't sound like a criticism, but if she had taken him I could learn from her experience.

'No, and neither would I,' she said. 'He's scared of the dark and loud noises.'

'I understand that,' I said. 'I'd choose the film carefully. But would you have any objection if I took him tomorrow?' It was appropriate to ask her.

'You can try if you wish,' she said a little stiffly. 'But I don't know how you think he's going to sit in a cinema for two hours when he doesn't even watch television for five minutes. And supposing he has a meltdown?' she asked anxiously. 'What will you do with all those people there?' Yet again it seemed that Reva had become imprisoned by Danny's condition as much, if not more, than he had, and was scared to try anything new with him.

'If necessary I'll have to carry him out,' I said. 'I wouldn't stay if he was upset.'

'Go ahead,' she said. 'Good luck.'

I thanked her and we said goodbye.

After Danny had fed George and we'd done a little of his homework (which he still liked to do as part of his evening routine, even though it was the school holiday), I talked to him about the cinema. I likened it to a very big television screen that we'd sit in front of to watch a film with other adults and children. I told him where the cinema was and that I was thinking of taking him tomorrow.

He was silent.

'Would you like to go to the cinema?' I asked him.

'Yes, thank you very much,' he said, which of course meant very little, being his stock phrase. But then there was a long pause when I knew Danny was trying to find the words he needed to reply. Finally he said, 'Children at my school go to the cinema.'

'Yes, I expect they do,' I said, delighted he'd answered with something appropriate. 'Do the children at school talk about the cinema and the films they've seen?'

There was another long pause before Danny said, 'They have seen the films *Chicken Run* and *Scooby-Doo*.'

'They were on at the cinema recently,' I said. 'Did they like going to the cinema?'

'Yes.'

Although Danny rarely spoke to the children at school and often appeared unreceptive and on the sidelines of their social interaction, he'd clearly been listening to what they said and taking it all in. I felt sad as I imagined him in the playground standing alone or with his classroom assistant, overhearing the other children chatting excitedly about what they'd been doing in their leisure time but never being able to join in.

'So we'll go to the cinema tomorrow afternoon,' I said to him. 'Then you will be able to tell your friends what you saw.'

He looked very thoughtful and after another pause said quietly, 'Yes, Danny tell friends he go to the cinema.'

The following morning when I went into Danny's bedroom I was expecting that he might have some questions about the cinema, having had time to process the information and compose them, but his bed was empty. I turned to the wardrobe, concerned that the door was closed and he might have shut himself in again, as I'd warned him not to. I opened the door, but the wardrobe was empty. Then I heard a noise under the bed. Turning, I knelt down and peered underneath. Danny was on his back, eyes open. I didn't think he'd been there for long as his bed was still warm.

'What are you doing under there?' I asked.

'I'm at the cinema,' Danny said.

'You're pretending to be at the cinema,' I said. 'You are really under your bed.'

'Pretending to be at the cinema,' Danny repeated. 'It's dark.'

'Yes, the cinema is dark,' I agreed. This, of course, was the only similarity between being under the bed and in the cinema, but it was significant that he'd latched onto the word 'dark' when I'd told him about the cinema.

'There's nothing to worry about,' I reassured him. 'It won't be very dark in the cinema, and you'll be with me the whole time.'

There was silence before Danny said, 'Danny hiding.'

'Yes, I know. Why are you hiding?'

'Danny hiding from Mummy.'

'I think you hide from Mummy a lot,' I said, as he began to crawl out. 'It worries her.'

'Danny hiding from Mummy now,' he said, and I realized he was referring to me as Mummy. How confusing it must be for him.

'Danny, love,' I said. 'I am your foster carer and you call me Cathy. Your mummy and daddy are at home. You saw Mummy yesterday, Tuesday.' I pointed to the children's calendar I'd pinned to the bedroom wall. 'You will see Mummy again tomorrow, Thursday. Then again on Saturday.'

Danny looked at the calendar and then at me, although he didn't make eye contact. There was a long pause as he concentrated on what he needed to say.

'Like my mummy,' he said at last, pointing at me.

'Yes, I am like your mummy,' I said, smiling. 'That's right. While you are with me I look after you and do the things for you that Mummy did.' Then, without thinking, I instinctively kissed his cheek. Surprisingly, he didn't recoil from the physical contact but suddenly threw his arms around my neck and hugged me. It was our first hug and I felt my eyes fill.

'Like my mummy,' he said. 'I love my mummy.' And I hoped Reva appreciated just how much love Danny had to give her. It was just very difficult for him to show it.

Chapter Twenty

Important

The trip to the cinema was a success overall, although it had its moments. Paula, Lucy and Adrian hadn't wanted to come, having other things to do, which was just as well in the end as they might have been embarrassed by some of Danny's behaviour. Danny was very good as I found a parking space and then held my hand as we walked to the cinema. He waited patiently while we queued to buy the tickets. I'd already explained the procedure and what to expect. We were seeing a Thomas the Tank Engine film, so there were many other children there too. Inside, he sat in the seat I showed him without a problem, but as the seats around us began to fill he grew anxious, and I swapped seats so he could sit at the end, next to the aisle. I continued to talk to him while we waited for the film to start, reassuring him and explaining more about the cinema and what was going to happen. I'd brought a bag of sweets that I knew he liked, but he didn't want one. As the lights began to dim I continued to talk quietly to him and placed my hand lightly on his arm. He was alert and vigilant but didn't appear anxious. However, when the first advertisement shot onto the screen with a loud whooshing noise, he screamed. Those sitting in front of us turned and stared.

'It's all right,' I whispered to him, lightly rubbing his arm. 'The advertisements are loud, but the film won't be so loud.' I don't know why they make the advertisements in cinemas so loud – even I find them uncomfortable sometimes. 'Put your hands over your ears while the advertisements are on,' I suggested.

He did so, relaxed at little, and then removed them at the start of the film when a large gleaming image appeared of his favourite character, Thomas the Tank Engine, grinning broadly. I watched Danny's reaction: his eyes rounded and his mouth dropped open, and for the rest of the film he was completely engrossed and enthralled. A few times, when Thomas was in danger and the action and drama intensified, Danny sat uncomfortably rigid, gripping the edge of his seat and grimacing, as though he too was experiencing Thomas's plight. So I whispered to him that it was a film and that Thomas would be all right in the end, which helped him relax a little.

Danny was still completely absorbed in the film as the credits rolled, but as the lights went up and the audience began to leave and the noise level grew, he couldn't cope. He covered his head with his hands and, dropping to the floor, curled into a ball and then tried to hide under his seat. I didn't know what his expectation was of the end of the film but clearly I hadn't explained it in enough detail. I apologized to those in the row trying to make their way out as they stepped over and around him. The cinema emptied quickly and as the hubbub died away I knelt down, talked to him quietly and was eventually able to persuade him to come out.

As we left I said to him, 'If we come to the cinema again you'll know what happens, so it won't be scary.'

Important

He didn't reply.

'Would you like to come to the cinema again?' I asked.

'Yes, thank you very much,' he said and, turning, tried to lead me back into the cinema.

'No, not now. We've seen that film,' I explained. 'Another time we can come and see a different film.'

'Yes,' he said, nodding enthusiastically. So I didn't think the experience had been too traumatic for him. Next time I might even try him with some popcorn.

It was raining when we arrived home, so George came into the house for his walk. Lucy and Paula asked Danny if he'd had a nice time at the cinema and he nodded, now more interested in George. Adrian was out, having gone to see a friend. Paula and Lucy stayed with Danny and George while I began preparing dinner, but as usual they called for me to come when the dustpan and brush was required. I pointed out to Lucy that if she was really going into child care she'd be clearing up much worse mess than a few pellets, and perhaps she should start getting used to it now, but she wasn't impressed.

When George tired and flopped out on the living-room floor Danny sat next to him. He took one of his Thomas the Tank Engine toys from his toy box and showed it to George, placing it in front of his nose. George sniffed it. Then Danny began telling him about his trip to the cinema: 'It was dark … lots of people … Thomas goes fast … chuff-chuff … fast … Thomas going down the hill … fast … very fast …' Danny's voice rose as he described the part of the film where Thomas's breaks had failed and he'd become a runaway train. This had been one of the scenes when I'd had to reassure Danny that Thomas would be safe.

'It's a film,' Danny now told George. 'Thomas safe. Not hurt.' Which was what I'd told him, and again I was reminded that Danny understood and remembered far more than he could communicate.

The following day, Thursday, Danny saw his mother for the second additional holiday contact. It rained all afternoon and was still raining when Reva brought Danny home. Danny went straight through to see George as Reva called goodbye. As usual I asked Reva if she and Danny had had a nice time and she nodded, a little like Danny did. 'He told me he went to the cinema,' she said.

'Yes?' I was expecting a bit more detail, possibly what he'd told her, but it wasn't forthcoming.

'See you Saturday then,' she said, and returned to her sports car, parked out the front, which had so impressed Adrian.

As it was raining George came into the house again, but I noticed Danny seemed subdued and also looked a little pale. I asked him if he was feeling all right and put my hand to his forehead, but he didn't appear to have a temperature. George seemed to sense that Danny didn't feel so good and after a quick run down the hall sat quietly on the living-room floor with his head resting in Danny's lap. It was uncanny and touching the way George tuned into Danny's feelings. It is said that animals can sense emotion and illness in their owners, and having seen George with Danny I believe it. I sat on the sofa watching them together while the dinner cooked; Danny quietly and lovingly stroking George's head, George relaxed and with his eyes slowly closing. Then Danny began talking to George.

Important

'I love you,' he said quietly. 'You're my best friend. And I'm your friend. We'll always be friends.' As usual Danny was more fluent when talking to George than he was with adults and other children. 'Daddy says he loves me,' he continued. 'But I don't think he does. He shouts at me when I get things wrong. He upsets Mummy and she shouts and cries. It makes me unhappy and gives me a tummy ache.'

I looked at Danny carefully as he continued to stroke George. Was that the reason he was pale and subdued? Because his parents had been arguing? 'Did you see Daddy today?' I asked lightly a few moments later.

Danny didn't reply but concentrated on George.

'Daddy shouts,' he told George. 'And Mummy cries. It's because of me. It would have been better if I'd never been born. That's what Daddy said. I have a brother and sister, but I'm not allowed to see them because I'm stupid. I wish I wasn't stupid. If I was smart like the kids at school Mummy and Daddy would love me, and I could live with them and we'd all be happy.'

I was shocked and greatly saddened. Had Reva and Richard any idea that Danny had been listening to them and taking it all in? I doubted it, or surely they would have been more careful in what they said. I couldn't pretend I hadn't heard, and Danny needed to know he wasn't to blame. I stood up, went over and sat on the floor beside him and George. Danny continued to stroke George and didn't look up. George opened his eyes and looked at me, almost as if he too understood the significance of what Danny had told him.

'Danny, love,' I said gently, touching his hand. 'You're not stupid, don't ever think that, please. Mummy and Daddy didn't mean what they said. They were arguing, and when people argue they get angry. They shout and say things they don't mean. All those wonderful patterns you can make. That shows how smart you are. I know you find it difficult sometimes to say what you mean, but Terri is going to get you some help for that. Mummy and Daddy love you lots. And they miss you. It's not your fault they argue and Mummy cries. Parents are really just big children and they get it wrong sometimes. They would be very, very sorry if they knew you were upset. They love you.'

How much of this Danny took in was impossible to gauge, but I hoped he believed what I'd said. The poor child was carrying the burden of everything that was wrong in his family, believing he was stupid and his parents didn't love him because of how he was. It was heartbreaking.

'We're not upset, are we?' he said to George, trying to put on a brave face.

'I would be if I'd heard those things said about me,' I said. 'Even if they weren't true. We like to hear nice things about us. That's makes us happy.'

Danny was quiet again, and then he stopped stroking George. Without looking at me, he asked, 'Do you love me?'

'Yes, I do,' I said, without hesitation. 'It's a different kind of love to the one Mummy and Daddy feel, because they are your parents and they have cared for you and loved you for a long time. Since you were a baby. But I love you, and so do Paula, Lucy and Adrian.' I believe we can never have too much love, and even if Danny returned to his parents and never saw us again, it would surely be positive for him to live his life knowing there were others in the world who loved him.

Important

As if to reinforce what I'd said, Lucy bounded into the living room in very good spirits. 'Hi, little fellow,' she said, going over and ruffling his hair. 'Good to have you home again. Missed you.' And this time Danny didn't recoil from her touch.

It was difficult writing up my log notes that evening, but I was duty bound to include what Danny had said. I wrote objectively and using the words he had spoken wherever appropriate. It wasn't for me to comment on Reva and Richard's behaviour, but without them realizing it their argument had emotionally abused Danny. Their comments about him had hurt him as much as, if not more than, any physical blow.

On Friday, continuing with my strategy of broadening Danny's experiences, I took him to an indoor activity centre that catered for toddlers and children up to the age of twelve. It was a thirty-minute drive away. Adrian stayed at home, as he had a friend dropping by, but Lucy and Paula came with me. I explained to Danny before we left where we were going and what to expect, but nevertheless he was very reticent to begin with. He sat with his hands over his ears, overwhelmed by the noise and movement going on around him, and refused to take off his shoes so he could go in the soft-toy area. The girls and I sat with him as he gradually grew accustomed to his new surroundings, and then Lucy and Paula demonstrated some of the activities in the soft-toy area. Eventually he was intrigued enough to venture in. Most of the children were younger than him in this area, so it was less threatening than where the bigger children were. After about half an hour we persuaded him to try the ball pond, which he did, and stayed there for another half an hour. Then he came out

Important

and said quietly to me that he'd had enough and wanted to go home. Most children would have happily spent all afternoon in the activity centre, but we recognized that Danny had done well to stay an hour. I was sure that if we came again he would be able to stay longer and try different things. When we asked him if he'd had a nice time and had liked the activities he said, 'Yes, thank you very much.'

At home he drew a detailed picture of the ball pond with its multitude of brightly coloured balls – only of course Danny's picture had the balls forming complicated coloured patterns, unlike the real ball pond where they fell randomly. It was truly a work of art and we praised him. When it was finished, I pinned it to the wall for all to see. 'Danny's picture,' he proudly told George.

On Saturday Danny had all-day contact with his parents again and as usual I took him. Until now the driveway had always been empty when I'd arrived. I'd assumed Reva's car and possibly Richard's were in the garages, although I'd never seen any sign of Richard. But this morning there was a car parked on the drive, and it wasn't Reva's sports car.

'Is that Daddy's car?' I asked Danny as I parked behind it.

'Yes,' Danny said.

We got out and as we crossed the drive I saw the outline of a man behind one of the downstairs windows. I thought that, at last, I might meet Richard.

Reva answered the door and was again reserved and a little standoffish. 'Thank you for bringing Danny,' she said formally. 'I'll bring him home at six o'clock.'

'Have a nice day then,' I said to them both. And we said goodbye.

If it was Richard, I wasn't given the chance to meet him.

When Reva returned Danny at six she didn't want to come in, and when I asked her if they'd had a good day she said, 'Yes, not too bad,' but didn't volunteer any details. With no feedback I didn't know if their day had been a success or not. Danny seemed his usual self, so I assumed there hadn't been a problem, but it was difficult to tell with Danny and some feedback would have been useful.

On Sunday Adrian and Paula went out with their father for the day, and Lucy went to a friend's house for a few hours to work on a joint project for school. I explained to Danny where everyone was and he too wanted to do some homework.

'Writing,' he said, and fetched his school bag.

He took out his pencil, which had a triangular gripper attached to it that helped him hold the pencil correctly so he could form his letters. I fetched some paper and we sat at the table, where I wrote the letters he had to practise as one of his learning targets and he copied them. He concentrated hard and it took him a long time to form each letter, and even after a lot of effort what he produced was more the standard of a three-year-old than a six-year-old. I praised him, though, for he had done his best.

We went for a little walk in the afternoon for a breath of fresh air and then Lucy returned home at four o'clock, followed by Adrian and Paula at five-thirty. They let themselves in but as usual I went to the front door to say hello to John, their father. It was important we kept our relationship polite and amicable for their sakes.

* * *

Important

On Monday morning, after a week's holiday from school, no one was very happy about getting up early and it took a lot of cajoling to make sure everyone left the house on time.

Danny was pleased to see Yvonne again, as she was him.

'Hello, sweetie,' she said. 'Did you have a nice half-term holiday?'

'Yes, thank you very much,' Danny said, and to our surprise he gave her a little hug.

'You're very honoured,' I said. I thought it was a testament to the trust he'd placed in her that he was able to do this.

At the end of the school day Danny's teacher, Sue Bright, came out with Danny, and my first thought was that something was wrong – that's often the reason a class teacher seeks out a parent or carer. But she approached me with a cheery 'Good afternoon, Cathy. How are you?'

'Very well, thank you,' I said.

'I wanted to check with you that Danny's review is still on for Wednesday. I'm on a training course tomorrow, so I won't be in school.'

'Yes, it is,' I said, relieved that this was the reason she wanted to see me. 'It's at ten-thirty at my house. Danny will be in school as usual.'

'Yes, Yvonne will be here with him. How long do you think the review will last? I have to arrange cover for my class.'

'They usually run for about an hour,' I said. 'Maybe a little longer.'

'Thanks. I'll allow an hour and a half.'

Sue then told me that Danny had had a good day and there was a new reading book in his book bag. We said goodbye, but as Danny and I crossed the playground I could see he was deep in thought, composing something he needed to say. His face was serious as he concentrated, his eyes were down and his hands made little jerky movements when he was thinking hard. Sometimes he flapped them.

Eventually he said, 'Do other children have reviews?'

'Only if they are in foster care,' I said. 'A review is a special meeting for children who live with foster carers. So that shows how important you are.'

'Important,' Danny repeated thoughtfully. Then there was a long pause before he said, 'I don't want to be important. I want to live with Mummy and Daddy like the other children do.'

There was little I could say.

Chapter Twenty-One

For the Good of the Child

knew as soon as I showed Reva into the living room for Danny's review that there was an atmosphere between her and Terri. She said a very frosty 'Good morning' to Terri without looking at her, and then chose the seat furthest away from her and completely ignored her. Sue, Jill and Ray (the independent reviewing officer, whom I'd met before at another child's review) were already present. It was only when Ray opened the meeting by asking, 'Are we expecting anyone else?' that the reason for Reva's hostility became obvious.

'If you mean my husband, Richard,' she said tartly, 'then no. He had to go to work.'

Ray hadn't specifically meant Richard – it was the question all reviewing officers ask at the start of the meeting – but Terri replied swiftly, 'He should be here, Reva.'

'He can't be if he's working,' Reva retaliated. 'Why don't you schedule these things for the evening?' She had a point.

'I've tried to see Richard in the evening,' Terri said. 'But he's not in then either.'

Ray looked surprised and somewhat bemused by their exchange. 'I'll record his apologies for absence,' he said, trying to smooth over hostilities. 'It isn't a problem. So let's start by introducing ourselves.' Introductions are normal practice at the start of a child's review and the reviewing officer, in this case Ray, would also be chairing and minuting the meeting. 'Ray Sturgess, independent reviewing officer for Danny,' he said, writing on the large notepad he had open on his lap.

'Jill – Cathy's supervising social worker,' Jill said.

'Cathy Glass, Danny's foster carer.'

'Thank you. You look familiar …' Ray said, glancing at me as he wrote.

'You were the reviewing officer for Alice, last year,' I reminded him.

'Yes, of course. Sorry, I see so many faces. Nice to see you again.' Then he looked at Reva for her introduction.

'Reva – Danny's mother,' she said stiffly.

'Thank you. I'll make a note of your husband's apology for absence now.'

'His name is Richard,' Reva said.

'And he is Danny's father?'

'Yes.'

Ray then looked at Sue, who was next. 'Sue Bright, Danny's teacher since he came to the school a year ago,' she said.

'Thank you.'

Lastly was Terri. 'Terri – Danny's social worker,' she said.

Ray finished writing and looked up. 'Thank you all for coming. This is the first review for Danny – who came into care on 1 February this year. The aim of this meeting is to make sure that everything is being done as it should for Danny, and that the care plan is relevant and up to date. I haven't had a chance to meet Danny yet, but I have made arrangements to see him in school after this meeting. I spoke to your head teacher yesterday,' Ray added looking at Sue. She nodded. 'Perhaps we can go there straight after this meeting?'

'Yes,' Sue said.

'Thank you. Danny is accommodated under a Section 20. Are there any changes to that?' he asked Terri.

'No,' she said.

'And Reva and Cathy have received copies of the care plan?' Ray asked, glancing at us.

'Yes, thank you,' I said. Reva nodded.

'Good. And the care plan is up to date?' he asked Terri.

'Yes,' Terri said. These were all standard questions.

'And contact remains unchanged? Tuesday and Thursday, four o'clock until six o'clock, and Saturday, ten till six. All contact is at the family home.'

'Yes,' Terri said.

'Good. I have received the review forms that Cathy and Danny were asked to complete,' Ray continued. 'And these are included in the minutes. Cathy, perhaps you would like to start by telling us how Danny has settled with you.' The foster carer is often asked to speak first at a child's review, because they are dealing with the child on a daily basis.

I sat upright. I had my fostering folder on my lap, but I knew what I wanted to say. I would give an honest account, but I would also focus on the positives. 'Danny has settled in very well,' I began. 'He eats and sleeps well, likes going to school and doing his homework. He has his pet rabbit here, George, which I think has helped him enormously.'

'And it's you and your three children living here?' Ray asked.

'Yes, Adrian is fifteen, Lucy thirteen and Paula eleven.'

'Thank you,' Ray said, making a note. 'And Danny gets on all right with your children? He is an only child at home.'

'Yes, although of course my children are much older than Danny, so there isn't really any sibling rivalry.'

Ray nodded as he wrote. 'What time does Danny go to bed?'

'I usually take him up at about seven o'clock,' I said. 'Then he's in bed between eight and eight-thirty, depending on whether he has a bath or not. It takes him a while to wash and change into his pyjamas. He likes to do it himself, in a set routine, but I stay with him and don't leave him unattended. He wakes between six-thirty and seven.'

'Any nightmares or bed wetting?' Ray asked.

'No,' I said.

'Danny used to wet the bed every night,' Reva said. 'But he stopped about six months ago when Richard told me not to buy him any more nappies.'

'The strategy seems to have worked,' Ray said encouragingly, smiling at Reva. The atmosphere lightened slightly.

'So Danny sleeps well,' Ray confirmed, looking at me to continue.

'Yes. He has a soft-toy rabbit, also called George, which he has in bed with him. He goes to sleep with the duvet pulled up over his head, but I uncover his face once he's asleep when I check on him. Sometimes I read him a story before we go up if he's not too tired.'

'And eating?' Ray asked as he wrote. 'Is Danny eating his meals?'

'Yes, but as in all things he needs a lot of time. He is very methodical and likes to cut up his food and arrange it before he starts eating. He's had quite a limited diet so I am gradually introducing new foods. He usually finishes all his meal, and he knows how to use a knife and fork.'

'That's good,' Ray said with another encouraging smile at Reva. She didn't respond. 'So what else can you tell us about Danny? Are there any health concerns?'

'He is special needs,' (which Ray would know), 'and finds new situations very difficult, even when they're explained in advance. I am slowly trying to widen his experiences, but it takes time. I have taken him to the park in the snow, and to the cinema and an activity centre. He coped pretty well.'

'And is his play age-appropriate?' Ray asked.

'No,' Reva said before I had a chance to answer.

'Perhaps Cathy could answer first, please, and then when she has finished her report you can tell us about Danny?' Ray put it nicely and she nodded.

'In some areas Danny's play is age-appropriate and even advanced for his years, especially in his art work and the patterns he creates – they are intricate and incorporate complicated colour sequences – but much of Danny's other play is more like that of a much younger child. For example, he can spend hours pushing a toy car around the floor without wanting to take the play further and create situations using the car. He doesn't role play. He can do some jigsaw puzzles, but he struggles with many other games that you would expect a child of six to be able to master, like Snap, for example. When he first arrived he played with Lego for a whole week and didn't want to play with anything else. He didn't build with the Lego bricks but arranged them into different patterns. Then, after that week, he played with something else for another four days. He seems to like the repetitiveness in games and tasks he is very familiar with.'

231

Saving Danny

Ray nodded.

'Danny likes his bath,' I said, moving on. 'I was going to ask if I could start taking him swimming. And perhaps he could join in the swimming lessons at school?'

'I don't mind,' Reva said with a shrug, which was a turnaround.

Ray looked at Sue. 'Can the school make the necessary provision for Danny to join his class's swimming lessons?'

'Yes,' Sue said. 'Yvonne, Danny's teaching assistant, will go in the water with him. We have offered this before.'

'Good,' Ray said, making a note. 'So let's make that one of the decisions of this review: that Danny will start swimming lessons at school.'

'If Danny starts swimming at school I don't think Cathy should take him swimming as well,' Reva said. 'It will be too much for him to cope with all at once.' Which was true.

Ray nodded. 'That's fine, and at the next review we can look into whether it is appropriate for Danny to go swimming in his leisure time with Cathy. But there is nothing to stop you from taking him swimming,' he said to Reva.

Reva gave a small, unenthusiastic nod.

'And can Danny tell you what he wants?' Ray now asked me. He would be aware that Danny had communication difficulties.

'Sometimes, but he struggles to express himself and needs a lot of time. To be honest, he finds it easier to talk to his rabbit, George, than to other children or adults.'

I saw Reva nod.

'Thank you,' Ray said to me. 'Is there anything else you would like to tell us about Danny?'

There was plenty I could say, but I knew that Ray would have seen the report from the social services and the school, and that I had to be sensitive to the fact that Reva was present. 'Danny is a lovely little boy,' I said. 'But because of his high level of needs he can also be very hard work. He requires a lot of time and patience, and needs preparing for even the simplest of events. He can easily become frustrated and then he screams and shouts. Sometimes he becomes overloaded, can't cope and has a meltdown. I'm learning to recognize the signs and can sometimes intervene in time to stop it, but not always. Danny has a lot to give, and although he can't express himself he takes everything in and feels things very deeply. I can only guess at how frustrating life must be for him. I do my best and hope I'm getting it right, but it's not always easy to tell.'

Ray nodded thoughtfully as he wrote.

'I was wondering', Jill said, looking at Ray and then Terri, 'if perhaps Cathy could meet with the educational psychologist or CAMHS [child and adolescent mental health services] to explore strategies that may help her to look after Danny.'

'Without me being present?' Reva interjected.

'I didn't mean to exclude you,' Jill said. 'But it might benefit Danny if Cathy was given some advice on managing his behaviour while she is the main carer.'

'I'm his mother. Why can't I go?' Reva said.

'You probably could,' Jill said, looking at Terri.

'Yes,' Terri said. 'But Reva, I'm still waiting to see you and Richard together so I can start a referral to the education psychologist to have Danny assessed. Once the assessment is made then it will become clearer what additional help Danny needs.' Then, looking at Ray, Terri said, 'Richard is still

233

opposed to his son being assessed and hasn't been able to meet with me yet. The department is considering its options, including applying for an ICO.'

I knew the significance of this and so did Jill. She threw me a worried look. ICO stands for Interim Care Order, so the social services were now very close to applying to the court for an order, which would assign parental rights for Danny to them.

'Perhaps Cathy and Reva could have an informal chat with the educational psychologist?' Jill suggested. 'I know the educational psychologist is very busy, but it might be worth asking. We could also apply to CAMHS, although I believe they have a long waiting list.'

'Will you follow this up then?' Ray asked Terri. She nodded and made a note.

'Cathy, can you tell us how Danny is after contact, and then we'll move on to Reva?'

'Danny is coping well with all the changes he has to make,' I said. 'He doesn't say much after contact, and usually goes straight out to see to George.'

'But he's not upset?' Ray asked.

'No. Well, apart from last Thursday when he was sad.'

'And do we know why he was sad?' Ray asked.

'Because Richard and I had an argument,' Reva put in, clearly annoyed.

There was silence.

'But normally Danny is all right after contact?' Ray asked me.

'Yes,' I said.

'And telephone contact?' Ray asked.

'There isn't any,' Terri pointed out.

'Danny hates the phone,' Reva said.

'I think it's the sound of it ringing that he doesn't like,' I said. 'He seems to have very sensitive hearing and will cover up his ears at loud noises. But I'm happy to try him with a phone call home if Reva would like me to.'

Everyone looked at Reva, who didn't immediately agree. Most parents would have jumped at the opportunity of more contact.

'Perhaps you'd like time to think about this?' Ray suggested to her. 'Then, if you would like to try telephone contact, tell Terri and she'll arrange it with Cathy.'

Reva nodded.

'Anything else you would like to add?' Ray asked, looking at me.

'It's not specifically about Danny, but I was wondering if I might buy a rabbit run for the garden so George can spend time out of his hutch when Danny isn't here.'

'If Danny says so,' Reva said. 'Ask him.'

'Thank you,' Ray said as he wrote. 'Cathy, one question I must ask you as a matter of course is: can Danny stay with you for as long as necessary?'

'Yes,' I said. The independent reviewing officer usually asks this at the child's first review.

Ray finished writing and then looked up. 'Reva, would you like to speak now? Are you happy with the level of care Danny is receiving at Cathy's?' This question is standard too, although I still feel uncomfortable as I wait for the parent(s) to reply.

'Yes,' Reva said.

'Do you have any concerns about the care Danny is receiving? Anything you would like to raise or discuss?'

'No,' Reva said.

'Is there anything you're especially pleased with?'

Reva shrugged. 'Not really.'

'Perhaps you'd like to tell us a bit about Danny now,' Ray said.

Reva shrugged again. 'I don't know what to say. I've said it all to Terri, and I gave Cathy notes on Danny when he first came here.'

'You mentioned earlier that you didn't think Danny's play was always age-appropriate. Perhaps you'd like to expand on that.'

'Not really,' Reva said. 'Cathy said it all.'

'And what about contact?' Ray asked. 'Are you happy with the level of contact at present and the way it is going?'

'I guess so,' Reva said.

'So the contact arrangements are working well?'

'Yes.'

'Do you have any concerns about Danny's health?' Ray now asked, working down a checklist of issues to be covered at the review.

'No,' Reva said.

'Are Danny's eyesight and hearing tests up to date?'

'I took Danny to the clinic about six months ago, but they couldn't do anything as he wouldn't let them touch him,' Reva said.

'So Danny hasn't had a recent health check-up? Hearing or sight test?'

'No,' Reva confirmed.

'And what about the dentist? Has Danny had a check-up recently?' When a child comes into care under a court order the foster carer usually arranges for these health checks, but if the child is accommodated under a Section 20 the responsibility often stays with the parents.

Reva shook her head. 'Danny wouldn't open his mouth for the dentist and then he screamed and lashed out.'

'Perhaps Cathy could take him,' Ray suggested to Terri. 'He should have a check-up.'

'Yes,' Terri said. 'That's fine with me.'

'Are you happy for Cathy to take Danny?' Ray now asked Reva. 'He could go to the clinic where you registered him.' Which most parents prefer.

'Yes,' Reva said. 'It's Yew Lodge clinic, in the same road as his school.'

I made a note.

'Is there anything else you can think of that Danny needs?' Ray now asked Reva.

'Not really,' Reva said. Usually parents have plenty to say at a review – it is, after all, their child, and even though they aren't actually parenting the child at the time they have worries and views about their care. But despite Ray's encouragement, Reva didn't want to say any more. I thought she seemed on her guard, as she had been recently with me, although the purpose of the review was to give all parties a chance to work together for the good of the child.

'And Danny's father, Richard,' Ray now said. 'Is he happy with the level of care Danny is receiving?'

'Yes,' Reva said tightly.

'And you both understand and agree with the care plan?' Ray asked. Reva didn't immediately answer, so Ray clarified: 'That Danny will stay here with Cathy until he is rehabilitated home to live with you and Richard in approximately three months' time.'

There was a long pause before Reva said, 'I don't know. I'll have to ask Richard.'

'Ask him what?' Ray said.

'If Danny can come home to live with us permanently.'

There was silence. I saw Jill and Terri exchange a glance. Sue was looking at Reva, also shocked by her comment.

'So you have doubts about Danny returning home?' Ray asked Reva.

'Yes,' Reva said.

'Can you tell us what your concerns are?'

Reva shrugged and looked close to tears.

Ray turned to Terri. 'I assume you weren't aware of this?'

'No,' Terri said. Then addressing Reva she said, 'This is the first I've heard of this. I need to meet with both of you as a matter of urgency.'

Reva's face crumpled. 'Why does everyone always blame me?' she said. 'It's not my fault Richard won't see you.' Grabbing her handbag from beside her chair she ran out of the room and down the hall. Terri followed her, but from the hall we heard Reva shout, 'Leave me alone, won't you!'

The front door opened and then slammed shut. Terri returned to the living room. She looked worried but was calm. I guessed as a social worker she'd had far worse situations to deal with.

'I'll phone her later,' she said stoically, returning to her seat. 'Sorry. I wasn't aware of this new development.'

Ray nodded. 'Can you telephone me when you've spoken to the parents.'

'Yes,' Terri said.

The rest of us were quiet, shaken by Reva's disclosure and sudden departure.

Ray took a breath and moved the meeting on by asking Sue for the school's report. Sue was as positive as she could be and said that academically and socially Danny was making steady but slow progress, and she hoped a referral to the educational psychologist could be made soon. She read out some recent test results, which highlighted just how far behind his peers Danny was. Ray asked her if she felt Danny would benefit from going to a special school. She said she thought he might, although of course it would need the educational psychologist to make that recommendation, and then the funding would have to be found, all of which would take at least a year. Sue explained how she adapted the class's work to suit Danny and showed us a piece of his written work. She mentioned the home school book and said that everything was being done to help Danny academically as well as socially. She concluded by saying that Danny was always in school on time and had a good relationship with his teaching assistants.

Ray thanked her and then asked Terri for her input. Given that the care plan was now in tatters, there wasn't an awful lot Terri could say. She confirmed that Danny had come into care at the request of his parents largely because Reva wasn't coping, and said she still hadn't met with Richard despite repeated requests to do so. She said that even before Reva's comments about whether Danny could go home, she and her manager had concerns over whether this could be achieved, at least in the proposed time scale. She said she felt there was a lack of attachment and that Richard appeared to have rejected Danny from an early age.

'When I return to the office I'll arrange a meeting with my manager,' Terri said. 'I'm not prepared to leave Danny in limbo while his parents decide if they want him back or not.' I could see Terri was annoyed, and understandably so.

Ray finished writing and looked at Terri. 'And you'll give me an update on what you decide after you've spoken to your manager, please,' he said.

'Yes, of course,' Terri said.

Ray then asked Jill to speak.

'I'll keep it short,' she said. 'As Cathy's supervising social worker I'm in regular contact with Cathy and I also observe her with Danny. She is a very experienced and well-qualified foster carer and is providing a high level of care for Danny. I have no concerns.'

Ray nodded and thanked her. This was all Jill had to say, as the other issues relating to Danny had already been covered in the review. Ray then began summing up the decisions of the review: that the care plan would be reviewed; Danny would start swimming lessons at school; Reva would consider telephone contact with Danny, and Terri would look into arranging for me to meet with the educational psychologist or CAMHS, as well as referring Danny to the educational psychologist for an assessment. Before Ray closed the meeting he set a date for the next review in three months' time.

'Hopefully it won't be necessary,' he said. 'And Danny will have returned home to his parents.' But I think we all knew that was wishful thinking.

Chapter Twenty-Two

No Cavity Club

I didn't *ask* Danny if I could buy a run for George as Reva had said I should, because as a responsible adult, and knowing Danny, I felt it was a decision I could reasonably make. I explained to Danny how it would be kinder to George and I involved him in the planning and took him with me to buy the run. Paula came too, and I had difficulty persuading her to leave the pet shop without one of the cuddly rabbits, hamsters, guinea pigs, gerbils or other cute small animals they had for sale. Once home, Adrian helped to assemble the run on the lawn, and from then on, when the weather allowed, George spent most of the day outside. Danny still took him for walks in the garden or brought him indoors if it was raining, but George was out in his run more than he was cooped up in his hutch; nibbling grass, running around or just sitting contentedly with his nose twitching in the air as he took in the different sights and sounds – a very happy bunny. He was pleased, and so was I.

Toscha and George continued to advance their friendship outdoors as well as in and sniffed each other, nose to nose, through the wire mesh of the run. Sometimes Toscha would sit pressed against the outside of the run – as close to George as she could get – and I guessed she was becoming as attached to him as we were.

Danny began swimming lessons at school the week after the review. Yvonne went in the water with him, but even so, that first lesson he was very anxious and only stayed in the water ten minutes before he began to show signs of stress. Yvonne and I agreed that this wasn't surprising, as the swimming pool was a whole new experience for Danny, and was very intense with the sound echoing, light bouncing off the water and the swimming teacher issuing instructions in a loud voice to the whole class. The following week Danny stayed in the water for fifteen minutes and by the end of March he was managing twenty, but Yvonne didn't extend it beyond twenty minutes as she allowed time for him to change in peace and quiet and at his own speed, before the rest of the class arrived in the changing room with their lively chatter and constant movement.

On the last Sunday in March I invited my parents to dinner again. Adrian, Lucy, Paula and I had been seeing them on Saturdays when Danny was on all-day contact, but I wanted to include Danny in as many family occasions as possible. This wasn't only to broaden his experience; it was also important that he got to know my parents, as it appeared he would be staying with us for some time – possibly for good, if he didn't return home and the social services decided it was the right place for him to be.

I began preparing him for their visit on Friday evening, by telling him that they were coming for Sunday lunch and what that involved. As far as I knew Danny had no experience of grandparents or their role apart from my parents' disastrous first visit. Reva's parents lived a long way away, and Terri had said that Richard never took Danny to see his parents. I explained in simple language to Danny my parents' relationship to me, where they lived, why we loved them so much and liked to see them regularly. On Saturday evening, after Danny had returned from contact and had seen to George, I explained to him in more detail what would happen when my parents arrived the following day: how they would ring the doorbell, come in and take off their coats and shoes, sit in the living room chatting with us, have dinner and then maybe play board games or card games with us in the afternoon. I told him much of this while he was getting ready for bed as I'd found before this was a good time to explain things in detail. It seemed that while he was occupied with the routine of washing and changing he was more relaxed and receptive to what I was saying. I concluded in his bedroom by pointing out Sunday on the calendar on his wall.

'They are coming tomorrow,' I said. 'The next day. One more sleep.'

'That's good,' he said, although I didn't read much into this as it had been his favourite phrase for the last few days.

Although Danny was as well prepared for my parents' visit as he could have been, he still hid behind the sofa when the doorbell rang. My heart sank. Thankfully he came out after about five minutes and began pushing one of his toy cars around the living room while making a low humming noise, which I knew he found comforting. He didn't want us to play with him, although we asked, and when my parents tried to initiate conversation with him – by asking him about school or George – he didn't reply, but just shook his head. They understood he wasn't being rude.

'It'll take him time to get to know us,' Mum said to Dad so Danny could hear. 'But I'm pleased Danny is able to play in the same room as us. I think that's wonderful.'

Dad agreed. I knew that Danny had heard their positive comments, although he didn't show it or reply.

Danny ate with us at the table, and we stayed at the table chatting quietly while he finished. But in the afternoon I began to see the tell-tale signs that suggested he was becoming overloaded and could be heading for a meltdown – windmilling his arms and looking slightly spaced out, and a small tic that sometimes developed by his eye. I told him we'd go into the front room for a while where it was quiet, and I'd read him a story. I offered him my hand and he came with me without a fuss. I read a couple of short stories and then Paula came in and said she would read to Danny so that I could go back into the living room. Danny didn't want to re-join us, so Lucy and Adrian also took turns to be with him, ensuring that unlike at my parents' previous visit I was able to spend time with them in the living room. When my parents were due to go Danny was still in the front room and didn't want to come out to say goodbye, so they called to him from the hall.

'Goodbye, Danny. We've had a nice day,' Mum said.

'See you again soon,' Dad added.

Once they'd gone Danny came out and I told him he'd done well, which he had.

'That's good,' he said, pleased.

I must admit it hadn't been the most relaxing day for me, as I'd been on alert for any sign that Danny's behaviour could deteriorate, but it had passed pleasantly and next time they came it would be a little easier still, until hopefully Danny would eventually be able to join in and enjoy my parents' visits as much as we did.

Continuing with my policy of broadening Danny's horizons through new experiences, the following Sunday I took him in the car to a park that had a café. He'd never eaten out socially with his parents and I thought this was a good place to start, as it was child-friendly and didn't have tablecloths or delicate flower centrepieces, which can lead to disaster for any parent. I explained to him beforehand where we were going, but when we got to the door of the café he stopped dead and couldn't go in. I took him to one side to stand in front of the bow window where we could see in below the café-style net curtains. I pointed out the tables and chairs and explained how the adults and children sitting at them were having something to eat and drink, which they were enjoying, and then when they'd finished they would leave and go home. None of which would be obvious to Danny. Goodness knows what those inside thought, seeing two faces peering in at them. But Danny was still reluctant to go in.

'We'll go inside and try it,' I said positively. 'If it's too noisy or hot we can come out and try again another time.' For I didn't want Danny thinking that if he refused to try something once that was the end of it.

He let me take his hand and we went in, up to the self-service counter. I took a tray and asked him what he would like to drink, and then read out the options from the menu on the wall. But he shook his head and began rocking anxiously on his heels.

'Don't worry. Would you like a hot drink or a cold drink?'

'Hot,' he said. Then, 'Chocolate.'

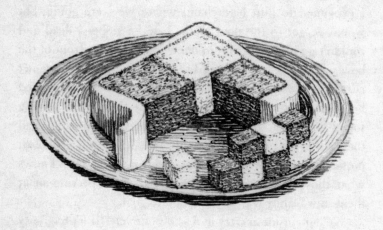

'Excellent.' He always liked that drink at home with me. I gave our order to the assistant behind the counter. Then Danny pointed to a slice of pre-wrapped Battenberg cake.

'That's good,' he said.

I smiled. I knew why he'd been drawn to that particular cake. Battenberg sponge has a distinctive pink-and-yellow chequered pattern. I placed the cake on the tray, took a plate and a knife and ordered a cappuccino for myself. Having paid, I carried the tray to a table. Danny looked anxiously around as we sat. It was quite noisy from the hum of voices and I wondered if he would cope, but the Battenberg diverted his attention. Very meticulously he peeled off the Cellophane wrapper and set it carefully to one side. Then, taking the knife, he began dissecting the cake, first into the different-coloured squares, and then he cut those squares into quarters. Finally he created a new pattern of yellow and pink sponge pieces before he began eating them. By the time he got around to drinking his hot chocolate it was cold, but he still enjoyed it. Danny seemed to prefer cold to hot, in food as well as drink. As we left I praised him; he'd coped well with another new experience. I said we'd come again another day if he'd like to.

'That's good,' he said.

What wasn't so good was our visit to Yew Lodge Clinic for Danny's medical. I'd taken children to similar clinics before, so I knew more or less what to expect and I explained to Danny what would happen. But when we arrived he refused to go in, perhaps remembering a previous visit with his mother, I don't know. I reassured him that there was nothing to worry about and I would be with him. Then I added that he needed to be quick as George would be waiting for his walk, and this swung it.

Fortunately we didn't have to wait long to see the paediatrician, Dr Holly Green. She was a lovely lady and couldn't have been more reassuring and patient with Danny, but he needed persuading and cajoling at every stage: to stand on the scales and be weighed – I had to stand on them first; to be measured – he didn't like the feel of the bar on his head, and I had to be measured first; and when she took a stethoscope from her desk drawer, despite explaining to Danny what it was for and letting him play with it first, he refused to undo his shirt.

'Just undo a few buttons then,' she said. Danny shook his head.

'Choose two buttons to undo,' I said. 'Which two do you want?' He looked down and pointed. 'Good. Can you undo them or do you want my help?'

He undid them.

As Dr Green placed the end of the stethoscope on Danny's chest it must have felt cold, for he shrieked and hid under the couch. I persuaded him out by reminding him that George was waiting for a walk, and then told him to choose a place in the room to stand or sit where the doctor could listen to his chest. He chose the doctor's chair and sat in it long enough for her to listen to his heart and lungs.

'Good boy,' I said.

'Well done, Danny,' she said.

Dr Green returned the stethoscope to her desk drawer and took out an otoscope, showed it to Danny and explained that she was going to look in his ears. It took three attempts, but she was able to see enough of both ears to pronounce them clear. It had taken over half an hour to carry out these simple checks. The doctor now sat at her desk and I sat in the chair next to the desk as she asked me some questions about Danny's diet, his general health and if he slept well. Danny stood beside me flapping his arms and making a low humming noise. Dr Green hadn't met Danny before, but she knew from his notes he had special needs. She concluded by saying he was healthy, although he was at the lower end of normal on the charts for height and weight, which I already knew. I asked her to send a copy of her report to the social services and to Danny's parents as well as myself, which was normal practice.

Danny's appointment to see the dentist was two days later, and it turned out to be the same dentist he'd seen with his mother. Both remembered their previous encounter, as did the nurse, and it hadn't been a good experience. Danny took one look at the dentist – 'Call me Tim' – and hid under the chair. Tim – young, fresh-faced and I guessed not long qualified – visibly paled and then asked who I was. I explained I was Danny's foster carer and that the social services had asked for Danny to have a dental check-up, as he was overdue for one. Tim clearly didn't know how to progress, so I said I'd found in the past with other children I'd fostered who hadn't liked coming to the dentist that if they could sit on an ordinary chair rather than lie on the dentist's chair it often helped. He nodded enthusiastically, clearly eager to try anything, and the nurse drew up the spare chair the parent usually sat on and placed it within reach of the instruments. I sat on the edge of the dentist's chair. Danny was still underneath.

'Come on, Danny,' I said. 'Sit on the chair and we'll have our teeth looked at together.'

There was silence from under the couch and then he was intrigued enough to look out.

'Come on, quick,' I said, patting the chair. 'Or we'll miss our turn, and Tim will have to see another person. We don't want that, do we?' I find that suggesting something is sought-after and shouldn't be missed is another useful piece of child psychology.

Danny slowly emerged from under the couch and I noticed there was a little impish grin in his eyes, making me think that some of his resistance might be a game to him, and not all trauma. He sat on the chair. 'Good boy,' I said. 'Now I'm going to open my mouth wide so the dentist can look at my teeth.' I opened my mouth so it formed a large O.

Watching someone open their mouth wide as I was doing is like watching someone yawn – you can't help but follow – and children are very susceptible to suggestion. Danny opened his mouth for as long as it took Tim to place the mouth mirror inside, and then he snapped it closed again.

'Ouch,' Tim said.

'Nice big wide open mouth,' I said, opening my mouth again. Danny followed suit. And as long as I kept my mouth open, so did he. Thankfully the examination didn't last too long.

'His teeth are excellent,' Tim pronounced.

'That's good,' I said.

'That's good,' Danny repeated.

'Well done,' the nurse said.

I wasn't surprised Danny's teeth were in good condition; he loved brushing them and did so thoroughly as part of his morning and evening routine. The nurse gave Danny a sticker and told him he'd done well. Then Tim said he thought I should have one too, so we left proudly sporting a sticker each showing a picture of a large molar with a smiling face and the heading: *Member of the No Cavity Club*. Danny wore his for two weeks until it lost its stickiness, when he placed it safely in a drawer in his bedroom. I took mine off that evening.

At the beginning of April Danny began speech therapy, once a week for half an hour, at school. He could have gone to the clinic, but it was decided it would be less disruptive for him to stay at school where he felt safe, and to see the speech therapist during morning break. There was no immediate improvement in Danny's speech, but I hadn't expected there to be. I knew it would be a long process, but at least it had started. Jill, as usual, telephoned me each week for an update, but I hadn't heard from Terri since the review. Neither had Jill. This wasn't unusual, as there are peaks and troughs of activity in fostering. There is often a lot going on when a child first arrives, and then it tends to settle down until a decision is made on whether the child can return home or needs to be found a new permanent home, either with a relative, via adoption or through a long-term foster placement. In Danny's case, however, I knew there was a time limit before the social services applied to the courts for an Interim Care Order. It wasn't fair on Danny to leave him in limbo indefinitely. Although he didn't say much, he would certainly be feeling the uncertainty of not knowing when or if he could return home, as well as the rejection of not being able to live with his parents. I sometimes try to put myself in the position of a foster child, and I really don't know how they cope with all the changes and uncertainty. They are true heroes, each and every one of them.

The routine of contact continued unchanged into April, and Reva maintained her distance and reserve with me. She was always polite but guarded. She didn't invite me into her house when I took Danny for contact, and didn't accept my invitation to come into my home when she returned him. She never volunteered any feedback after contact, and if I asked her if it had gone well she always said, 'Yes, fine.'

While I was widening Danny's experiences I was also broadening my own, specifically in the school playground while waiting for Danny at the end of school. He'd made his mother stand on a spot well away from the other parents, possibly trying to replicate his own feelings of isolation. But this was never going to suit me. I like company, so I'd been gradually inching my way across the playground towards where the other mothers waited. Danny appeared not to notice my migration until one afternoon I began actually talking to another mother, whose son was in Danny's class and also had special needs and found it difficult to make friends. Danny didn't say anything immediately, but as we left the playground he said, 'You talked to Simon's mummy. Why?'

'Because she is a nice lady and she wanted to talk to me and be friends. I think Simon would like to be friends with you too.'

Danny didn't reply, but I could see he was thinking hard. Then two days later Yvonne came out of school with Danny on one side of her and Simon on the other. They were all smiling.

'The boys have something to tell you,' Yvonne said as the three of them approached us.

'Yes,' Simon said, grinning broadly. 'Danny is my best friend.'

And without hesitation Danny said, 'Simon is my best friend.'

It was one of those moments that stays with a parent or carer, and I knew that Simon's mother, like me, would remember it longer than the boys did. Clearly it would take time for them to build on this to make a lasting friendship, but it was a good start and I was very hopeful. Spring had arrived, the days were lengthening and the skies were more blue than grey. Although Danny was hard work, I felt he was making progress and that his parents would see this. I was therefore completely unprepared for what happened next.

Chapter Twenty-Three
History Repeating Itself?

It was Thursday and I was in the kitchen clearing up after dinner while I waited for Danny to be returned home from contact. Paula, Lucy and Adrian were in their rooms finishing their homework. When the doorbell rang just after six o'clock I assumed it would be Reva with Danny, but as I opened the door I saw a tall, smartly dressed man standing beside Danny.

'Reva's ill,' he said in a rich, cultured voice. 'She asked me to bring Danny to you.'

'Thank you, and you are?'

'Reva's husband, Richard.'

'Oh,' I said, mildly surprised. 'Pleased to meet you.' I didn't add 'at last'. 'I hope Reva is better soon. Come in.'

'I won't, thanks,' he said. 'I've only just returned from work.'

Slim, with blond hair and blue eyes similar to Danny's, he wore a stylish tailored suit. I could immediately picture the handsome couple he and Reva made together. Danny adopted his usual routine, yelling, 'George!' and shooting down the hall to the back door.

'Danny!' Richard shouted after him. 'Come here, now!'

'It's all right,' I said, slightly taken aback by the ferocity of Richard's tone. 'Danny always sees George when he first gets in. It's part of his routine.'

'Who's George?' Richard frowned, puzzled.

'His rabbit?' I said, bemused he didn't know.

'Oh yes. I'd completely forgotten the rabbit was here too. Well, thanks. I'll be off then.'

Not so fast, I thought. 'Richard, I think it would be really nice for Danny if you could manage to stay for a few minutes while he feeds George and settles him for the night. Danny doesn't see much of you and I know it would mean a lot to him if you could.' In truth Danny rarely mentioned either of his parents, but I'd put that down to his communication difficulties rather than any lack of feeling. And this was an opportunity too good to miss – not only for Danny, but also for me to have a chat with Richard. He was, after all, Danny's father, even though he appeared to have minimal input in his life. 'Just five minutes,' I added. 'I appreciate you need to get home.'

It would have been ill-humoured of him to refuse outright, so with a tight nod he stepped in.

'Thank you,' I said, and closed the door.

'George!' Danny yelled from the kitchen.

'Sorry,' Richard said as he followed me down the hall. 'I've told him before not to shout like that.'

'It's OK. He's excited,' I said. 'Although I am teaching him to speak more quietly when necessary, and so is his teacher.'

We entered the kitchen. 'Daddy!' Danny exclaimed, surprised at seeing his father. He was at the back door yanking on the handle, waiting for me to open it.

'Daddy is going to stay while you feed George,' I said, with a smile. 'Then he will say goodnight and go home.' I didn't want Danny thinking his father could stay indefinitely and then being upset when he didn't.

'Daddy,' he said again, unable to believe his good fortune. 'Daddy feed George.'

'I'm watching,' Richard said flatly.

I went over and opened the back door. Danny shot out first. The sun had only just set and with the added light coming from the kitchen window it was easy to see the hutch and George inside, with his nose pressed against the wire mesh, waiting for Danny. Although I put George in his run during the day when the weather was good, I always returned him to his hutch before Danny came home so I didn't disturb his routine. Richard stood awkwardly by the hutch with his hands in his trouser pockets as Danny opened the hutch door.

'Have you seen the way Danny relates to George?' I asked him. 'It's really beautiful to watch.'

'Not really,' Richard admitted, slightly uncomfortable. 'I work late most evenings, so he's usually in bed by the time I get home.' And what's wrong with the weekends? I thought but didn't say.

Danny put his face to George's as he hugged him. 'Have you had a good day?' he asked the rabbit, using a phrase he'd learnt from me.

George replied by sniffing and then licking Danny's ear as though he was whispering something to him. It must have tickled Danny, for he giggled. I glanced at Richard, who was watching them, expressionless, apparently unmoved. Then, following his usual routine, Danny checked George's water bottle, which was still half full, and then took the food bowl from the hutch and set it on the floor.

'I'm going to get your dinner,' he told George, and closed the hutch door.

'Show Daddy what you do,' I encouraged Danny.

Was it my imagination or had Richard winced when I referred to him as Daddy? Without saying anything, Richard followed Danny indoors to the cupboard under the stairs. Continuing his well-practised routine, Danny set down the bowl, opened the cupboard door, unsealed the bag of rabbit food, carefully measured out three scoops and then resealed the bag. He picked up the food bowl and I closed the cupboard door.

'Well done,' I said, as usual taking every opportunity to praise Danny. Richard didn't say a word.

As Danny carried the food bowl through the kitchen a few pieces of rabbit food fell onto the floor. 'Danny, be careful,' Richard admonished unnecessarily harshly.

'Don't worry,' I said. 'I'll clear it up later.'

Outside, Danny carefully set the food bowl on the ground beside the hutch so he could open the hutch door where George was still waiting patiently. I felt sure that what followed next – when Danny said goodnight to George – would move Richard; it was one of the reasons I'd wanted him to see it. Danny began gently stroking George's head and face, then he rested his cheek against George's, giving him a hug as he did every night and enjoying the feel of his soft, warm fur against his skin. After a few moments Danny raised his head slightly and whispered to George, as he always did in the evening, 'You're safe with me. Thump if you want me. I'll hear you. I'm up there in my room.'

I glanced at Richard, who did seem slightly taken aback at how much Danny was able to say, apparently having no idea of the relationship Danny had with George. Danny then kissed George's cheek in preparation for him going to bed. 'Goodnight, George,' he said.

As usual George responded by 'kissing' Danny's cheek.

'I love you, George,' Danny said. 'You're my very best friend.'

Richard remained expressionless.

Danny now picked up George's food bowl, placed it carefully inside the hutch and then closed the door. 'Night, George. I love you,' he said again, and drew the plastic sheet down over the hutch.

I turned to Richard and to my surprise his eyes had suddenly filled.

'It's very moving,' I said, and I touched his arm reassuringly. He turned away, clearly not wanting Danny or me to see his emotion.

'Let's go in,' I said to Richard. 'I'll make you a coffee.'

'You go in,' he said, his voice trembling. 'I'll follow in a minute.'

Danny was already on his way in and I went after him, leaving Richard on the patio. It wasn't until Danny and I were in the hall that he asked, 'Daddy?'

'He'll be in soon,' I said. 'I want you to get ready for bed now. I know it's early, but I need to talk to your daddy. Then he will say goodnight to you before he leaves.' I intended to ask Lucy or Paula to stay with Danny while he got ready for bed so I could sit with Richard for a while. I felt bad he was upset – that hadn't been my intention; I just wanted him to see how loving and caring Danny was with George.

As we went upstairs Danny suddenly stopped and asked, 'School book?'

'Maybe later, if we have time,' I said. 'Things are a bit different tonight.' I sincerely hoped Danny could accommodate the changes, as a tantrum now certainly wouldn't help.

Upstairs I found that Paula hadn't finished her homework yet, but Lucy had and was happy to stay with Danny while he got ready for bed. I told her only that Danny's father had brought him home and was downstairs and I wanted to talk to him. 'Call me if you need me,' I added.

Downstairs again, I went into the kitchen. The back door was still open and Toscha was just coming in. I found Richard where I'd left him, on the patio and returning a handkerchief to his jacket pocket.

'Tea or coffee?' I asked him.

'Coffee, please.'

He came into the kitchen.

'Danny is upstairs getting ready for bed,' I said. 'One of my daughters is helping him. I've told Danny you'll say good-night to him before you leave.'

'Thank you,' Richard said, subdued.

'Why don't you take a seat in the living room while I make the coffee?' I suggested. 'There's no one in there.'

I showed him through to the living room. 'Do you take milk and sugar?' I asked.

'Just milk, please.'

As Richard sat on the sofa I saw his gaze fall on the photograph of Danny on the mantelpiece. When I returned with his coffee, he asked, 'Where did you get that picture from?'

'I took it,' I said, passing him his cup of coffee. 'I like to have a photograph of the child I'm looking after in here with all the ones of my family. It makes them feel part of the family

259

and more at home. I've given Reva a copy, and of the others I've taken of Danny.'

Richard took a sip of his coffee. 'You've certainly got quite a collection of photographs,' he said.

'Yes. I like the reminders of all the children. Danny has a photograph of you and Reva in his bedroom.'

'Did Reva give you that?'

I nodded. 'I always try to obtain a photograph of the family for the child. It helps to keep the bond going between contacts.'

'So you've been fostering a long time?' Richard asked, setting his cup lightly in its saucer.

'Nearly fifteen years now,' I said.

'It must be hard work.'

'It has its moments.' I smiled. 'But I enjoy it. You couldn't foster if you didn't.'

He paused thoughtfully and then said, 'Danny is hard work, isn't he?'

'He can be at times,' I agreed. 'He needs a lot of patience.'

Richard looked relieved at my acknowledgement. 'Sorry for breaking down out there,' he said. 'I'm usually the strong one.'

'I didn't mean to upset you,' I said. 'I just thought it would be nice for you to see Danny with George. It's very emotional to watch them and see how Danny relates to George, given how difficult he normally finds it to express himself.'

Richard nodded. 'Reva used to say that Danny talked more to George than he did to us. I didn't really believe her, until now. It's not very flattering, is it? Having your son talk to a rabbit, rather than his parents.'

I smiled kindly. 'Danny finds communicating very diffi-cult. He doesn't mean to be unkind.'

Richard took another sip of his coffee. He looked at me and I saw the strong family likeness in his gaze, though without Danny's reluctance to make eye contact.

'When you said earlier that Danny doesn't see much of me, you were right,' Richard said. 'Reva accused me of having an affair, but I'm not. I think deep down she knows why I stay away so much. I know my behaviour must seem callous to you, but try not to judge me. It was a very difficult decision to put Danny into care.'

'I'm sure it was,' I said. 'I certainly wouldn't judge you.'

'I would, if I was in your position and didn't know the whole story. The social worker certainly judges me, and she's never even met me.'

'You haven't met with her yet?' I asked, gravely concerned.

'No, and I don't intend to. I'm not having her digging into my past and telling me I've failed. It's got nothing to do with her.'

I chose my reply very carefully. 'I'm afraid Danny's future does have quite a lot to do with her,' I said. 'Danny won't be returned home unless the social services are satisfied that their concerns have been addressed. You need to start cooperating and meet with Terri.'

'And who says I want Danny to return home?' Richard asked abruptly, his face tense. 'I struggle to be in the same room as him, and can't bear to hear him call me Daddy. I think it would be better if he didn't return.'

I went cold. Richard concentrated on his cup as Lucy's voice floated down from upstairs praising Danny as he went into the bathroom. Richard leant forward and set his cup and saucer on the coffee table.

'There! I've said it,' he said.

'But surely with support, and once Danny has been assessed, you could find a way forward?'

Richard was shaking his head. 'Too many memories, too much baggage, far too many reminders of things I'd rather forget. It's not fair on Danny.'

'Memories of what?' I asked.

There was a long silence before Richard said, 'Robert.'

'And Robert is one of your children from your first marriage?' I assumed this, for it was the first I'd heard of him.

'No, he was my brother. He died two years ago.'

'Oh. I'm sorry,' I said.

'There's no need to be. It was a release in the end.'

I waited as Richard summoned his thoughts, clearly about to tell me more.

'Robert was eighteen months older than me,' Richard began sombrely. 'But mentally he remained like a three- or four-year-old throughout his life. He nearly died at birth and to be honest it would have been kinder if he had. The toll it took on my parents, looking after him for all those years, was unbearable to watch. Robert was still in nappies when he died aged forty-three, and he took a teddy bear to bed with him every night. He never learnt to speak properly but made noises and pointed to get what he wanted. He had uncontrollable tantrums. A grown man, shouting and screaming and writhing around on the floor! My parents are only in their mid-sixties, but they look much older. They insisted on caring for Robert at home, but it wore them out. And all for what? I don't think Robert had the least idea who we were. If my parents had put him in an institution he wouldn't have been any the wiser and it would have given them the chance of a life. So don't judge me, Cathy, because I know what's in store if Danny comes home, and I can't put Reva through that. It would be kinder all round if Danny was looked after by someone like yourself, who has the time and patience to give him what he needs.'

I was stunned and horrified, not only by Richard's rejection of Danny, but by the reasons he'd given for leaving him in care. 'Does Terri know about Robert?' I asked him.

'Not unless Reva has told her, and I don't think she has.'

'That's a great pity,' I said. 'She could have put you both right on Danny's condition. He isn't disabled like Robert was, not at all. From what you've told me, Robert had profound learning disabilities. Danny appears to have mild to moderate learning difficulties, and possibly autism. Danny can learn, but it takes him time. Look at everything he has achieved. He can dress and wash himself, brush his teeth, eat with a knife and fork, look after George, use the toilet and he's learning to read and write. I know it takes him time, but he gets there in the end. And he hears, sees and feels things just the same as other children, but he can't tell you. You saw the way he talked to George. It's all in there inside Danny, but it needs to be unlocked. Danny has nowhere near the level of disability that Robert had, and he'll go on to lead a full and rewarding life, I'm sure. Once Danny is assessed he can be given the help he needs. It will also reassure you and Reva that there is nothing badly wrong with him.'

There was a small silence before Richard said, 'I can see Robert in Danny. I lived with him all those years. I can't take the chance. Supposing Danny doesn't progress, which I don't think he will. It'll be too late then. Reva isn't coping now. She'll be suicidal if things get worse. I'm not convinced Danny has anywhere near the level of awareness you attribute to him. I'm sure in time he'll forget us.'

I tried to stem my rising anger. I was appalled. Richard had diagnosed and labelled Danny, and had decided there was no hope and he'd be better off in long-term care. There was nothing to lose by speaking out.

'Danny might just be suffering from mild autism,' I said. 'You won't know unless you have him assessed. And of course he won't forget you. You're his parents and he loves you. He's very aware and takes everything in. Do you have any idea how upsetting it is for him when you and Reva argue? He told George you shout at Mummy and it makes her cry and gives him a tummy ache. He also heard you say that you wished he'd never been born. Danny knows you hide him away from your family, and won't let him see his step-brother and sister. And as far as I know you don't let your parents see him at all.'

'That's to protect them,' Richard said defensively. 'I'm not putting them through all that again. They saw Danny until he was two, but when it became obvious he wasn't developing normally I stopped taking him to see them. It's for their own good.'

'Have you ever asked them for their opinion? Perhaps they would have liked the opportunity to play a part in their grandchild's life. They could have given you and Reva some support as well. They must be very kind, loving and commit-ted people to have cared for Robert all those years.' Richard kept his gaze down, staring at a point on the floor.

'Danny knows he is different,' I continued. 'And he dearly wishes he wasn't. He tells George how much he would like to be the same as all the other children at school. He also told

George that if he wasn't stupid Mummy and Daddy would love him and he could return home, and you'd all live happily together. You want to listen to what Danny tells George sometimes – it can be very revealing. I expect your other two children are bright and reaching all their developmental milestones, but Danny isn't stupid. He's just different. Inside he's a loving, caring, sensitive little boy who finds life very difficult. He thinks you don't love him – his own father! How sad is that?' I stopped as my voice caught and I blinked back my tears.

There was silence for a moment and then Richard said, 'I have told him that his father loves him. Reva said I should.'

'And you think that's good enough for Danny? Where's the passion in your love for him? He's your son and he desperately needs to feel your love and know he is wanted, but he can't tell you that. Try to put yourself in his position. It must be devastating.'

Richard suddenly stood. 'I think you've said enough. I'm going now.' And he headed for the living-room door.

I realized I'd gone too far. 'I'm sorry,' I said, following him. 'I feel for Danny and want what is best for him, that's all.'

'And you think I don't?' he snapped, rounding on me. 'I shouldn't have come in.' He continued down the hall to the front door. 'Tell Danny I said goodbye.' He opened the door and went out, pulling it closed behind him.

'Daddy?' a little voice called from the top of the stairs. 'Where's my daddy?'

Chapter Twenty-Four
Significant Development

I swallowed hard and tried to compose myself. 'Daddy's had to go, love,' I said as Danny came down the stairs in his pyjamas and dressing gown. 'He said to say goodbye to you.'

'Daddy gone?' Danny asked, navigating the last two steps.

'Yes, love.'

Lucy was on the stairs behind him. 'Danny thought he'd see his father before he left,' she said. 'That's why he got ready so quickly.'

My heart went out to him, and of course I felt responsible for his father's abrupt departure. 'I'm sorry,' I said. 'Daddy had to leave in a hurry.' I couldn't say he'd see him again soon, for the chances were he wouldn't.

'Daddy had to leave in a hurry?' Danny repeated.

'Yes, love.'

And the look of abject disappointment on his little face was far sadder than any tears he could have shed.

* * *

Significant Development

It wasn't Danny's bedtime yet, so I took him into the living room and read him one of his favourite books, *The Very Hungry Caterpillar*. Then he wanted to do his homework, so I heard him read and we practised the new words he had to learn. He didn't mention his father again, but I guessed he was thinking and feeling plenty. Although Danny hadn't heard the conversation I'd had with Richard, I thought there was a good chance he realized his father's sudden departure had something to do with him. He'd been blamed for so much in the past, and I appreciated how easy it must have been for Richard and Reva to believe that Danny wasn't aware of the dramas going on around him simply because he didn't show his feelings. I slipped my arm around his shoulders and he didn't pull away. After a few minutes he relaxed against me so that I could cuddle him properly. It was the first proper cuddle he'd let me give him, and I was sure it was a result of this latest rejection by his father.

The following morning, as soon as I returned home from taking Danny to school, I telephoned Jill and told her what had happened: that Reva had been unwell the day before, so Richard had brought Danny home, the conversation we'd had and how Richard had walked out. I'd already written a short note in my fostering log the previous evening, but I now told Jill the full story, as I should.

'I don't think Terri is even aware that Richard had a brother,' Jill said. 'I guess it explains some of Richard's attitude towards Danny, although it's been very detrimental to their relationship. I'll phone Terri when we've finished and pass on what you've told me. I'll also ask her if contact is going ahead on Saturday; given what Richard has said, it sounds like it might not. Either Terri or I will get back to you. And, Cathy, don't beat yourself up. You did what you thought was right, and it might have brought Richard to his senses. It was worth a try.'

I thanked Jill, although it didn't make me feel any better. I knew I hadn't succeeded in getting through to Richard, and as a result of what I'd said he'd stormed out without saying goodbye to his son. I hoped Danny would get the chance to see his father again soon, but I wasn't convinced. Richard had seemed resolute in his decision not to have Danny return home, in which case it was likely he and Reva would stop contact too.

Terri telephoned in the afternoon having spoken to Jill. She'd also telephoned Reva and confirmed that contact would be going ahead as usual on Saturday. Richard was away for a few days and Reva said she was recovered and well enough to have Danny. She told Terri she'd guessed something had happened at my house, because when Richard got home he'd hardly said a word and hadn't wanted his dinner. Later she'd found him sitting alone in Danny's room before he packed a weekend case and said he was going away for a few days. He'd left without saying where he was going.

'I'm meeting with Reva next week,' Terri continued. 'I've asked her to tell Richard. It's essential he's there as we shall be discussing Danny's long-term care arrangements, although I'm not holding my breath. Once I've seen Reva I'll arrange a planning meeting. As Richard and Reva seem to be saying that Danny will stay in long-term care, and they're cooperating, there's no immediate need for me to take out a Care Order.' This was normal practice.

Significant Development

Terri finished by asking how Danny was and then wishing us a nice weekend. We said goodbye. I didn't have any firm plans for the weekend. I thought we'd see how the weather was and then decide.

That evening, as I waited in Danny's bedroom while he fastidiously went about his night-time routine of meticulously folding his clothes and adjusting his duvet, soft-toy George, the lights and anything else that came into sight, I heard an owl hoot – 'Twit' – in the distance. Danny heard it too and frowned, puzzled. I explained to him that it was an owl calling out to another owl, and that if we heard a 'twoo' it was the other owl replying. We both listened hard and for some moments all we heard was the 'twit' of the first owl, then magically a second owl replied, 'Twoo.'

Danny's mouth dropped open in wonder.

'Two owls,' I said, smiling.

'Two owls,' Danny repeated.

I'd heard owls before in the distance at the rear of my house, but it was a rare occurrence, and I hadn't heard a pair for many years. Danny went to the window to look out, but it was too dark to see. I explained to him that the owls were probably a long way off, but their calls could carry through the night air. As we listened their twit-twoos were repeated a few more times and then they stopped. Danny was disappointed, so I said they'd probably gone to sleep and eventually persuaded him into his bed.

'Twit-twoo,' he said, imitating the noise of the owls as he snuggled into bed. 'Twit-twoo,' he continued as he pulled the duvet over his head. 'Twit-twoo, twit-twoo.'

Danny's twit-twoos continued as I said goodnight and then came out of his room and closed the door. They followed me across the landing and downstairs, and continued for about half an hour. We all knew when Danny was asleep, for the twit-twoos abruptly stopped: 'Twit-twoo', then silence. I went up to check on him and as usual took the duvet away from his face. His lips were still pursed as though he was about to make a twit-twoo noise, and a faint smile had stayed on his face, so I guessed that he'd liked the owls very much indeed.

The following morning we were all woken by the sound of Danny twit-twooing from his bedroom, much to the irritation of Lucy, Paula and Adrian, who were hoping for a Saturday morning lie-in. I went into Danny's room where I found him at the window looking out and twit-twooing for all he was worth.

'Danny, owls only make that noise at night,' I said. 'And if they do make it during the day it's very, very quiet, like this.' I demonstrated a quieter version of twit-twoo and he copied me.

The more subdued twit-twoos continued as he dressed and washed and came downstairs. They stopped long enough for him to eat his breakfast, before resuming as we got ready to leave the house for contact. They continued for most of the car journey and I must admit that by the time I pulled onto the driveway at his house it was getting on my nerves, as I thought it would Reva's if it went on all day.

'Danny, love,' I said as I cut the engine, 'I think you should stop that noise now. Then tonight we can listen carefully to see if we can hear the owls again.'

He fell silent.

'Good boy,' I said.

Significant Development

Danny remained owl free as we walked across the drive, but as his mother opened the door he greeted her with a very loud, 'Twit-twoo! Twit-twoo!'

'Oh, Danny's being an owl!' she said good-humouredly. 'Twit-twoo to you too.'

I explained to Reva how we'd heard the owls the night before. 'I hope the novelty wears off soon,' I said with a smile.

'I've heard worse,' she said easily. She seemed in a pleasant mood.

I asked her if she was fully recovered now from her illness and she said, 'Yes. Thank you for asking. I'll bring Danny back as usual at six o'clock.'

We said goodbye and I returned home.

When Reva brought Danny back that evening she was still in good spirits and surprised me by volunteering some feedback on what they'd done during the day.

'As Danny liked the noise of the owls so much I took him to the bird sanctuary at Kettle Green,' she said. 'They have some rescued owls there.'

'I know the place,' I said. 'Fantastic. Did it go well?'

'Yes, quite well,' she said. 'It made a change. We usually stay at home on Saturday. I've told Danny I'll take him out again next Saturday, if he's good.'

'That'll be nice,' I said. Although I was confused. Why make the effort to take Danny out now, after she and Richard had decided Danny would be staying in long-term care? Perhaps Reva was relieved that the decision had finally been made and was now starting to regain her old self-confidence. I invited her in but she said she wanted to go home, as there was a film on television she wanted to see.

'Richard's away, so I'm having a relaxing evening after a busy day,' she said cheerfully.

Interestingly, Danny hadn't immediately rushed off to see George but instead was standing in the hall watching his mother. When she said goodbye she reached out to hug him and very briefly he returned the gesture, before yelling, 'George!' and running to the back door.

'I'll see you on Tuesday then,' Reva said with a smile.

'Yes. Enjoy your evening.'

'And you.'

Although it was good for Danny that Reva had taken him out and was planning to again, her surge of enthusiasm had really come too late. The level of contact would remain the same for now, but after the planning meeting it would gradually be reduced to allow Danny to loosen his bond with his parents in preparation for bonding with his forever family – the one who would look after him permanently. Whether it was my family or not would be for the social services to decide. If I was asked to keep Danny long term I'd have to discuss it with Adrian, Lucy and Paula first, for it was a huge commitment that would affect us all, although I thought I knew what their feelings would be. They were as attached to Danny as I was. However, social services might well decide that Danny's long-term interest would best be served in a family where there were no other children, so he could receive more attention and the help he needed to reach his full potential. Whatever happened, though, contact would soon be reduced to a few times a year, and I hoped Reva (and Richard) were aware of that.

* * *

Significant Development

As Danny had had a full day out on Saturday, I kept Sunday reasonably relaxed. The weather was good so I took him to a local park for an hour or so in the morning. Lucy came with us; Paula and Adrian were out with their father. We returned home for lunch and then spent most of the afternoon in the garden, with George out of his run. When Danny and George had had their fill of chasing each other around the lawn they sat together as they often did, and Danny talked to George as he petted him. I was gardening but also furtively listening, and I heard Danny tell George about the owls he'd seen with his mother at the bird sanctuary. 'One had a sore leg,' he told George. 'But don't worry, it will soon be better.' Which I assumed was what his mother had told him. Danny also told George that his mother had given him some sweets for being good and he was happy.

On Monday we fell into our weekday routine and the week progressed as usual. Danny had contact on Tuesday, when Reva took him for a walk in the woods, but it rained so they didn't stay long. Reva told me this when she returned Danny, but the next day I overheard Danny telling George, 'Daddy came to the woods with Mummy and me. We had fun.'

As far as I knew that was the first time Danny had seen his father since the incident at my house, and it was certainly the first time he'd ever mentioned having fun with him. While I was pleased they'd spent some quality time together, again I felt it was too little too late, and I assumed that, like Reva, Richard must also be relieved that the decision on Danny's future had been made.

I hadn't heard anything further from Terri or Jill – I wouldn't, unless there was some news. However, Jill telephoned on Friday while I was out and left a message on the answerphone to say she was going away for a long weekend and would be back in the office on Tuesday, and that I should phone the agency's out-of-hours number if there was an emergency. Homefinders, the agency I fostered for, was very good with their out-of-hours service; there was always someone on the end of the phone, day or night, all year round, even on Christmas Day and public holidays.

It was May now and summer was just around the corner. The air was much warmer and the days were quickly lengthening, so we were able to spend more time in the garden, especially in the evenings. The following week, on the Wednesday morning, I was in the garden hanging out the washing when I heard the phone ring. I went in through the patio doors and answered it in the living room. It was Jill, and I could tell from her voice she had something important to say.

After a very brief hello and how are you, she said, 'I've just finished speaking to Terri. There's been a significant development, and it involves you.'

'Oh?' I said, immediately concerned.

'It's OK,' Jill said. 'You haven't done anything wrong. I'll explain. Apparently, the weekend after that scene at your house Richard went away. He saw his parents and finally told them that Danny was in foster care. They had no idea and were very shocked, as you can imagine. His mother said he should have asked them for help. Then Richard admitted he was planning on leaving Danny in care, and both his parents were horrified. They telephoned Terri and said they wanted to look after Danny. They asked to have him straight away. Richard's mother was very upset on the phone to Terri and

274

cried. Not only because Danny was in care, but because Richard had believed all those years that Danny had the same condition as Robert. It's impossible, because Robert had cerebral palsy – he was brain damaged at birth as a result of oxygen starvation, so it's not a genetic condition.'

'Has his mother told Richard this?' I asked.

'Yes. She has now. She told Terri that she realized it was a conversation she should have had with Richard a long time ago, but it had never occurred to her that Richard believed Danny had inherited a condition and was the same as Robert. She and her husband had thought the reason Richard had stopped taking Danny to see them and never invited them to their house was because Reva didn't like them. She had no idea it was because he was trying to protect them from Danny. She also told Richard that they never regretted their decision to look after Robert and care for him at home, even though it had been very hard work.'

'They sound like a lovely couple,' I said.

'Yes,' Jill agreed. 'She was adamant that Danny shouldn't stay in care and should live with them. Terri said she'd have to talk to her manager, and then explained that they would need to be assessed as kinship carers, even though they were Danny's grandparents. They weren't very happy about this, but agreed to do whatever it took to have Danny live with them. However, the next day Richard telephoned Terri and said that, having spoken to his parents and after a long discussion with Reva, they'd decided they wanted Danny home to live with them. But of course you and I know it's not that simple. Although Reva has stopped drinking, Terri had other concerns and she called a meeting for Reva, Richard and his parents.

'This is the outcome,' Jill continued, 'it's possible that Danny may be able to go home, but not straight away, and only after certain conditions are met. Firstly, Richard and Reva have to agree to Danny being assessed by the educational psychologist and accept the help that is recommended. Danny is to have regular contact with his grandparents, and Terri has also told Richard she would like Danny to see his step-brother and step-sister sometimes, although she can't force that. Reva has to attend a parenting course for children with special needs. Terri would like Richard to attend too, but she accepts that he has to work, so it may just be Reva. Also – and this is where you come in – Terri would like both Richard and Reva to spend time shadowing you at your house. Again, because of Richard's work commitments, it's likely to be mainly Reva, but Terri has said that Richard must come to you at least once, preferably twice. She's been so impressed by the way you handle Danny, she thinks Reva and Richard would learn a lot by watching you. So be flattered, my dear.'

'I am,' I said, astounded by all Jill had told me. 'What an incredible turn of events.'

'Yes. Terri will be asking you, Richard and Reva for feedback as we go along, and once Danny is home – assuming he goes home – she will be visiting and monitoring him there.'

'I see,' I said. 'So when will all this start?'

'Friday. Danny will have contact as usual tomorrow, and then either Reva or Richard will come to your house on Friday, early evening, for at least two hours. Contact will take place as usual on Saturday, and Terri has made it clear to Richard that he needs to be there – she wants to see commitment from him. Then, so that Danny's rehabilitation home isn't too protracted, Terri wants either Richard or Reva or both to spend at least two hours with you on Sunday. She's leaving the exact times for you to arrange between yourselves. The following week one of them will come to you on the evenings Danny doesn't have contact, and again on the Sunday.'

'So he'll be seeing them every day?'

'Yes. That's the idea. Then, if Terri is satisfied, the plan is to move Danny home on the following Monday – in twelve days' time.'

Chapter Twenty-Five
Stay Calm

I'm not sure who was the more nervous when Reva arrived on Friday for her first visit to 'shadow' me – her or me. We'd agreed she would come at five o'clock, which would give Danny a chance to settle after school, and would also include dinner – an important thing for Reva to see, as prior to coming into care Danny had eaten his meals alone. I'd already decided that I wouldn't be lecturing Reva or overtly instructing her – I didn't think that was required – but I'd try to show her through example, then let her parent Danny, and I'd be on hand to help if necessary.

I'd explained to Danny that his mummy would be coming to see us and would stay for dinner and then go home, because she wanted to spend more time with him. I couldn't tell him the real reason – that it was in preparation for him hopefully returning home – because it wasn't definite he *would* be going home. I thought it would be less disruptive to Danny if I kept everything as normal as possible while Reva was with us, so, following his usual routine, he was in the garden with George when she arrived. Paula was out there too. I offered Reva a drink and she had a glass of cold water, which she took into the garden. She said hello to Paula and Danny.

'Mummy!' Danny exclaimed slightly surprised.

'Hi, were you expecting me?'

Danny gave a small nod and returned his attention to George. He hadn't come over to hug his mother and she didn't go to him. As one of Reva's concerns had been Danny's lack of affection towards her, I thought it would be a good idea if she began initiating it, as I had started doing, instead of relying on Danny – though of course keeping within the boundaries of what he felt comfortable with.

'I would just give him a kiss on his head if he doesn't want a hug,' I suggested to her.

She went over and lightly kissed the top of his head. Danny responded by kissing George's head. Well, it was a start!

Paula stayed for a while and then went indoors and I continued chatting to Reva about things in general, trying to put her at ease as Danny played with and petted George. Presently I went indoors to put the finishing touches to dinner while Reva stayed in the garden with Danny. I could see them through the kitchen window as I worked, and very slowly they lost their awkwardness, Reva was talking more to Danny and he was nodding, although I couldn't hear what she was saying. Adrian and Lucy came down from their rooms to see when dinner would be ready and then went into the garden. Once dinner was ready I called everyone. Danny knew to put George in his hutch first, and when he came in he automatically took the stool to the sink to wash his hands ready for dinner.

'Good boy,' I said, hoping Reva would realize how important it was to praise Danny.

The start of the meal was quiet and uncomfortable, but then Reva broke the ice by asking my children what they planned to do when they left school, and conversation began. As the meal progressed I had the feeling that Reva had been used to socializing in her work, meeting and greeting clients, attending business lunches and similar, for she knew how to keep a conversation flowing and put others at ease. I thought, not for the first time, that she must once have been a very confident and accomplished lady, but had been brought down by Danny's high level of needs and challenging behaviour. I noticed as we ate that she kept glancing at Danny, who, as usual, was cutting up his food and arranging it around the edge of his plate.

'Come on, eat up,' she said to him. Then to me, 'He's still playing with his food then? I wondered if you'd managed to stop that.'

Feeling his mother's criticism, Danny immediately grew anxious and ate even more slowly.

'I haven't tried to stop it,' I said to Reva. 'I think that at Danny's age if it helps him to eat then it isn't a real worry. If he doesn't grow out of it, it's something that can be addressed when he's older.' Reva had paused in eating and was looking at me intently, so I felt I should explain further. 'I've found through fostering that it's usually impossible to correct or modify all aspects of a child's behaviour at once, so I concentrate on what I think is most important. Danny has far fewer tantrums now, is talking more and hasn't had a meltdown here or at school in weeks. He's also enjoying activities that would previously have petrified him. So I think he's doing well.'

Reva gave a small nod and returned to her food.

We all stayed at the table until Danny had finished and I praised him for having a clean plate.

'Well done,' Reva added. I could see from Danny's expression that his mother's praise was worth far more than mine, which was how it should be.

As soon as he'd finished eating he was down from the table and wanting to feed George as he normally did. I suggested to Reva that she might like to go with him while I cleared the table.

'I feel I should help you with the dishes,' she said politely.

'Don't worry. It's fine,' I said. 'Adrian, Lucy and Paula will help me. It's more important you spend the time with Danny.'

She went with Danny as he collected George's food bowl from the hutch and then returned indoors to the cupboard under the stairs. 'One, two, three scoops,' I heard Danny telling his mother.

'Good boy,' I called from the kitchen.

'Yes, good boy,' Reva repeated.

I wished she'd praise him more; I'd have to mention it.

I left them alone to feed and settle George for the night and then, when they returned and Danny had gone into the living room and couldn't hear us, I explained to Reva why I took every opportunity to praise Danny, even in the actions he was used to getting right. 'Children can never have enough praise,' I said. 'It builds their confidence and self-esteem. It also makes them more open to suggestions for correcting their negative behaviour, which is helpful in a child like Danny.'

'That makes sense,' Reva said amicably.

We went into the living room and, following his usual routine, Danny fetched his school bag from the hall but now presented it to his mother. I could see she was pleased. Danny hadn't really said much to his mother or paid her much attention, but I knew he was coping with this very new situation in his own way. It must have been strange for him to suddenly have his mother here without a plausible explanation. I left Reva with Danny, listening to him read, while I went to clear up in the kitchen. The doors were open so I could hear Danny, first reading and then practising the words and numbers from his learning targets, but I couldn't hear any responses from Reva. Presently I went into the living room. 'He's doing well, isn't he?' I said enthusiastically to Reva.

'Yes,' she said. 'I hear him read at contact sometimes.'

'That's good,' I said. But had she told him how well he was doing? Not from what I'd heard. Danny needed so much encouragement. I didn't want to labour the point further that evening, so I said, 'Lovely reading, Danny,' and hoped Reva would pick up the message.

When Danny had finished his homework he put his school bag in its usual place in the hall, and as he did Reva took the opportunity to speak to me. I could see from her expression she was worried. 'He's still so far behind in his learning,' she said. 'It worries me. Do you think he will ever catch up?'

'I don't know,' I said realistically. 'But the educational psychologist's assessment will give you a better indication. She'll also make recommendations of the type of help Danny needs. I think what's more important is that Danny reaches his full potential, which, with help, I'm sure he will do.'

'You're always so positive,' Reva said with a small smile. 'I saw that the first time I met you – at that meeting at school. Richard and I are more positive now, but I still worry what the future will hold for Danny.'

'That's only natural,' I said. 'The future is a scary place, so let's concentrate on the present.' And if it sounded like a lecture then so be it. I was entitled to give one.

I now told Reva that I'd introduced a bedtime story into Danny's routine as it was a nice way of relaxing at the end of the day, before having his bath and then going to bed.

'Do you find there's time?' she asked. 'Everything takes him so long.'

'I know,' I smiled. 'That's why we start the bedtime routine early.'

She nodded. 'I'll have to rethink our routine around dinner and Richard coming home.'

I told Danny that his mother would read him a story tonight, and he chose a book and then settled beside her on the sofa. I sat in the room with them. Reva read to him for fifteen minutes until it was seven o'clock and then told him it was time for her to go. She'd been with us for two hours, as Terri had suggested, and it was long enough. I could see Danny was getting tired, and if he got overtired his behaviour would deteriorate. We hadn't really done an awful lot, but everyone was more relaxed now, and another evening we'd include Danny's bath and bedtime routine. Reva stood as Danny returned the books neatly to the bookshelf and then she said goodnight to him, kissing him on the head. To our surprise he threw his arms around her and hugged her tightly.

'That's lovely,' she said, clearly moved and holding him to her.

They hugged for a while longer, but when she tried to move away he tightened his grip. 'Mummy stay,' he said. 'Mummy stay.'

While it was nice for Reva to have this spontaneous display of affection from a child who normally had so much trouble expressing it, I could see it was going to be very difficult for

Danny to say goodbye. He buried his head further into her skirt and clung tighter.

'Mummy has to go now,' she said, still holding him and giving him mixed messages. 'But I'll see you tomorrow, and Daddy will be home too.'

Danny didn't move.

'Danny, give Mummy one last hug and then say goodbye,' I said.

He clung to her and Reva began easing him away, but as she did he screamed, 'No!'

She looked to me for help.

'Danny,' I said, going over and touching his arm to gain his attention. 'It's time for Mummy to go. Do you want to say goodbye to her in here or come with us to the front door?'

There was silence before he said, 'Front door.' Slowly he relinquished his grip on her skirt.

'Good boy,' I said. 'Excellent choice. Well done.'

'Yes, well done,' Reva said.

And I made a mental note to tell her about the closed-choice technique on her next visit.

Reva's first visit had gone pretty smoothly and Danny had been on his best behaviour – partly, I thought, because the situation was new and he was unsure and treading carefully. Her second visit – on Sunday – proved more challenging. As we'd arranged she arrived at two o'clock. She was expecting Richard to join her, and so was Danny, for Richard had told Danny the day before at contact that he'd see him on Sunday at my house. As Reva came in she explained to him that Daddy had had to go and see his parents as his father had been taken ill in the night, but he hoped to join us later.

Stay Calm

Danny clearly didn't understand why his father hadn't arrived with his mother (as he'd promised to) and preferred instead to visit a man Danny had no knowledge of, having not seen his grandparents since the age of two. He grew increasingly agitated.

'Daddy coming? Daddy coming?' he demanded of his mother.

'I hope so,' she kept telling him. 'We'll have to wait and see.'

Eventually I settled him with a brightly coloured puzzle in the living room. We were indoors, as the weather wasn't good. As Danny played I took the opportunity to quietly explain to Reva why Danny had reacted as he had and why it was so important to give him clear, concise information in short chunks that he could manage. Danny wouldn't be able to conceptualize terms like 'I hope so' and 'We'll have to wait and see'. I also explained the closed-choice technique and some other parenting strategies I'd found useful: using the child's name at the beginning of a sentence to get their attention; referring to oneself in the first person – 'I' – rather than the third – for example, 'Mummy'. 'I have to go now' is so much stronger and more immediate than 'Mummy has to go now', and therefore more likely to produce the desired result. It would also help Danny to use it. Reva said she wanted to learn all she could and had applied to go on the parenting course Terri had recommended. She asked me how I dealt with Danny's tantrums and meltdowns, and I told her, explaining the main difference between the two: a tantrum is an angry episode designed to get what a child wants, or to avoid doing something they have been asked to do but don't want to. While a meltdown, often triggered by sensory overload, results in the child losing all control. There are, however – as Reva had seen in Danny – some similarities in the way a tantrum and a meltdown manifest themselves, and also in the way one deals with them.

Ten minutes later Danny provided me with the opportunity to put my words into practice. The landline rang and when I answered it I wasn't completely surprised to hear Richard, for he was well overdue now. 'Sorry, Cathy,' he said. 'I'm going to have to postpone my visit today. I've only just left my parents' house and I'm at least an hour's drive from where you are.'

'You're still welcome to come,' I said. 'I'm not going out and we don't have to stick exactly to the two hours. It can be a bit longer. How is your father?'

'A lot better, thanks. He was very bilious in the night and I think it scared mother. He's stopped being sick now, but I think I'd rather leave my visit to you until next week.'

'All right, if that's what you prefer,' I said.

'Thanks. Could I have a word with Reva?'

'Yes, of course.' I passed the phone to her.

She listened to what Richard had to tell her, and then he must have asked to speak to Danny, for taking the handset from her ear she said to me, 'Do you think Danny would cope with saying hello to his dad?' Reva had always said Danny was afraid of the telephone, and I'd assumed it was the noise it made when it rang.

'It's worth a try. Ask him,' I suggested. Danny was playing on the floor not far from us and without doubt had heard what his mother had said.

'Danny, would you like to talk to Daddy on the phone?' she now asked him.

'Yes,' he said without hesitation. He immediately stood and went over to the phone. Which made me think we should have tried telephone contact sooner.

Reva passed the handset to Danny and he put it to his ear but didn't speak.

'Say hello to Daddy,' Reva prompted.

'Hello, Daddy,' Danny said in a small voice, concentrating hard.

He listened to what his father said – which I guessed was an explanation as to why he wouldn't be coming this afternoon and, hopefully, an apology too – but didn't say anything. Then Richard must have said goodbye, for Danny said a very quiet 'Goodbye' and returned the handset to his mother.

'Well done, Danny,' I said to him. 'You used the telephone.'

'Yes, well done,' Reva said.

But Danny didn't look pleased. He was standing beside his mother as she said goodbye to Richard, agitatedly snapping his fingers and humming.

'Daddy?' Danny asked her as she replaced the handset.

'Daddy can't come here today,' she said. 'But you'll see him tomorrow.'

The average child of six, while disappointed, would have understood and coped with the change in arrangements, but for a child like Danny it was just another confusing broken promise in a world of confusing people who said things they didn't mean.

'Daddy! Daddy!' he demanded, clenching his jaw and stamping his foot.

'Daddy can't come,' Reva said, immediately growing anxious.

Danny gritted his teeth, stamped his foot hard and then kicked his toy box before throwing himself on the floor and screaming. Reva looked petrified. 'It scares me when he does that,' she admitted.

'That's the purpose of it,' I said. 'A tantrum is designed to get what the child wants. Some tantrums are best ignored – if a child is demanding sweets, for example – but I think Danny needs some more explanation.'

I went over to him and knelt beside him.

'Go away! I want Daddy,' he shouted, trying to kick me.

Reva gasped.

I put my hand lightly on Danny's leg to stop him and kept out of reach of his flailing arms. 'Danny, don't kick,' I said firmly. 'It hurts. I can understand why you're angry, but you mustn't kick.' He turned his head away from me, closed his eyes and screamed. I waited until he stopped. 'Daddy wanted to see you today but he couldn't,' I said calmly. 'I know you're sad he couldn't come; Daddy is sad too, but it wasn't his fault, so don't be angry with him. You'll see Daddy tomorrow at home.' I paused. He was listening. 'Soon it will be time for Mummy to go, so I want you to get up now and choose a game to play with her.' He grew still, although his fists were still clenched and his eyes shut.

'I know Mummy would like to play a game with you,' I said. 'But there won't be time if you stay here on the floor.'

'I would like to play a game with Danny,' Reva said. But Danny didn't move.

'Perhaps Mummy would like to choose a game,' I suggested.

'Yes, I would,' she said, relaxing a little now Danny was over the worst. 'I like the game Four in a Row. We used to play that.'

'It's in Danny's toy box,' I said.

Stay Calm

Reva stood and went towards the toy box. Danny heard her move and immediately his eyes shot open and he was on his feet. Rummaging in the toy box he took out the game and gave it to his mother.

'Thank you. Well done,' she said.

'Thank you. Well done,' Danny repeated, and Reva smiled.

'Tantrums usually start and end quite quickly,' I said to Reva as Danny sat beside her on the sofa ready to play the game. 'But it can take some time for a child to recover from a meltdown. The main thing is to stay calm.'

'Stay calm,' Danny repeated, and planted a big kiss on his mother's cheek.

Chapter Twenty-Six

Saving Danny

O n Monday, while Reva and I were upstairs going through Danny's bath and bedtime routine, Danny pointed to the toilet and said to his mother, 'George scared.'

'Yes, he is,' Reva said, shooting me a pointed look.

I now remembered that Danny had said the same to us when he'd shown George around upstairs. He hadn't wanted to show him that room but wouldn't tell us the reason.

'Why is George scared?' I now asked Reva.

'Shall I tell Cathy?' she asked Danny.

Danny nodded.

'We'd just got George, he was only small, and at the time I was trying to toilet train Danny. One afternoon when my back was turned Danny decided he'd toilet train George. He must have tried to sit George on the toilet, and either George slipped from Danny's grasp or jumped. I found poor George under the water, just in time. Thankfully Danny hadn't flushed it,' she added with a brief smile. 'Neither of them has forgotten that episode. George won't go near our downstairs toilet, even now.'

'Danny sorry,' he suddenly said, showing empathy and concern.

'I know you were, love,' Reva said, kissing his head. 'I didn't blame you.' Then turning to me she added, 'You need eyes in the back of your head with Danny.'

'I know,' I said. 'You have to be so vigilant. I ask one of my children to watch Danny if I'm not in the same room as him, but it must've been difficult for you without Richard at home much.'

'It was,' Reva said. 'Richard didn't appreciate just how difficult it was. But he does now.'

Reva's visit on Monday went well, then on Tuesday Danny had contact at home as usual and from what Reva said that had gone well too. When Reva arrived on Wednesday she was clearly in very good spirits and came in with a lightness in her step that I hadn't seen before. She said she felt far more confident now parenting Danny, but also it was her wedding anniversary, and that morning Richard had given her a beautiful necklace – the one she'd previously found the receipt for and which had led her to assume (together with Richard working late) that he'd been having an affair. She said he'd also given her a card in which he'd written some lovely words. I said I was pleased for her and congratulated her on their wedding anniversary. Yet while all this was very positive, the fact remained that Richard hadn't come to my house as he was supposed to and we were running out of time.

I said as much to Reva. 'There's only Friday and Sunday left if Danny is to return home as planned on Monday.'

'Richard *will* come on Friday,' Reva said. 'He's promised. He'll be here at six o'clock. He won't let you down.'

I didn't point out that it wouldn't be me he would be letting down, but her and Danny. 'Richard does understand how important it is as part of the process for Danny going home that he comes, doesn't he?' I said, labouring the point.

'Yes,' Reva said. 'He's completely committed to having Danny home, and he has been seeing Danny at every contact. But Richard works long hours. I also think he might be a bit nervous of meeting you again.'

'Why?' I asked.

'He's not used to being told off,' she said with a smile.

'Oh, I see,' I said. 'Well, tell him I don't bite.'

'It didn't do him any harm. In fact, you did us a big favour,' Reva said. 'If it wasn't for you speaking to him, he wouldn't have had that conversation with his parents, and we wouldn't be in the position we are now, working towards Danny coming home. I can't believe how close we came to losing our little boy.' Reva's eyes filled. 'So a small dent in Richard's ego won't do him any harm.' She kissed my cheek.

Yet despite Reva's assurance and faith in Richard, I remained concerned that something could still come up at work to prevent him from coming on Friday, which would jeopardize Danny returning home on Monday.

I needn't have worried, for at exactly six o'clock on Friday the doorbell rang and when I answered there was Richard, looking very smart in an open-neck shirt, casual jacket and trousers.

'Promise you won't tell me off again?' he said, grinning boyishly.

'Not unless you deserve it,' I said. 'Good to see you again, Richard. Come in and make yourself at home.'

He kissed my cheek as he came in and appeared far more relaxed and at ease than the last time we'd met.

'Daddy!' Danny yelled, running the length of the hall into his arms.

Richard scooped him up and held him high above his head and they both laughed. What a difference to their last meeting, I thought, when Richard had barely been able to look at his son and couldn't wait to get away.

'We've had dinner, but I can easily fix you something,' I offered.

'I'm good, thanks, Cathy. I left work early so I've had time to go home first, change and grab a bite to eat.'

Richard set Danny down and then slipped off his jacket and hung it on the hall stand.

'Daddy,' Danny said, tugging at his arm.

'So, Mister,' Richard said, turning to Danny, and using the same term Lucy sometimes used, 'Mummy tells me we do your homework first and then I read you a story before you have your bath.'

Danny looked impressed, and also a little bemused.

'I take it George has been fed?' Richard asked me.

'Yes. Danny does that straight after his dinner.'

'Great. Come on then, little man, let's get that homework done and we may have time for a game as well as a story.'

Danny didn't need telling twice and, picking up his school bag, he slipped his hand into his father's and led him down the hall into the living room. I went with them but left them to it once they were settled. 'Call me if you need me,' I said.

'Thank you, Cathy.'

* * *

Over the next hour – as Danny did his homework, played a game of toy cars with his father, which involved Richard on all fours making brum-brum noises, and then listened to a bedtime story – I kept largely out of their way. The door to the living room was open so I could hear them, and I was on hand to help if necessary. I popped in every so often, but clearly Reva had passed on much of the work we'd been doing together, and other than getting Danny over-excited (when I had to calm him down), there were no problems. Richard's attitude to Danny was so very different from the last time I'd seen them together, when he'd appeared distant and afraid to engage with his son. Now I saw the commitment Reva had spoken of. Richard was embracing parenting Danny and accepting his quirks and differences. I also saw a very different side to Richard the person as well as the father – good-humoured and ready for a joke. Adrian, Lucy and Paula were in the house and at various times went into the living room to say hi to Richard. Each time Danny pointed to his father and said proudly, 'My daddy.'

At seven o'clock Richard came to find me. He was holding Danny's hand. 'I think it's time for Danny's bath,' he said.

'Yes. I usually take him up about now.'

'Lead on then, please,' he said, 'and show me what to do.' Then to Danny he said, 'I'm going to bath you today.' Excellent, I thought, and Danny grinned, just like his father.

'Be prepared – it does take a while,' I said lightly as we began upstairs.

'I know,' Richard said. 'Reva used to tell me what a battle it was to get him into bed. She was exhausted by the end of it, but then I was never home to help her. I will be in future. I didn't realize how much she struggled. I put all her problems down to drinking.'

'And she's stopped drinking now?' I asked.

'Oh yes. Reva was never a heavy drinker. She began drinking as a way of coping, but of course it just made her feel worse. Most of our arguments were a result of that.'

I nodded.

Richard and I stood on the landing and continued talking while Danny used the toilet and washed his hands. 'Good boy,' I said as he came out. We waited some more as he collected his pyjamas from his bedroom and I praised him again.

Danny was pretty excited as the three of us went round the landing to the bathroom – he skipped and hopped and jumped.

'Steady on, Mister,' Richard said. But I could see he was pleased that Danny was so happy at having his father there.

In the bathroom Danny spent some time meticulously folding his pyjamas and adjusting his towel on the towel rail until it was to his liking. I saw Richard watching him, but he didn't comment.

'Patience is the key,' I said quietly with a smile.

'I know, I'm learning,' Richard said.

I put the plug into the bath and turned on the taps. 'I always run the water to the right temperature,' I said. 'And I never leave Danny unattended in the bath, not even for a minute.'

Richard looked serious. 'Reva says he tries to drown himself.'

'It's more of a game,' I said. 'But I don't encourage it, and it frightens Reva.'

'That's why she didn't want him to go swimming, but I understand he's doing all right in swimming at school.'

'Yes. He really enjoys it now. You could try taking him swimming when he's home, or even to the seaside,' I suggested. 'There are so many new experiences Danny hasn't tried yet.'

'There's a lot we can and will be doing,' Richard confirmed, which I was pleased to hear.

Danny usually undressed himself, but now his father was here he wanted his help and held up his arms so that Richard could take off his jersey.

'What do you say to Daddy?' I asked Danny, as usual trying to encourage him to talk more.

'Daddy do it,' he said.

'Good boy,' Richard and I chorused together.

Richard helped Danny out of his jersey and then his vest, and then Danny took off his other clothes by himself. Once the bath was full I turned off the taps and tipped in Danny's bath toys. Richard put his hands under Danny's armpits and lifted him over the edge of the bath into the water. He landed with a large splash, which splattered water down the front of Richard's smart shirt.

'Best not to wear your good clothes for baths and hair washing in future,' I quipped.

'Point taken,' Richard said good-humouredly.

Danny sat happily in his bath and began playing with his toys. 'I usually wash his back and hair while he is occupied playing,' I explained to Richard.

Rolling up his shirt sleeves Richard knelt beside the bath. 'It's a long time since I gave you a bath, Mister,' he admitted to Danny.

Danny laughed, but I think it was in response to the duck he was playing with rather than what his father had said, for I doubted 'a long time' was a concept for him.

I passed Richard the sponge and bath lotion and he began gently washing Danny's back, then his neck and chest. 'Give Danny the sponge and he'll do the rest,' I said to Richard. When Danny had finished washing he meticulously squeezed out the sponge and set it on the side of the bath. 'Good boy,' I said.

'Now his hair,' I said to Richard, who was looking as though he'd finished. 'Wet his hair with this.' I passed him the plastic beaker, and also Danny's face flannel. 'Hold the flannel against his forehead; it'll keep the water out of his eyes.' For a moment Richard looked between the flannel and the beaker as though he didn't know what to do. 'Come on,' I said jokingly. 'It's not rocket science.'

'But you know us blokes can't multi-task,' he laughed. Danny laughed too.

Richard did as I suggested and, placing the flannel against Danny's forehead with one hand, began scooping up water in the beaker with the other. Danny was so engrossed in playing with his toys that he didn't appear to mind his father's rather clumsy attempts at hair washing. Once Danny's hair was thoroughly wet I passed Richard the bath lotion. 'Just a little squirt onto his head,' I told him.

Richard applied the bath lotion to Danny's hair, but as he began massaging it into Danny's scalp it must have felt different to his mother's or my touch, because Danny looked up, startled. 'Daddy washing my hair?' he asked, touching his father's hand on his head to make sure.

'Yes, I am,' Richard said. 'Keep nice and still. Good boy.'

Telling Danny to keep still if he had other plans was like asking an eel to stop wriggling. As Richard tried to shampoo Danny's hair he kept ducking and moving his head from side to side so that his father had to chase it around. Danny laughed loudly and Richard smiled. It was lovely to see father and son having fun together, and to see Richard playing so unreservedly. He didn't seem to mind that the front of his shirt was covered in globules of foam. But I also knew how frustrating these games could be if you were tired and just wanted to get Danny into bed at the end of a busy day.

'I'll wear my wetsuit next time,' Richard joked.

'Like my diving man,' Danny said.

Once Richard had finished shampooing Danny's hair I passed him the plastic beaker and flannel again and he carefully began rinsing the lotion from Danny's hair. 'I've tried using the shower head and that shampoo shield,' I said, 'but Danny doesn't like them. I've found this method works best.'

Richard nodded and concentrated on rinsing Danny's hair.

'Good boy,' I said.

'Me or Danny?' Richard laughed.

'Both of you,' I smiled.

I'd just reached for Danny's towel so that Richard could towel-dry Danny's hair in the bath before he got out when, without warning, Danny threw himself back and went under the water. Richard started. I guessed it was the first time he'd seen Danny do this.

'Stay calm,' I said quietly to him. 'He'll come up soon.'

We waited, both looking at Danny, who had his eyes and mouth shut and lay motionless under the water. After what seemed like an eternity he rose like a fish breaking through the water. 'Danny drowning!' he exclaimed, and looked at his father for his reaction.

While Richard's face didn't register panic or alarm as Reva's had, I could see it had shocked him.

'Do you know why he does it?' he asked me.

'No. Do you?'

He shook his head as Danny jettisoned himself back into the water again. He stayed under for longer this time and when he came up he looked directly at his father and said firmly, 'Danny drowning,' as if challenging Richard to say different.

'No, you're not drowning,' I said evenly, as I'd said before when Danny had done this. 'You're playing.'

Richard had gone very quiet and his face was set and serious. I wondered if he was going to tell Danny off. I didn't want such a positive bath-time experience going sour, so I thought it was time to bring it to a close and get Danny out of the bath. 'Danny, it's time to dry yourself,' I said.

Danny threw himself under the water for a third time, staying submerged for as long as he could hold his breath, and then came up spluttering and gave the same challenging look. 'Danny drowning!' he said to his father.

He was just going under for a fourth time when Richard suddenly leant forward and, plunging his hands into the water, grabbed Danny and scooped him up. Danny looked surprised but didn't cry out. I quickly put the towel under his dripping body and Richard wrapped him in it. He then sat cross-legged on the floor with Danny in his lap and cradled him like a baby. 'You're not going to drown, Danny,' Richard said, holding him close. 'Daddy is saving you.'

Danny looked up questioningly. 'Daddy saving Danny?' he asked in a small voice.

'Yes, I'm saving you,' Richard said, kissing his forehead. 'There's nothing for you to be afraid of any more. I love you. I'm sorry I haven't been there for you, but I will be in the future. I promise you I will.'

Danny stared up at his father thoughtfully, as though he was finding this difficult to believe. 'Daddy loves Danny?' he asked after a moment.

'Yes,' Richard said, his voice catching. 'I love you more than you can ever know.'

'Danny loves Daddy,' he said. 'Danny happy.' He reached up and gently wiped the tear away from his father's eye. 'Don't cry. We're happy.'

'I promise you, we will be,' Richard said. And I knew he meant it.

Chapter Twenty-Seven
Another Story ...

I couldn't tell Danny that he was going home until Terri telephoned me to confirm that he was, so Danny went to school on Monday morning as usual, and when I collected him I was able to tell him the good news.

'Danny going home?' he repeated. 'Danny going home?'

'Yes, Mummy and Daddy are coming to collect you from my house in an hour,' I explained as we walked to the car. 'I've packed all your clothes and toys ready.'

'George?' Danny asked, immediately concerned.

'Yes, of course, George will be going home with you.'

Danny thought for a moment and then asked, 'In your car?'

I was amazed that Danny had remembered I'd collected George in my car. He hadn't been part of the process. 'No. Your daddy is bringing his car and your mummy is bringing her car too. The hutch will go on the back seat of your daddy's car.'

Danny thought again. 'Two cars?'

'Yes. Your mummy's and daddy's.'

'Danny going home,' he repeated quietly. 'Danny going home.'

* * *

Saving Danny

As soon as I'd received Terri's telephone call to say that Danny was definitely going home that day I'd begun to pack his belongings. They were now all bagged and boxed in the hall. George was in his hutch out the back, sitting on clean hay, and I'd collapsed the run so it would fit in Richard's car as well. Richard had taken the day off work to bring Danny home. Terri had left it to us to arrange the time of Danny's departure, and when I'd spoken to Richard and Reva that afternoon I'd asked them to come at 4.30 p.m., after Lucy, Adrian and Paula had arrived home from school, so that they had a chance to say goodbye to Danny. My children knew it was likely Danny would be returning home today, so they weren't completely surprised when they came in from school to find his luggage in the hall.

'Danny going home,' he told each of them as they arrived.

'Yes. Are you happy?' Paula asked him.

Danny gave a very small nod. I guessed his leaving was bittersweet for him too.

We assembled in the living room and gave Danny his leaving present – a DVD and a large book on rabbits. It had stories and facts about rabbits and beautiful colour photographs of different rabbits, some of whom were just like George, although none were quite as big as him. We also gave Danny a card with a rabbit on the front and I read out the words we'd written inside.

'Thank you very much,' Danny said, clearly pleased.

'You're welcome,' I said.

'You're welcome,' Danny repeated.

We stayed in the living room looking at the pictures of the rabbits in Danny's book until the doorbell rang at 4.30.

'Mummy? Daddy?' Danny asked me, looking up.

'Yes. They're here now to take you and George home,' I said.

Danny came with me down the hall, still clutching his gifts and card. I was pleased he liked them – I thought he would. 'Look!' he exclaimed as I opened the door, and he held them up for his parents to see. 'Presents!'

'Fantastic,' Richard said. 'We'll look at the film once we're home.'

As Richard admired the book and DVD, Reva said quietly to me, 'How was Danny when you told him he was coming home?'

'Very pleased and excited,' I said. 'But it will be strange for him to begin with, even though he's going home.'

'Yes, Terri told me to be prepared for a backlash,' Reva said. 'She's coming at the end of the week to see how we're all getting on.'

'Don't worry. You'll be fine,' I said. 'Just try to relax. No one gets parenting right all the time.'

Terri had advised us to keep the goodbyes short so it wasn't upsetting for Danny. Adrian, Lucy and Paula came out of the living room and said hello to Reva and Richard. Then Richard said to Danny, 'Let's get cracking, Mister. You've got a lot of gear here.'

Danny grinned but looked confused. It must have been difficult for him to understand why he was suddenly going home, although I'd done my best to explain. The girls and I helped Reva load her car while Adrian went with Richard and Danny to load George in his hutch into Richard's car. It took us about fifteen minutes before everything was in. Then Danny clambered into the small back seat of his mother's sports car – there was no room in Richard's car – and he sat nestled between his luggage. As we stood on the pavement ready to say goodbye I could see Adrian admiring Reva's car. Richard must have seen this too, for he said to Adrian, 'You don't want one of those, they're completely impractical.'

'I wouldn't mind a chance to find out,' Adrian returned with a smile, and Richard laughed.

We weren't saying a final goodbye to Danny, for it had been decided by the social services that I, and my children if they wished, could visit Danny at home once a week for the next month so we didn't simply disappear from his life. However, Danny was leaving our family, which was a huge loss, and of course we all felt very emotional. When a child has lived with you and been part of your life and you've nurtured and cared for them, it's only natural that you grow to love them. It's impossible not to. So that when they go – even, as in Danny's case, when they are returning home – it's hard. You have to put on a brave face for the sake of the child and wish them well. It was OK to tell Danny we'd miss him, which we had done, but we couldn't burst into tears. Although, as I looked in through the open passenger door and saw him sitting on the back seat, so small and vulnerable, clutching his presents and cards, I was very close to it.

'Take care, love,' I said one last time. 'You've been great. We've loved having you stay. You're a treasure.'

'Thank you very much,' Danny said. I felt my bottom lip tremble.

I kissed him, straightened and moved away from the car so that Adrian, Lucy and Paula could say goodbye. Reva closed the car door and before she and Richard got into their cars they both thanked us all for looking after Danny. They hugged the girls and shook Adrian's hand.

Then Richard gave me an extra hug, and I felt the warmth of his sincerity. 'Thank you for everything, Cathy. It's very much appreciated.'

'I'm glad everything worked out for you all,' I said.

'Thanks to you,' he said. Then to my children, 'Look after your mum. She's special.' Which was kind of him, and they smiled.

Richard and Reva got into their cars and started the engines. Richard pulled away first and then Reva followed a moment later. We waved to Danny and he grinned and waved back. We continued waving until they were out of sight, then we slowly returned indoors. No one spoke and the atmosphere was sombre, as it always was after a child left. I usually suggested a small outing or a treat to take our minds off our loss, and I now asked Paula, Adrian and Lucy if – once they'd done their homework – they'd like to go out for something to eat. They agreed, although without a lot of enthusiasm. I said it was better than sitting at home moping, so they went upstairs to get ready. We should have been used to children leaving us by now after so many years of fostering, but I don't think you ever get used to it. You adjust to the child's absence and hope that they stay in touch, and even if they don't you never, ever forget them.

I went into the kitchen mindful that George, whose cage had sat just outside, against the back wall, had also gone. He'd been such a personality and part of our lives that I knew we'd miss him too. No more putting him in his run, seeing him in the garden, clearing up his pellets in the house or hearing him thump when he thought he heard danger. He'd been so good for Danny and without doubt had helped him settle, as well as being a trusted confidant. I put the kettle on to make a coffee and while it boiled I opened my mail, which I hadn't had time to do that day with all the packing. One of the letters was from CAMHS (child and adolescent mental health services), with the appointment I'd been waiting for; too late for me, but I'd pass it on to Reva and Richard to use. I took my coffee into the living room, where I sat on the sofa and waited for the children to get ready. The room seemed very bare now all Danny's toys had gone. There'd always been a puzzle or brightly coloured pattern laid out on the floor, often the same pattern for days, subtly altered by Danny from time to time to form a new one. Now the carpet appeared plain and drab.

My parents hadn't had a chance to say goodbye to Danny, for once his rehabilitation home had begun there hadn't been an opportunity with every day full. I'd thought about trying to squeeze in a quick visit but decided it would be more than Danny could cope with, given everything else that was going on in his life. I'd also considered the possibility of him saying goodbye to my parents over the telephone, but as he'd only used the phone once before, I thought that too could have been unsettling for him. They knew he was being prepared to go home; I'd telephone them now and tell them that the move had gone well, and also arrange to see them the next weekend. Then, when I next saw Danny, I'd pass on their best wishes, which doubtless they'd want me to. However, before I got the chance to make the call, the telephone rang. I reached out and picked up the handset from the corner table. I wasn't surprised to hear Jill's voice. She always telephoned just after a child had left to ask if the move had gone well and if we were all right. I told her the move had gone to plan and we were OK. But Jill now asked another question.

Another Story ...

'Cathy, I appreciate Danny has only just left, but could you take a thirteen-year-old girl straightaway? Her present foster carers have said she must leave them this evening. They can't take any more. We daren't put her with a new carer. Her behaviour is too volatile and they wouldn't cope. Could she come to you in an hour or so? Sorry, but we're desperate.'

My heart sank. Sometimes fostering feels like a production line of desperate social workers trying to find homes for distraught children. 'Jill, the room isn't ready yet,' I said. 'I haven't even stripped the bed. And I've promised to take Adrian, Paula and Lucy out. Can't she come tomorrow?'

'The social worker said the girl's behaviour was so bad that the carers had given an ultimatum – that the girl had to go by eight o'clock this evening. But I'll phone the social worker now and tell her that you can definitely take her in the morning. Perhaps the carers will feel they can keep her for one more night if they know there's an end in sight.'

'Thank you, Jill.'

I replaced the handset and gazed across the room. It wasn't the first time I'd been asked to take a child at very short notice, as an emergency, but that was usually when the child was in imminent danger and had to be removed from home quickly. What would I do if the carers couldn't be persuaded to keep the girl for one more night? Cancel going out with my family, or stand my ground like they were doing and insist she could come to me in the morning? I appreciated the carers must be at their wits' end, but I wanted to spend the evening with my children, not dealing with a disturbed teenager, who by the sound of it would need all my attention. Yet to say no would have been unprofessional and no good for the girl or the carers. I finished my coffee and waited for the telephone to ring.

Ten minutes later Jill telephoned again. 'The carers have agreed to keep Joss for one more night as long as she goes first thing in the morning.'

I breathed a sigh of relief. 'Thank you, Jill.'

'No, thank *you*. Joss has been kicking off big time and has already had a lot of moves. She had a shocking experience as a child and …'

But that's another story.

Epilogue

I visited Danny every Saturday for the next month. Paula came with me the first time, Adrian the second, Lucy the third and then we all went together for our fourth and final visit. My children were all impressed by the grandeur of Danny's house, but of course to Danny it was just home – and a much happier home now that he had been accepted for who he was, especially by his father, who was going that extra mile to make up for lost time. On each of our visits we spent some time outside in the garden with George and Danny and also indoors, where Danny showed my children his extensive collection of games, puzzles and toys, while I talked to Reva and Richard.

They told me they were now in regular contact with Richard's parents, who were fantastic with Danny, which wasn't surprising given all the years they'd spent looking after Robert and coping with his profound learning disabilities. Richard told me he'd talked to Danny about his step-brother and sister and was planning on taking him along when he next saw them. 'We'll make it a short visit to begin with,' Richard said. 'So it's not overwhelming for Danny.'

'Showing Danny some photographs of your children may help to prepare him,' I suggested.

'Yes, I will nearer the time. Terri suggested that too,' Richard said.

On one of my visits Reva told me that her parents were going to come for the weekend and also that she'd telephoned her sister, whom she hadn't seen for over two years. They'd had a good chat and Reva had apologized for not keeping in touch, explaining that she and Richard had come through a difficult patch, although she didn't go into details. She said she and her sister were planning to meet up with the children when the schools broke up for the long summer holiday. 'I'm sure her kids are still angels,' Reva said with a smile. 'But now I feel more confident in managing Danny's behaviour I'm not so worried. If he does have a tantrum or a meltdown, I'll just have to take him somewhere quiet until he's over it. I spent too long worrying about what other people might think. I'm not making the same mistake again.'

Danny didn't say much during our visits, but he seemed happy enough. Terri was visiting and monitoring the family, although now I was no longer Danny's foster carer I wouldn't be given any updates. On our final visit Reva, Richard and Danny waved us off at the door, and it was a poignant moment for us, knowing that we wouldn't hear any more about Danny unless his parents stayed in touch.

I didn't hear anything further from Richard or Reva for about four months, and then I received a letter from Reva with a lovely photograph enclosed of Danny and his father together on a beach, building sandcastles. *Great day out!* Reva had written on the back of the photograph, along with the date. In the accompanying letter she wrote that they were all well and hoped we were too. She thought I would like to know that

Epilogue

Danny's assessment by the educational psychologist had begun, but her report and recommendations wouldn't be available for some months. She said Danny still loved colourful patterns and his bedroom walls were now covered with his drawings. The parenting course she'd signed up for would begin in January, and she finished the letter by thanking me again for looking after Danny.

I added the photograph to our family album, and sent Reva a notelet thanking her for both the letter and the picture, and wishing them all well.

I didn't hear any more – I wasn't expecting to, as I thought Richard and Reva would want to get on with their lives and put a very difficult period behind them. Then, eighteen months later, I was in a popular pub restaurant one evening celebrating a friend's birthday when who should walk in but Richard and Reva with another couple. I waited until they were seated – at a table on the far side of the room – and had ordered their drinks, then excused myself from my friends and went over. Reva saw me first and was immediately on her feet. She came out from behind the table and hugged and kissed me.

'Cathy, how lovely to see you. I'm so sorry I haven't been in touch. I feel awful, but the time has just slipped away.'

'Don't worry. I know the feeling,' I said, smiling. 'It's good to see you.'

'And you.'

Richard stood and shook my hand warmly. 'Lovely to see you again, Cathy. So the kids have let you out for the evening.'

'Just for the evening,' I said with a laugh.

Saving Danny

'Danny still talks about you,' Reva said. 'I'll tell him I've seen you. He will be pleased. We had the assessment.' She lowered her voice so those around couldn't hear. 'Danny is on the autistic spectrum and has been identified with mild to moderate learning difficulties, but he's doing incredibly well. He's still at the same school and working on a special learning programme. And guess what,' she added with a satisfied smile. 'I've returned to work part time!'

'That's fantastic,' I said. 'I am pleased for you. You're both looking very well, but I won't keep you. I just wanted to say hello.'

'I'm glad you did,' Richard said.

We said goodbye and I returned to my seat. During the evening I occasionally glanced over to their table. They were laughing and joking and appeared to be very relaxed. Reva looked noticeably more vibrant and self-assured, and I was pleased everything had worked out. They were obviously happy, and I knew Danny would be fine, for happy parents tend to make happy kids. The assessment had been important in identifying Danny's difficulties and forming a platform for his learning programme, but more importantly Danny had been accepted by his parents for who he was. A fantastic kid with his own unique personality.

For an update on Danny and the children in my other fostering memoirs, please visit: www.cathyglass.co.uk.

Cathy Glass

———

One remarkable woman, more than **100** foster children cared for.

Learn more about the many lives Cathy has touched.

The Child Bride

A girl blamed and abused for dishonouring her community.

Cathy discovers the devastating truth.

Daddy's Little Princess

A sweet-natured girl with a complicated past

Cathy picks up the pieces after events take a dramatic turn.

Will you love me?

A broken child desperate for a loving home

The true story of Cathy's adopted daughter Lucy.

Please Don't Take My Baby

Seventeen-year-old Jade is pregnant, homeless and alone

Cathy has room in her heart for two.

Another Forgotten Child

Eight-year-old Aimee was on the child-protection register at birth

Cathy is determined to give her the happy home she deserves.

A Baby's Cry

A newborn, only hours old, taken into care

Cathy protects tiny Harrison from the potentially fatal secrets that surround his existence.

The Night the Angels Came

A little boy on the brink of bereavement

Cathy and her family make sure Michael is never alone.

Mummy told me not to tell

A troubled boy sworn to secrecy

After his dark past has been revealed, Cathy helps Reece to rebuild his life.

I Miss Mummy

Four-year-old Alice doesn't understand why she's in care

Cathy fights for her to have the happy home she deserves.

The Saddest Girl in the World

A haunted child who refuses to speak

Do Donna's scars run too deep for Cathy to help?

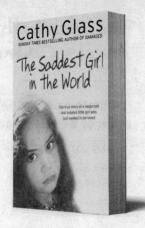

Cut

Dawn is desperate to be loved

Abused and abandoned, this vulnerable child pushes Cathy and her family to their limits.

Hidden

The boy with no past

Can Cathy help Tayo to feel like he belongs again?

Damaged

A forgotten child

Cathy is Jodie's last hope.
For the first time, this abused
young girl has found someone
she can trust.

Inspired by Cathy's own experiences...

Run, Mummy, Run

The gripping story of a
woman caught in a horrific
cycle of abuse, and the
desperate measures she
must take to escape.

My Dad's a Policeman

The dramatic short story
about a young boy's
desperate bid to keep his
family together.

The Girl in the Mirror

Trying to piece together her past, Mandy uncovers a dreadful family secret that has been blanked from her memory for years.

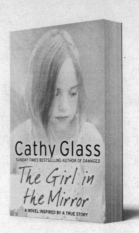

Sharing her expertise...

About Writing and How to Publish

A clear and concise, practical guide on writing and the best ways to get published.

Happy Mealtimes for Kids

A guide to healthy eating with simple recipes that children love.

Happy Adults

A practical guide to achieving lasting happiness, contentment and success. The essential manual for getting the best out of life.

Happy Kids

A clear and concise guide to raising confident, well-behaved and happy children.

Be amazed
Be moved
Be inspired

———

Discover more about Cathy Glass
visit www.cathyglass.co.uk

Moving Memoirs

Stories of hope, courage and the power of love…

If you loved this book, then you will love our Moving Memoirs eNewsletter

Sign up to…

- Be the first to hear about new books

- Get sneak previews from your favourite authors

- Read exclusive interviews

- Be entered into our monthly prize draw to win one of our latest releases before it's even hit the shops!

Sign up at

www.moving-memoirs.com